IMAGES
of America

ONARGA

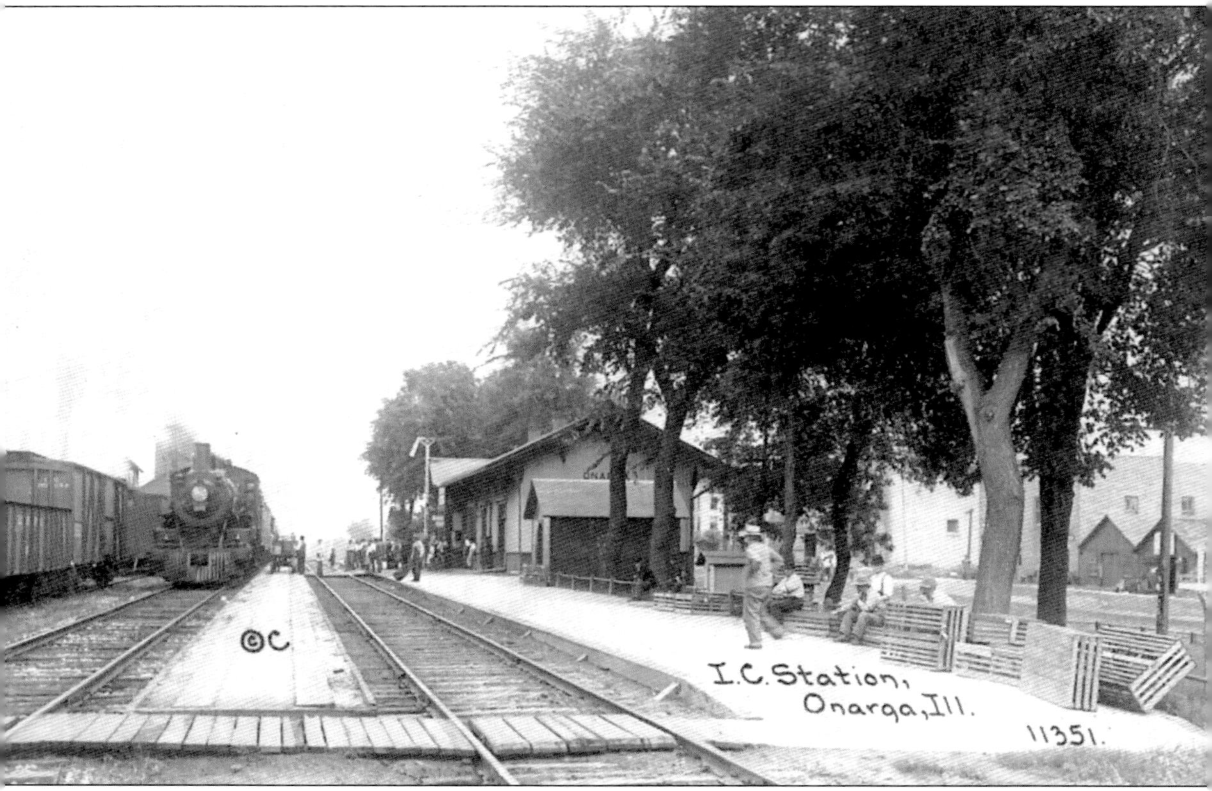

The Illinois Central Railroad laid tracks through Onarga in the summer of 1853. The Onarga passenger and freight depot was built in 1866. The original building was 24 by 78 feet and was lengthened and remodeled sometime between 1879 and 1900. The three Onarga station signs were painted directly on the building on both ends and on the front of the depot. This photograph was taken in 1915 and shows men loading mail on a southbound train.

On the cover: On July 19, 1867, the directors of the Union School District 1 contracted with Ralph McKenney, Cyrus Austin, and R. B. Cultra for the erection of a 32-by-50-foot, two-story brick schoolhouse. This was the first village school. The brick schoolhouse was completed that year and was dedicated on January 6, 1868. The total cost of the school and furnishings was $5,749.57. An addition with an unusual mansard roof was built in 1872, and a gymnasium was added in 1939. (Courtesy of the Onarga Historical Society.)

IMAGES
of America

ONARGA

Onarga Historical Society

ARCADIA
PUBLISHING

ISBN 978-0-7385-6060-1

Published by Arcadia Publishing
Charleston SC, Chicago IL, Portsmouth NH, San Francisco CA

Printed in the United States of America

Library of Congress Control Number: 2008940508

For all general information contact Arcadia Publishing at:
Telephone 843-853-2070
Fax 843-853-0044
E-mail sales@arcadiapublishing.com
For customer service and orders:
Toll-Free 1-888-313-2665

Visit us on the Internet at www.arcadiapublishing.com

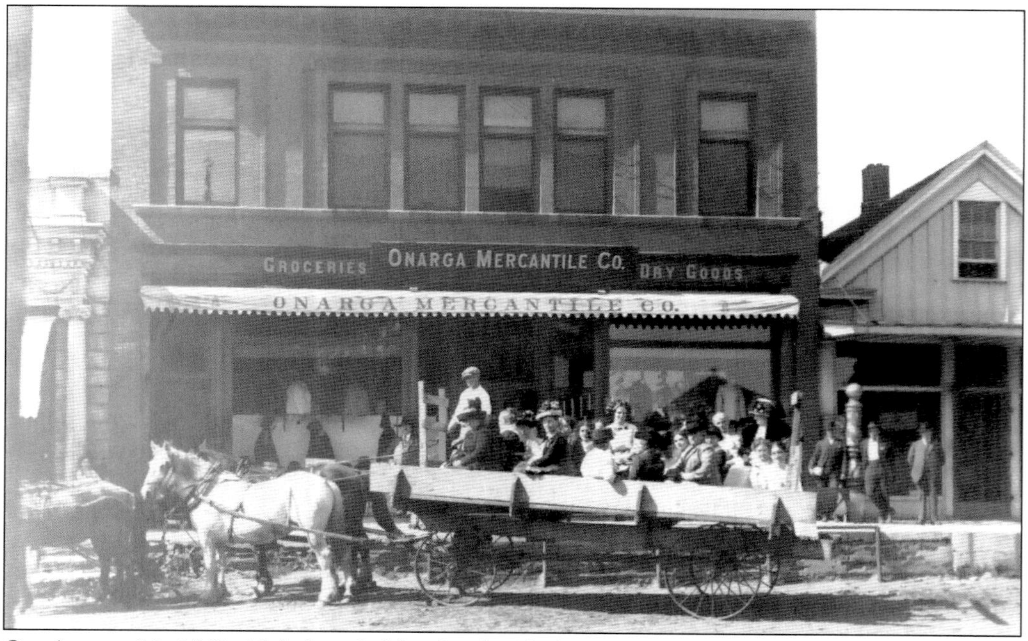

On August 26, 1862, 25 ladies, led by Sarah Clark, entered Thomas R. Barnes's saloon and destroyed all his liquors. Barnes, defending his business, used a hay fork. Two other saloons in town agreed to close business. A suit with Barnes as plaintiff was brought against 48 citizens of Onarga. On April 24, 1863, the court rendered a judgment for Barnes in the amount of $300. This could possibly be Sarah Clark and her temperance followers.

Contents

ACKNOWLEDGMENTS

The following publications were invaluable resources: *History of Iroquois County* by H. W. Beckwith, 1880; *Portrait and Biographical Record of Iroquois County, Illinois* 1893; *Past and Present, Iroquois County, Illinois* 1907; *History of Iroquois County, 1818–1968; 100 Years of Learning at Grand Prairie Seminary and Onarga Military School, 1863–1963; Christmas Greetings from the Onarga Post No. 551 of the American Legion*; *Onarga Military School, Book of Views*, 1924 and 1925; "Allan Pinkerton's Larch Farm" by Russell Palmer; "Larch Farm: A Resort in the Prairie," the *Daily Times*, Watseka; "The Pinkertons of Onarga" by Don L. Long, the *Daily Times*, Watseka, December 2 and 3, 1967; "Allan Pinkerton and the Larch Farm: A Collection of Writings" by Patricia Dissmeyer Goff, 2000; and *Timothy Webster: The Story of the Civil War Spy and His Family* by Patricia Dissmeyer Goff, 2000.

Special thanks to the friends of the Onarga Historical Society for their invaluable research and those persons who contributed photographs, family history, and items of interest pertinent to this publication. Special thanks also to the Iroquois County Old Courthouse Museum and Genealogical Department.

INTRODUCTION

Gurdon S. Hubbard, an American Indian trader employed by the American Fur Company, owned by John Jacob Astor and Company, settled Iroquois County in the winters of 1821–1822. And, except for the United States surveyors, who were in Iroquois County by May 15, 1822, Hubbard was also the first white man known to have been over the land that became the town of Onarga.

Of course, long before the white man traveled through and settled on the Grand Prairie, the American Indians lived in wigwams and hunted deer, elk, and buffalo on the grassy plains. They fished the abundant streams. Large colonies of bees were discovered all through the timber area, wild artichokes grew along the edge of the prairie, and the timber ground was covered in acorns. Wild hogs were plentiful along the streams of the timber first brought to the area by Hubbard in 1826.

The Butterfield Trail, or Butterfield's Trail, over which all our early settlers on the Upper Spring Creek came, was named for Benjamin Butterfield in the year 1831. This trail followed the general course of Spring Creek, past the point known as Leonard, continued north past the present sites of Plato and L'Erable and then extended to a point near Joliet, where it forked with both forks leading to Chicago. For many years, Butterfield Trail was one of the main routes from east central Illinois to the Chicago area, and it is written that for 20 years following the close of the Black Hawk War, Butterfield's Trail was the greatest route for cattle and hogs in the state of Illinois.

In June 1834, the last band of American Indians, numbering 30 or 40, living on Spring Creek left the area. The only American Indian camping ground, out of the timber area, eventually became the tiny village of Onarga.

The settling of Onarga grew quite rapidly when it became known that a railroad was to be built. The very first train, the Illinois Central, went through Onarga on December 2, 1853. It traveled from Kankakee to Spring Creek, a distance of 31 miles. Onarga was laid out in the fall of 1854 by David A. Neal, vice president of the railroad, on a comparatively high ridge. One of the reasons Onarga was chosen as the location for the Illinois Central Railroad was because of the high sandy ground. Onarga is approximately 100 feet above the level of Lake Michigan, 23 feet above neighboring town Gilman, which lies to the north, with Del Rey to the south and Ridgeville to the west. By 1855, some 20 families had settled here. Just a year later, Onarga boasted 64 houses, six stores, three schools, one church, one hotel, two sawmills, and two gristmills. The Illinois Central had a very large part in the early growth of Onarga.

In 1864, Allan Pinkerton, the renowned detective, purchased 254 acres, located about a mile north of Onarga on the line of the Illinois Central Railroad. Pinkerton, determined to carry out an idea that had long occupied his mind, began operations in 1873 to cultivate a prairie farm that would be the acme of western rural development. And, after seven years of labor and a lavish expenditure of funds, the Larch Farm became the model farm of Iroquois County. When Timothy Webster, ace spy, was hung as a spy in Richmond, Virginia, Pinkerton had his body returned to Onarga and buried in the Onarga Township Cemetery.

On June 18, 1931, an 18-foot, 138-electric-light sign was erected on the west side of Route 25 (now Route 45) out of the generosity of the CIPS Company, and in cooperation with the Onarga Village Board and the Lions Club. The blue and white porcelain decorative sign weighing 800 to 900 pounds was double-faced and spelled out *Onarga*. The newspaper article said, "A good sign creates the impression that here is a town that is proud of its name and one which undoubtedly possesses an up-to-date spirit among its citizens. This blazing beacon advertises the fact that this village is alive and that it has a name which it is proud to display before the passing world." This admirable sign still stands in the village of Onarga and still advertises to the world that we are proud of our town and our name. We have enjoyed a very rich history, and it is our privilege to share not only our written narrative of events, from our inception to our 100th birthday, in these 10 chapters, but the superb selected images as well.

—Cheryl Rabe
President, Onarga Historical Society

One

Early Settlers

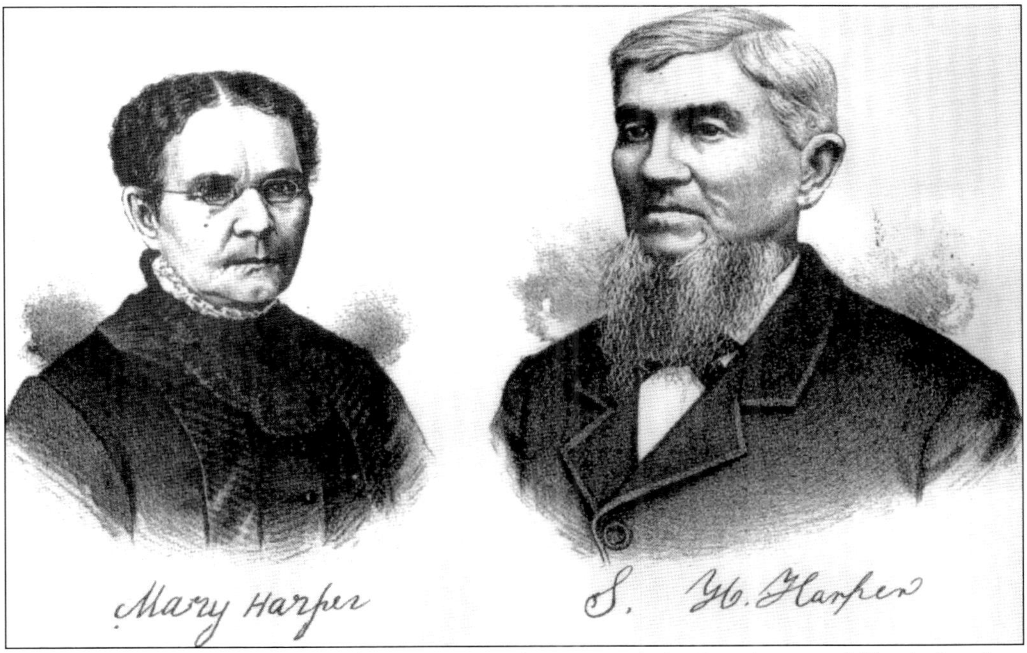

With a party that also included his parents and sisters and the Pangborn and Skeels families, Samuel H. Harper (1814–1889) arrived to settle southeast of Onarga along Middle Spring Creek in the fall of 1837. The Harpers and Pangborns spent the first winter living in a 16-foot square cabin that had been vacated by the previous owner of the claim. Samuel H. Harper made his first claim for 160 acres of government land in 1839 and engaged successfully in agricultural pursuits throughout his entire life.

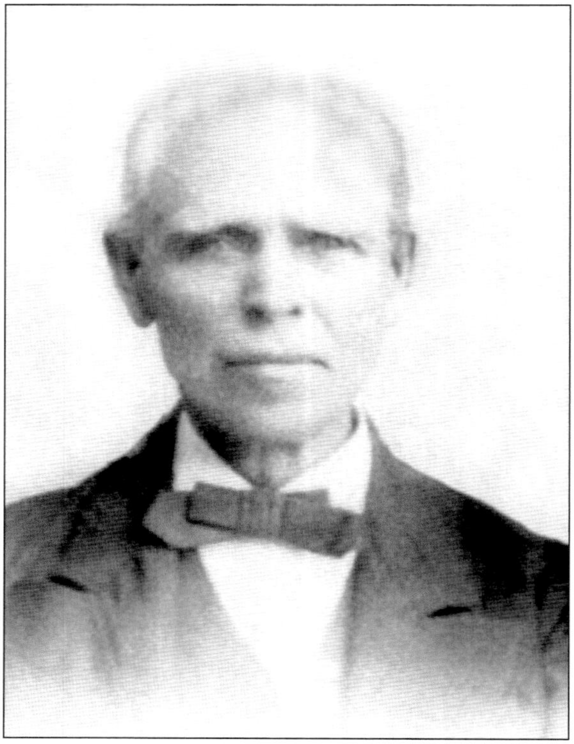

Thomas M. Pangborn (1806–1892) married Samuel H. Harper's sister, Jane (1812–1902), in 1832 and made his first trip to Spring Creek in 1834 or 1835. He was accompanied by his brother Ransom. Pangborn's father and a younger brother Cyrus would come to settle on part of the Pangborn claim in 1845. Thomas was elected associate judge of Iroquois County in 1853 and served until 1857. He also served as overseer of the poor. He and his wife were among the earliest members of the Methodist church where he served as class leader for over 30 years. Thomas taught school for a short time and was one of the original public school trustees, serving in the position for 19 years.

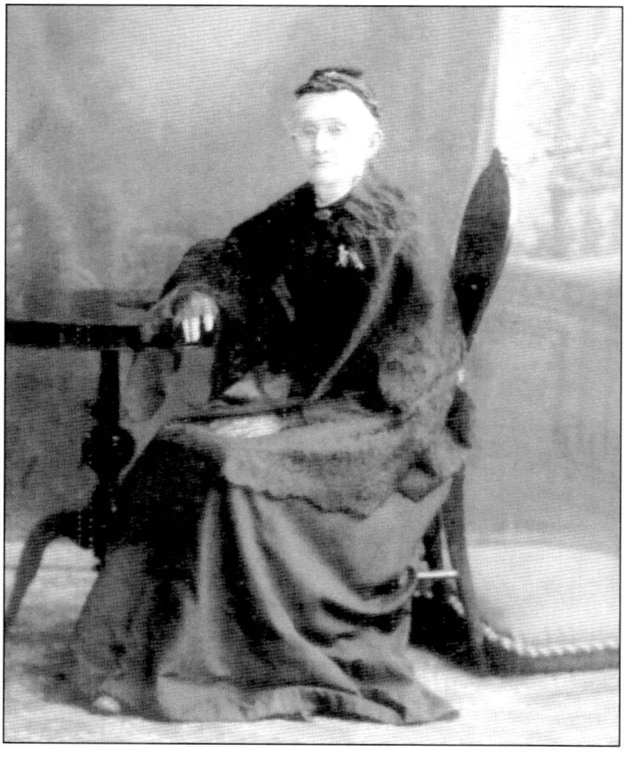

Experience Lehigh (1801–1860) and her husband Abram (1794–1836) left Perrysville, Indiana, to settle along Spring Creek close to Del Rey in 1835. Their son Frederick was the first white child born on Spring Creek on August 14, 1835. When Abram died in 1836, Experience was left a widow with eight children. Her claim on Spring Creek near Del Rey consisted of 120 acres of unbroken prairie and 194 acres of timberland. With the aid of her older sons she turned this claim into a successful farming and lumber business.

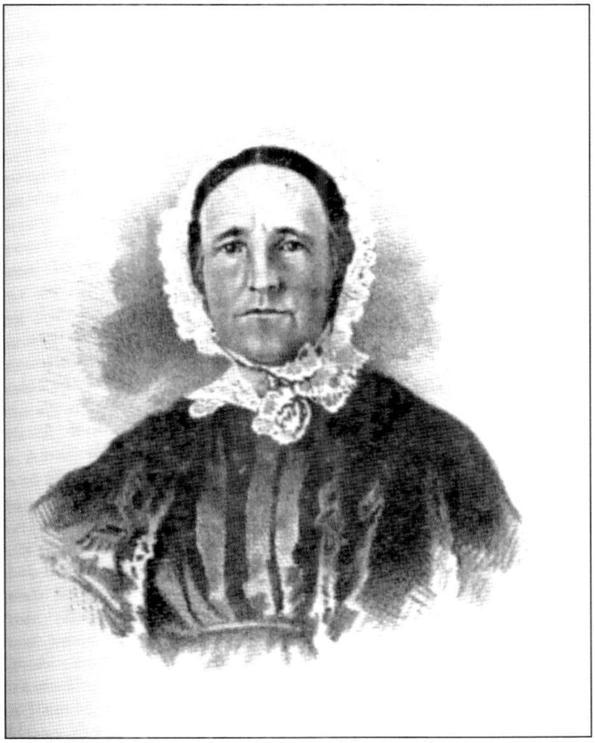

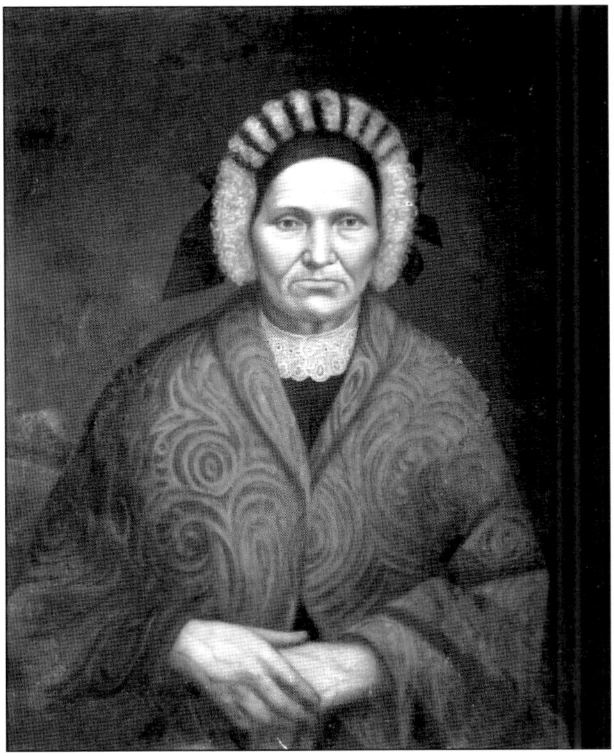

Maria Ayres Lindsey Boyd (1810–1883) was the wife of Ira Lindsey (1790–1844). Ira settled southwest of Onarga in the fall of 1834 and purchased over 800 acres of land during the years 1835 to 1837. In 1843, he built the first permanent buildings—a brick house and large frame barn—along Spring Creek near Del Rey. Ira served as the first grand juror from Onarga and was the first justice of the peace west of Spring Creek. Maria later married Dr. Lemuel Boyd, one of the first postmasters at Del Rey in 1854 and the first Onarga assessor elected in 1856.

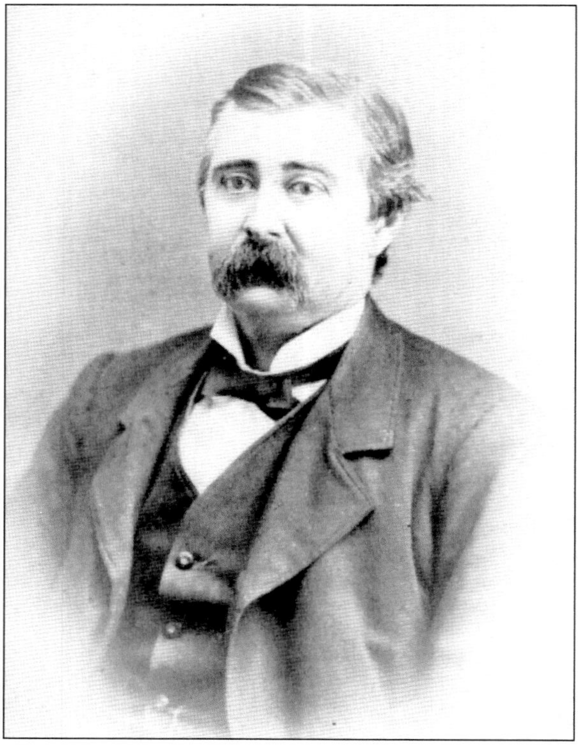

Elkanah Doolittle (1829–1897) was a civil engineer involved in the construction of the Illinois Central Railroad. In 1856, he was appointed as the first Iroquois County engineer. He was elected Onarga town clerk in 1857 and Iroquois County surveyor in 1858. He and his mother were founding members of the Onarga Episcopalian Church. After serving in the 20th Connecticut Infantry during the Civil War, he returned to Onarga and began farming on his old homestead. He also partnered in several business ventures during the 1870s. Pictured below is his second wife, Miranda Pangborn Doolittle, the daughter of Thomas Pangborn.

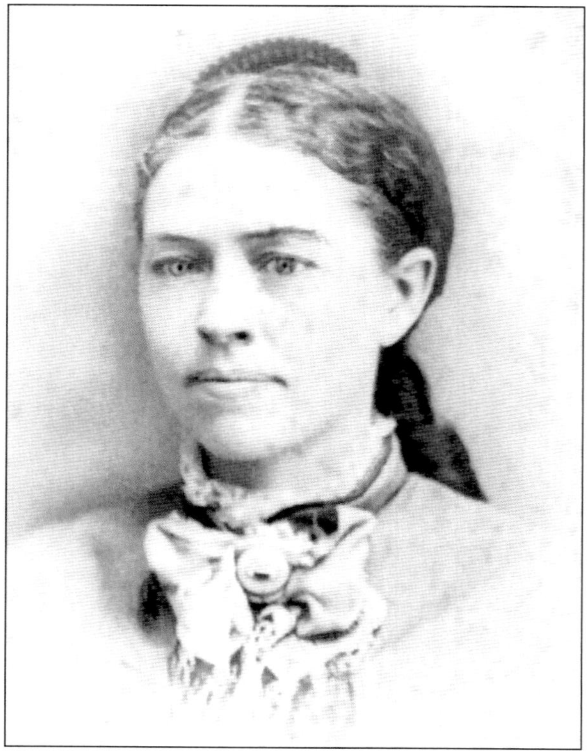

Addison Lockwood (1829–1882) came to Onarga around 1850 and taught school from 1850 to 1860. In 1854, Onarga was laid out by David A. Neal, vice president of the Illinois Central Railroad. That same year, Lockwood moved a log schoolhouse to his claim on what is now West Seminary Avenue. This became the first building in the village of Onarga.

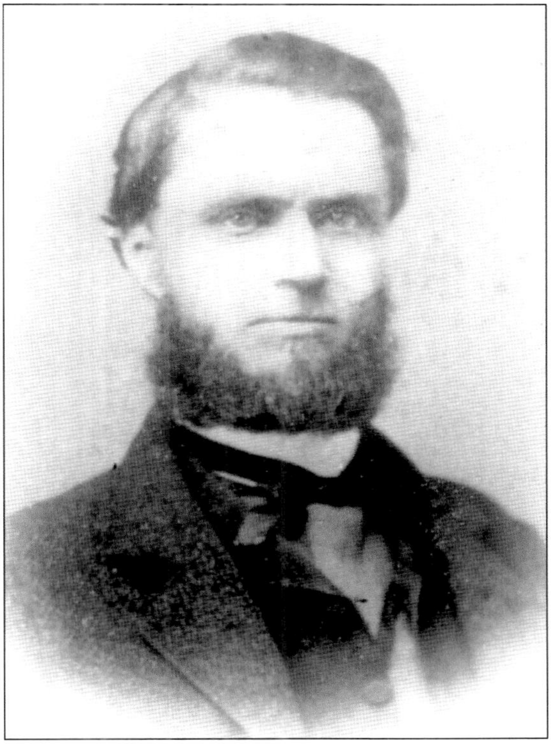

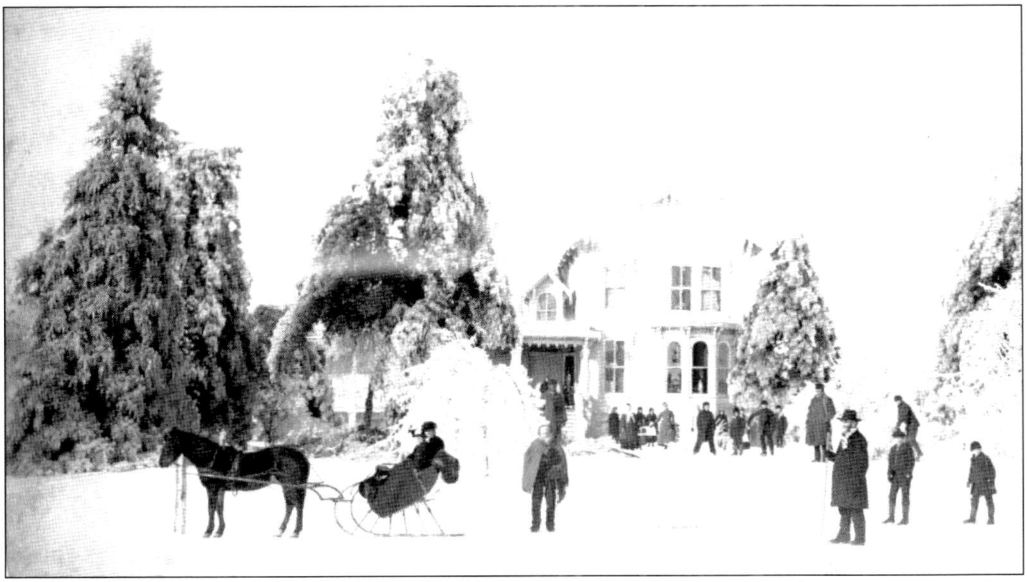

This photograph of Moses Haynes Messer (1829–1900), civil engineer and surveyor, was taken sometime after 1871 on the lawn of the William Pierson home. Messer is standing, wrapped in a shawl, behind the sleigh. In October 1855, he arrived to set up his surveying office. He served as Iroquois County surveyor from 1859 to 1865 and was responsible for platting a great deal of the county. He also served as Onarga justice of the peace from 1856 to 1868, Onarga school director from 1862 to 1871, and United States Internal Revenue assessor from 1862 to 1865.

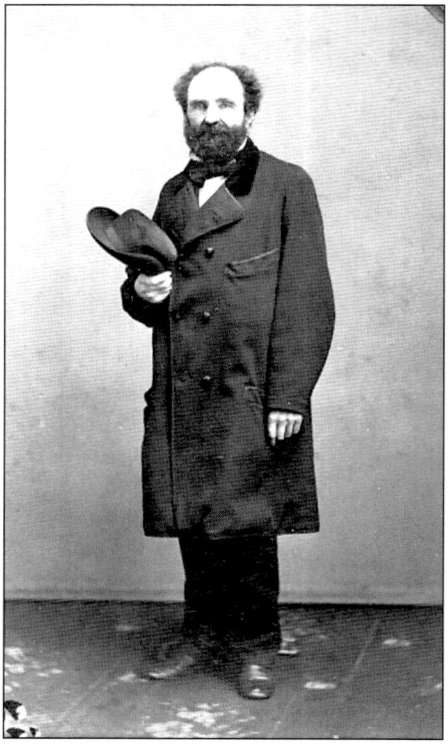

William Porter Pierson (1811–1909) did not arrive in Onarga until 1854 but was probably the first major businessman to locate permanently in the area. He had actually intended to stay only temporarily in Onarga and move on to Champaign once the Illinois Central Railroad line extended that far. Fortunately, he changed his mind and opened his lumber business in Onarga. He later expanded the business to include hardware, farming tools, coal, and flour. He also purchased grain and erected buildings for his own use and to rent to others.

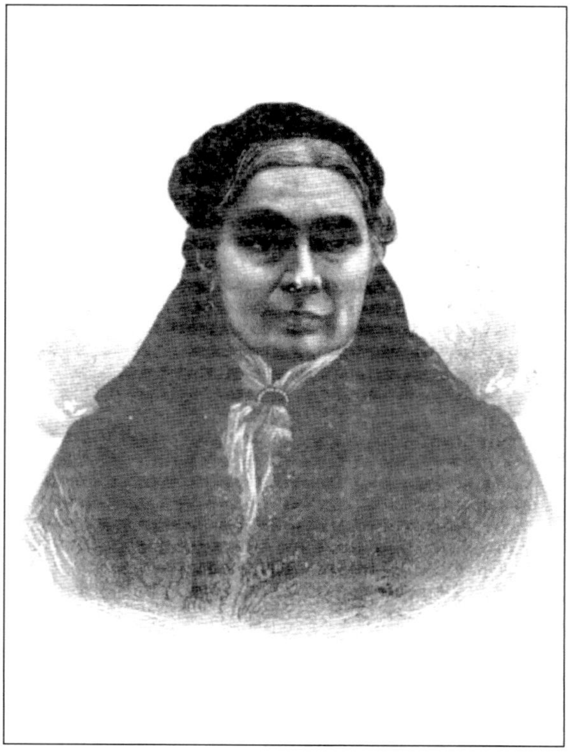

William Pierson married Mary Tucker Condit (1821–1890), the daughter of a Presbyterian minister, in 1853. No children were born to the Piersons, but they opened their home to at least 20 orphaned children, raising and educating them as their own. Shortly after arriving in 1854, Mary began teaching Sunday school classes in her home. In 1857, both Piersons became founding members of the Onarga Presbyterian Church.

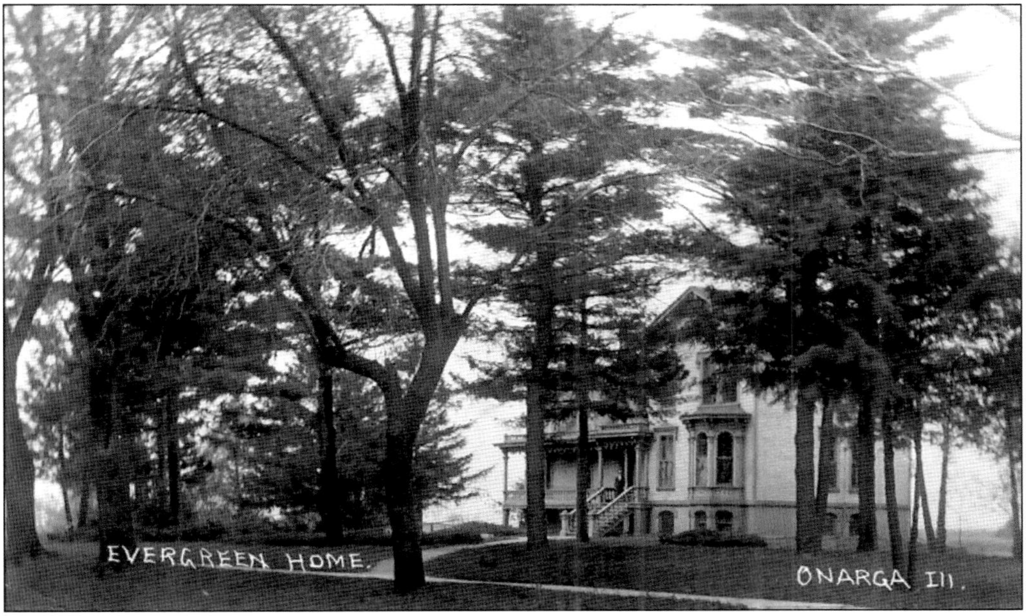

When the Piersons first came to Onarga, they boarded for a short time in the home of Judge Thomas Pangborn. They later moved into what had been the Lockwood cabin. In the summer of 1857, Pierson built a small home not far from his business on what is now Chestnut Street. The Piersons lived in that modest, little house until the house pictured here—which they called Evergreen Home—was built in 1871. It was located on what was then the southwest edge of town in a grove of evergreens that Pierson had planted shortly after settling in Onarga. This house still stands and is occupied on what is now South Evergreen Street.

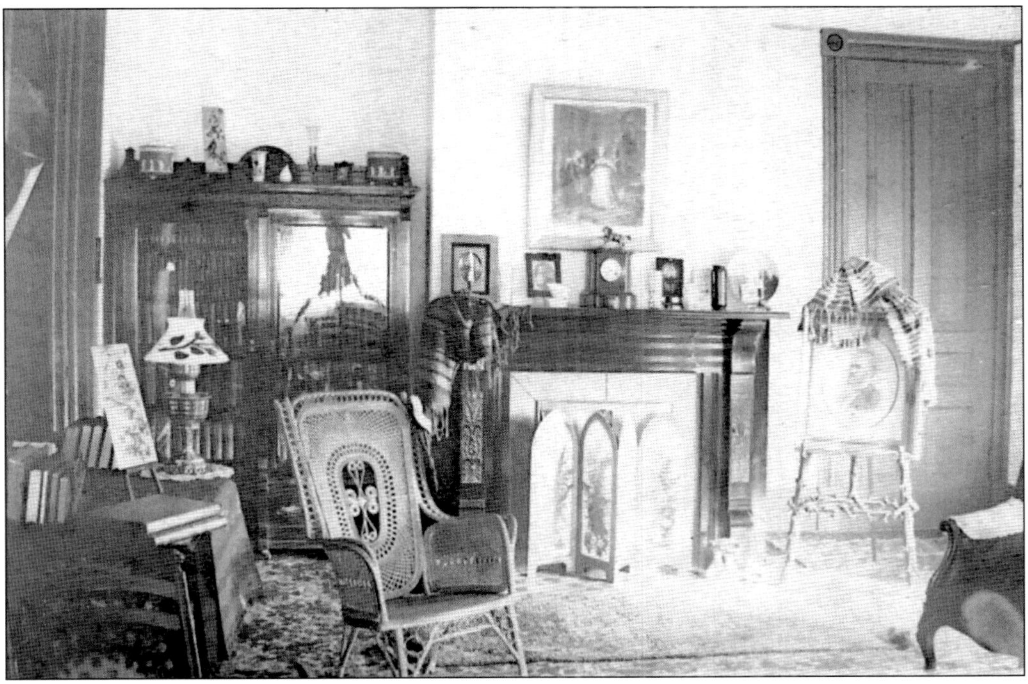

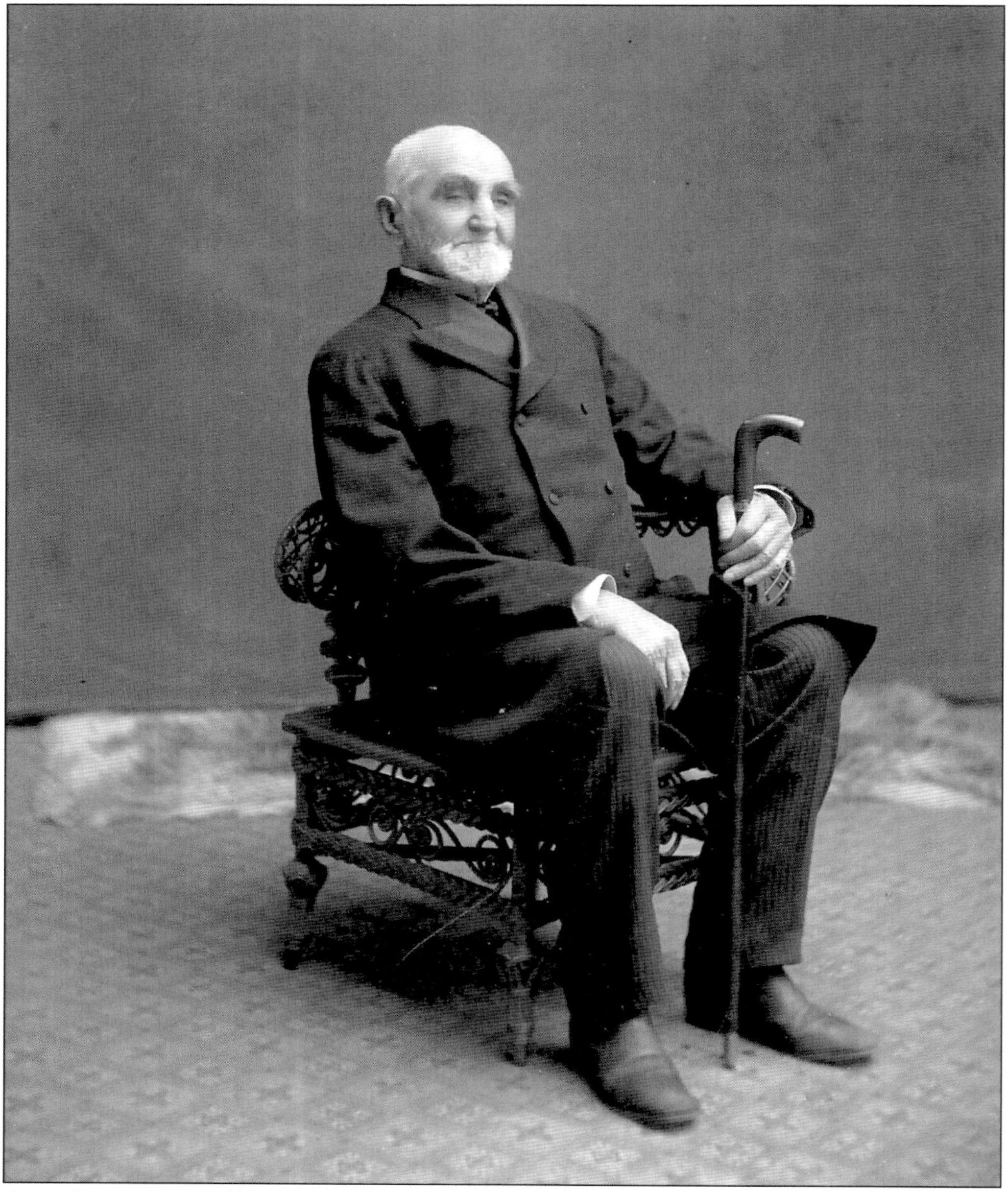

As early as 1866, William Pierson's health began to fail, and he began to withdraw from the active management of his business. During the fall and winter of 1870–1871, he left his wife in the care of her relatives in New York and began an extensive European tour. When he returned from this tour in the spring of 1871, he retired completely. The Piersons continued to be an active part of their church and community until Mary Pierson died in 1890. William spent his remaining years at Evergreen Home in Onarga. Although he was almost completely deaf in his later years, he remained active, stating when interviewed on his 97th birthday that he took a walk almost every day. William Pierson died at Evergreen Home on June 10, 1909. This picture appeared with his obituary in the June 18, 1909, issue of the *Leader and Review*. His obituary filled four columns and had the title line "Onarga's oldest pioneer passes away."

Two

Grand Prairie Seminary and Onarga Military School

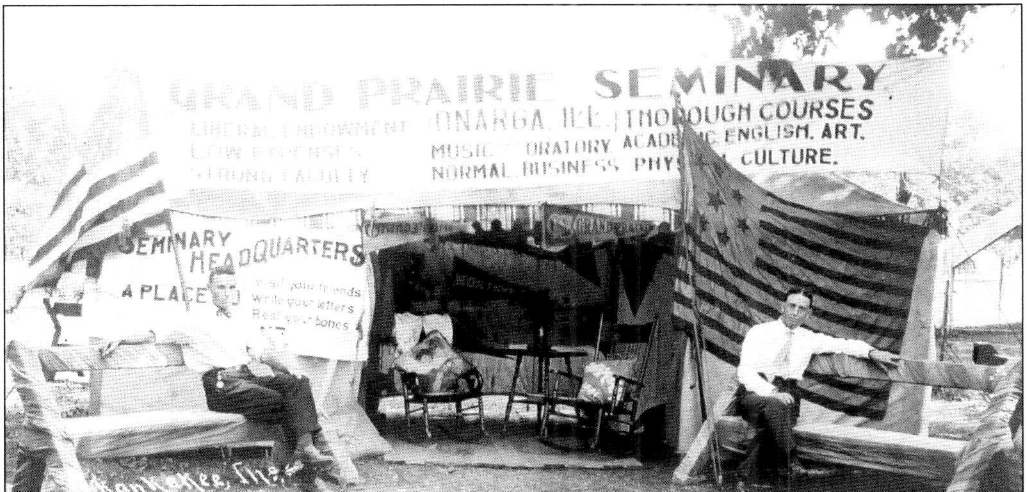

The early immigrants to the area considered education a valuable asset. On June 10, 1863, an educational convention was held in Onarga with Rev. P. T. Rhodes presiding and the driving force. Representatives from several villages near Onarga—Buckley, Sheldon, Chebanse, Fairbury, Ash Grove, and Kankakee—met to discuss the possibilities of an educational institution. Onarga, on the final vote, cast at midnight, received 13 of the 22 votes cast with the remaining 9 votes cast for Kankakee. Tradition has it that the ladies of Onarga plied the visitors with wonderful food and large saucers heaped with ripe strawberries served with fresh cream.

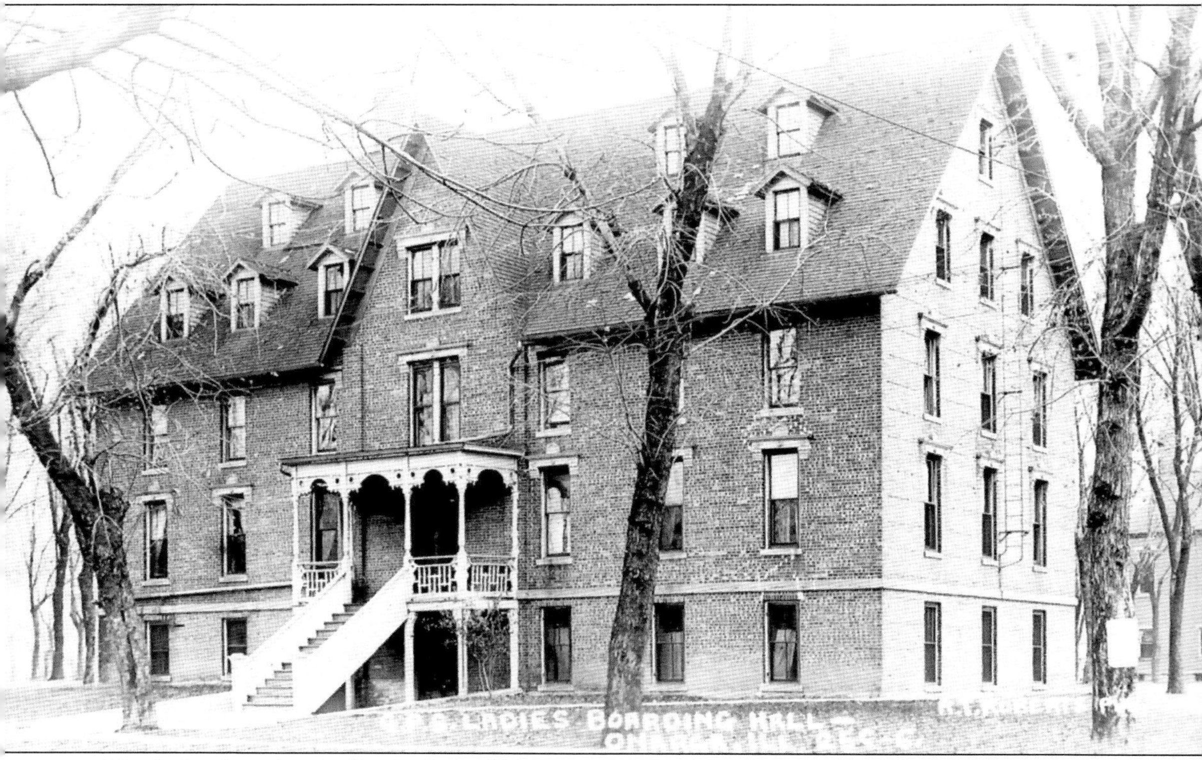

The ladies boarding hall, which could house 60 women, was constructed and put to use in 1888. This building was constructed in modern style with commodious rooms supplied with heavy furniture and was heated by steam. It was 72 by 36 feet. The ladies were housed for 40¢ to 60¢ per week, and meals were included for $2 per week. This was a major improvement as it was a big problem to house and feed over 300 students in private homes. To board with a private family including room, heat, and light ran $2.50 to $3.50 per week. The new building not only gave some relief in that line but was also a very attractive inducement to parents who wished to send their daughters to Grand Prairie Seminary.

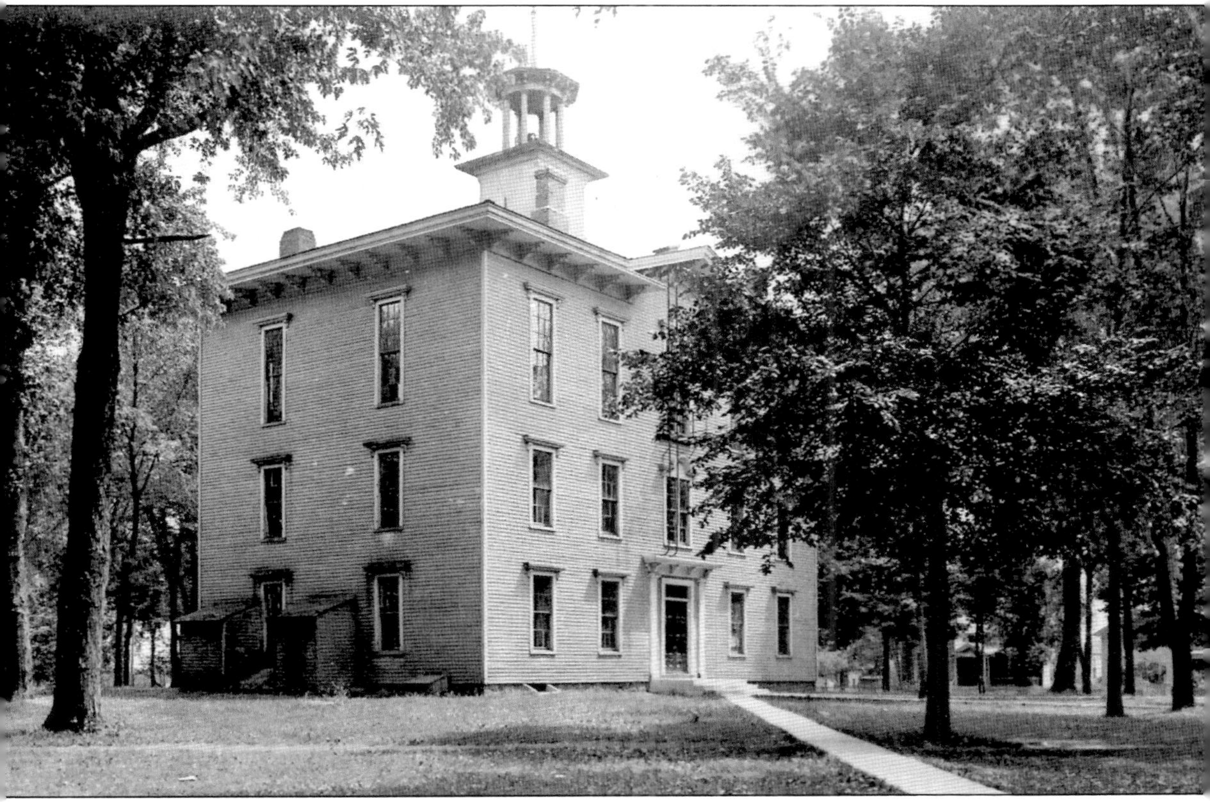

The Onarga citizens subscribed $7,000 toward a three-story-high building, which was the very first one constructed on the Seminary Block. The building was erected in 1864 and was called the Recitation Hall. The main school building in course of construction was 40 by 60 feet and was three stories tall. The total cost was $11,000, including the fencing of the grounds. The student body in 1864 consisted of 136 members. The building included five classrooms, two literary society rooms, a laboratory, a library, and a chapel. The first faculty consisted of only nine persons. These teachers each taught several subjects or acted as administrators. Classical, scientific, normal, music, and commercial were the courses of study at that time. The amount of tuition ranged from $2 to $12 for each 12-week term with three terms per year. By the end of 1872, the Grand Prairie Seminary catalog listed 83 ladies and 92 gentlemen as students—a total of 175.

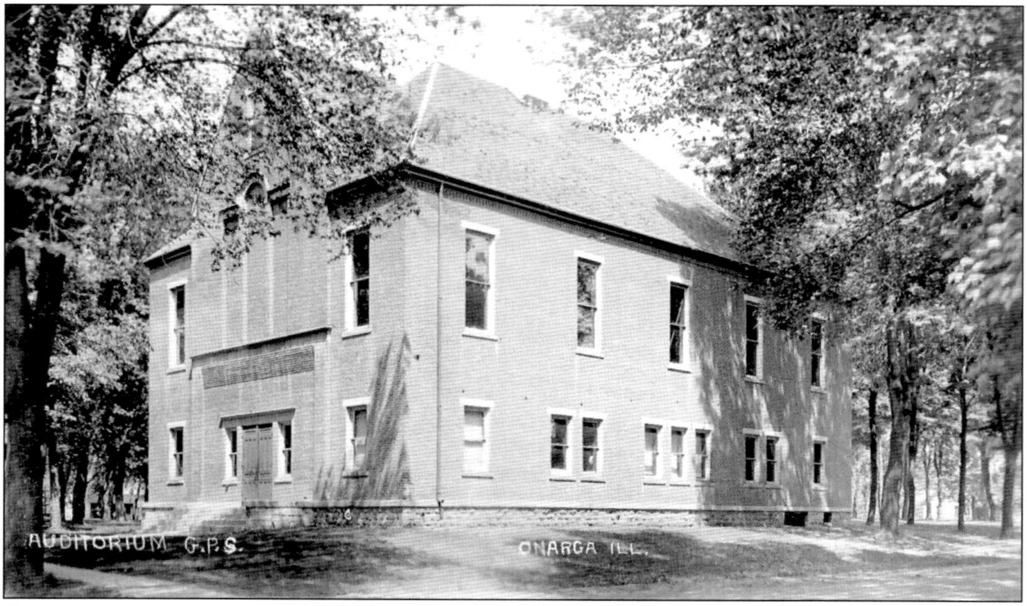

A two-story conservatory, also known as the auditorium, was constructed in 1892. This building, made of brick and stone, was considered one of the finest in the state. The chapel in the conservatory would seat up to 700. Students were not only required to attend church twice on Sunday, but also to attend chapel every day. From the beginning, music received its share of attention. Vocal culture, theory, and composition were prominent features of the school. Hilft and Gilbert's minstrel shows were popular. The photograph below depicts the stage area of the conservatory. It is important to note the picture (center of stage) of P. T. Rhodes, founder of Grand Prairie Seminary.

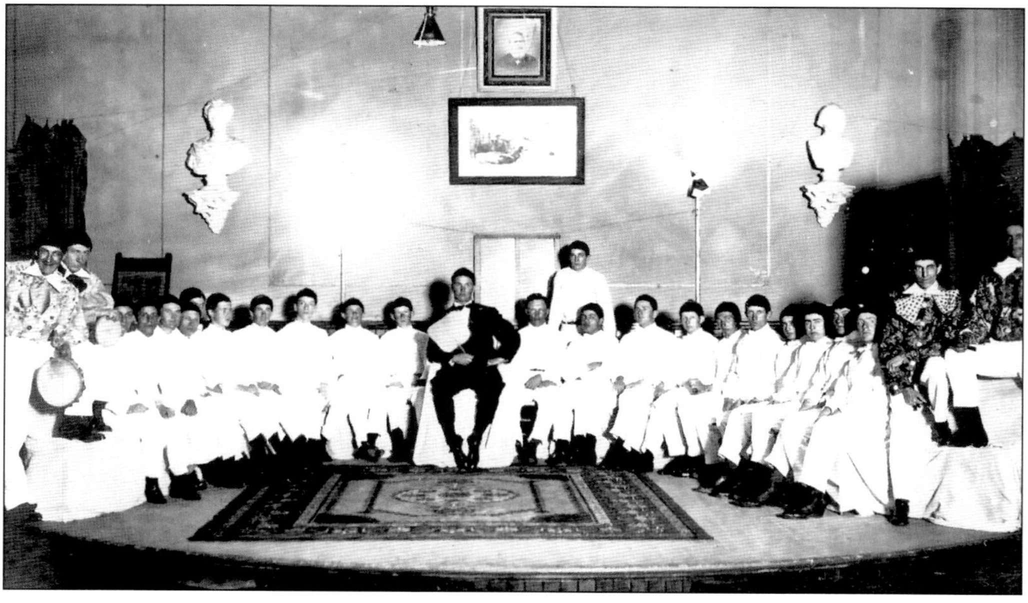

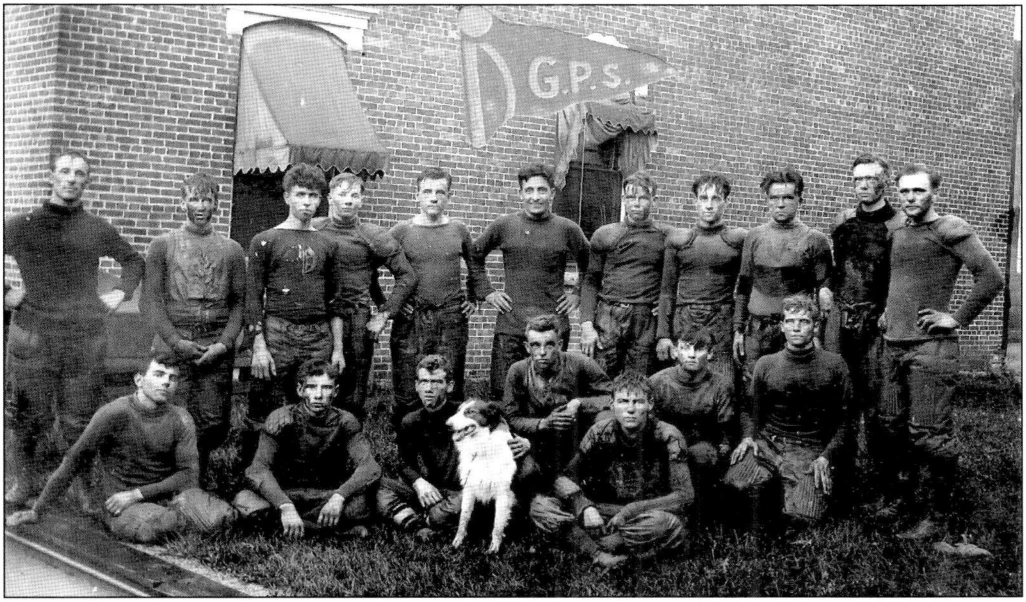

The above postcard sent from Onarga on September 3, 1911, at 7:00 p.m. from "Messrs Lamarre and Flagrole," Court House, Kankakee reads, "Excuse me if I send only one card to you both as I am in hurry to catch train. We beat this bunch 22 to O. Feeling fine . . . not a scratch. Aurevoir, Harris." Quoting a poem, entitled "Our Football Team," "We have a Seminary football team that's very hard to beat. We're going to play the game this year and every team defeat. Our little ends are hard to beat when running with the ball. They make the scores for Grand Prairie Seminary and rivals take a fall!" Note the Grand Prairie Seminary football team's mascot and the purple and gold Grand Prairie Seminary sticker. The various sports teams contributed their share of favorable publicity for the seminary and won a high place in the sports world of that day. The subjects of the picture below are the ladies' basketball team at Grand Prairie Seminary with teachers Miss Gilbert and Professor Ranne.

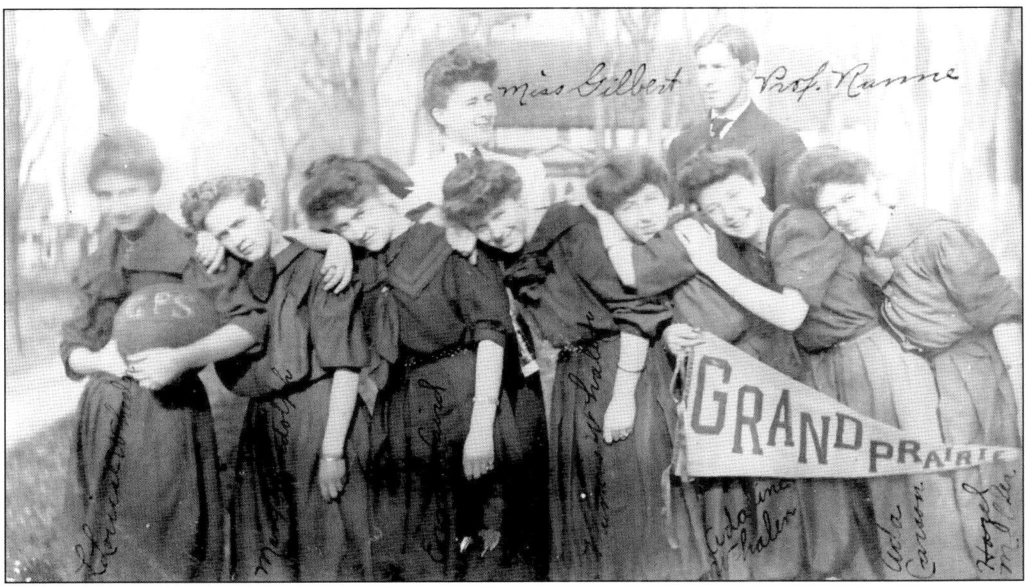

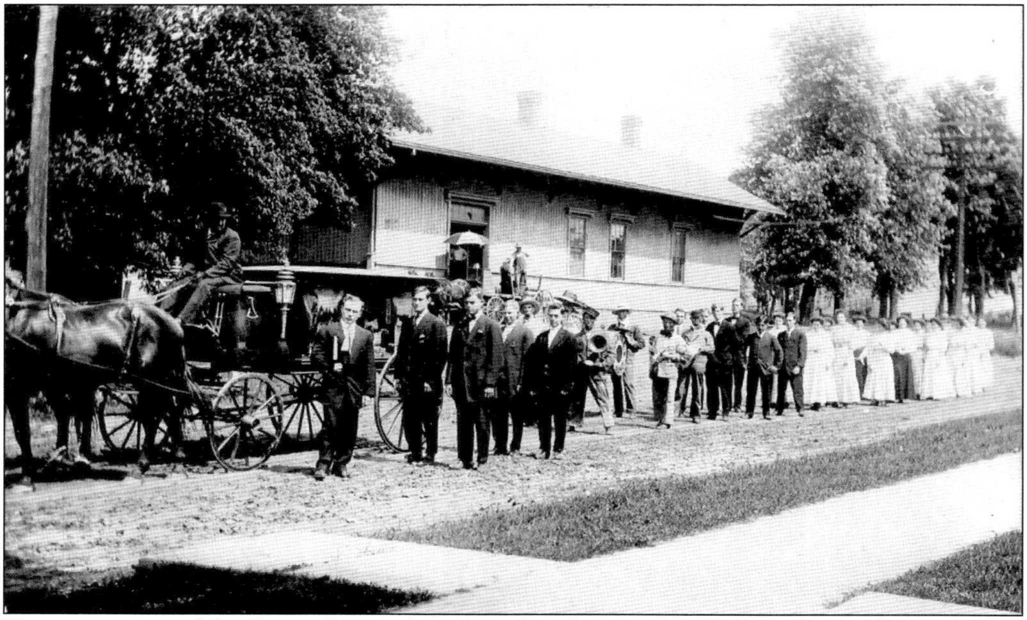

This is a picture of the Grand Prairie Seminary class day procession, around 1909, featuring Sam Moon's Funeral Car with Charles Schultz driving. Note the Onarga Band immediately following the funeral car. It was the custom for the outgoing senior class to "bury" the junior class. The funeral procession photograph was taken on Chestnut Street (Onarga's main street) in front of the Booth and Stitt Building. The photograph below shows the Grand Prairie Seminary junior class represented by the burning coffin. This photograph was taken in front of the Grand Prairie Seminary Auditorium Building located on the Seminary Block.

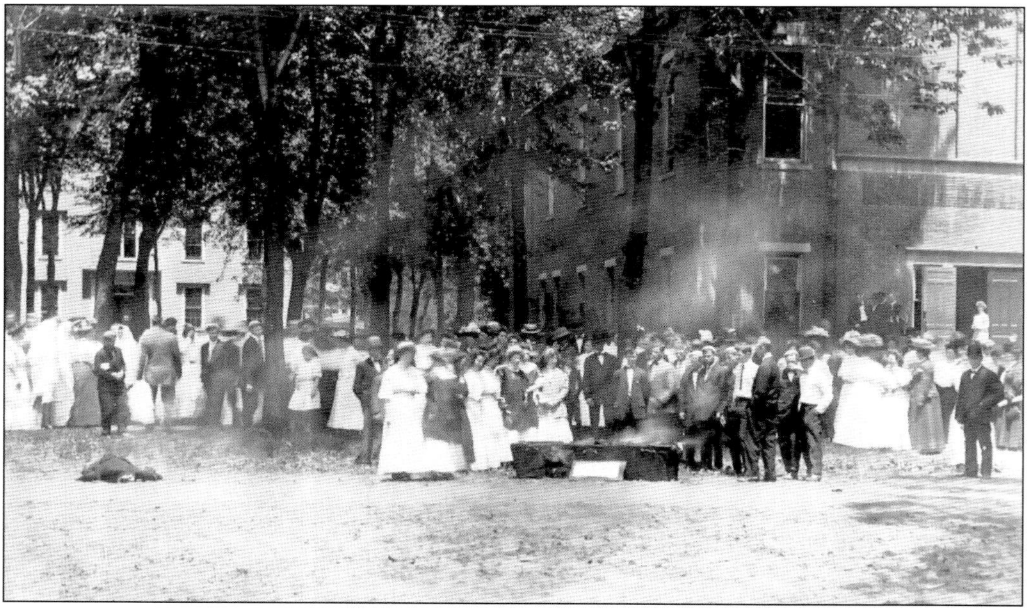

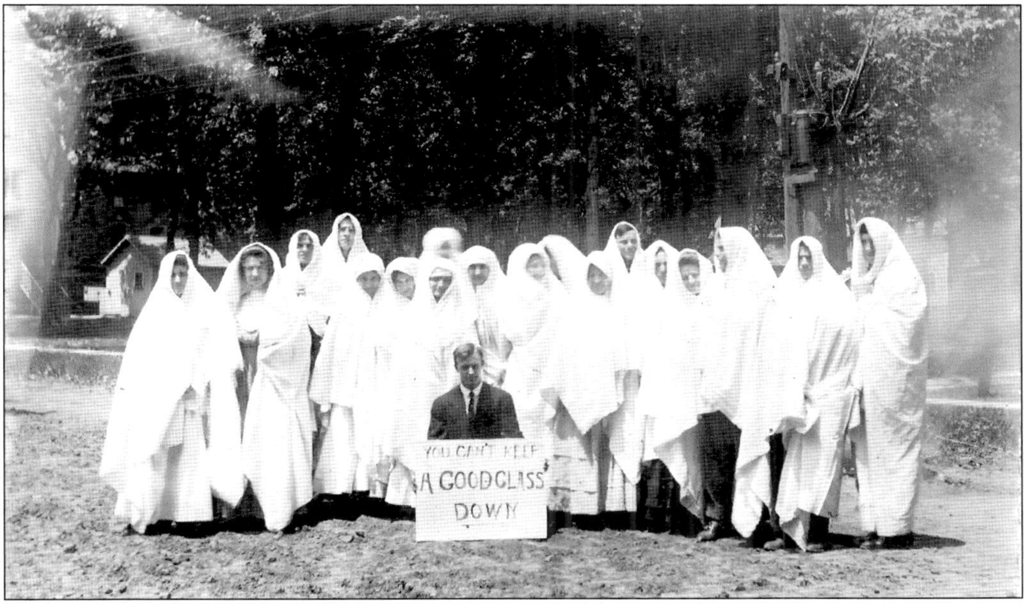

"You can't keep a good class down!" The above photograph shows the Grand Prairie Seminary junior class posing as ghosts as the senior class "buried" them, as was tradition. Of course, the class reappeared as "Seniors" at Grand Prairie Seminary. Grand Prairie Seminary achieved great renown as a high-grade seminary. This school continued until the year 1918, when it opened as a school for boys stressing military training. World War I was on, and many changes were in progress, especially in the rapid growth of accredited high schools, all of which contributed to the decreasing number of students at Grand Prairie Seminary. The photograph below depicts the 1909 student body of Grand Prairie Seminary taken on the east side of Chestnut Street. The card reads, "Oh, you kid! Write me please! Faye."

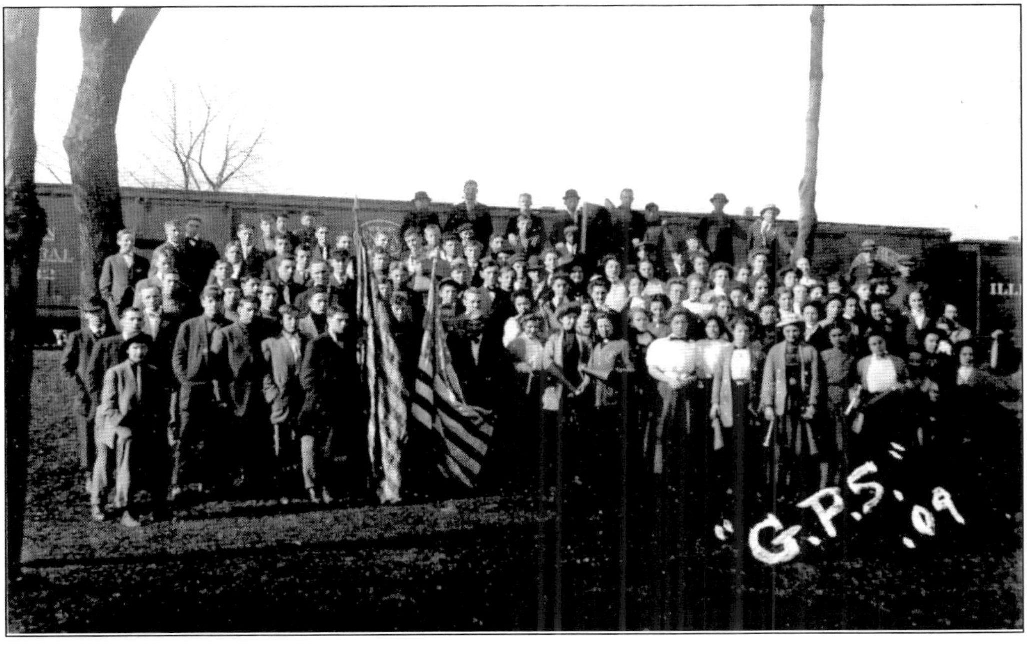

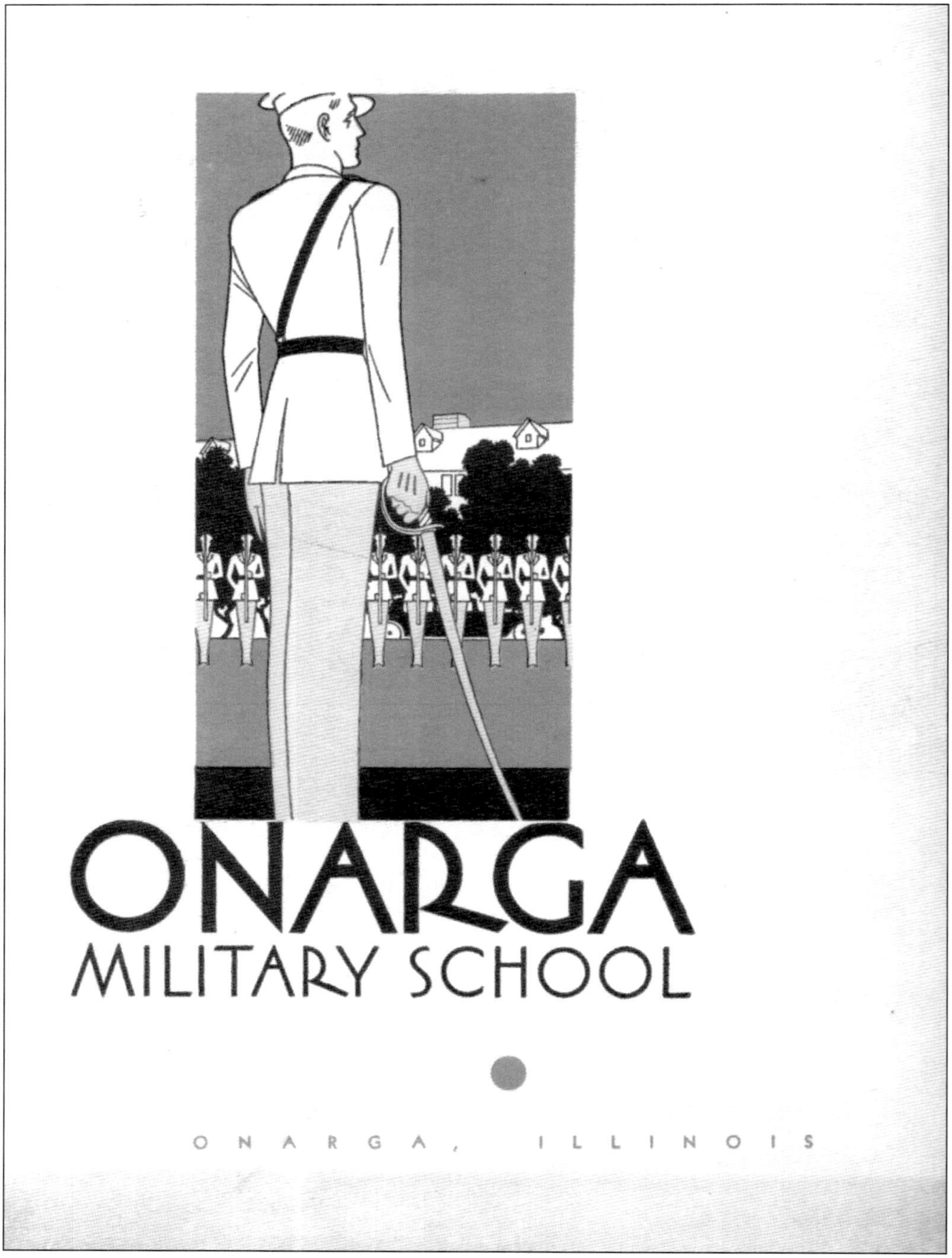

The Onarga Military School was in operation from 1919 through 1971. This is the front cover of the 1930s catalogue for the school. The brochure advertises that good citizenship and 100 percent Americanism are taught through a modified form of military training and that Onarga Military School graduates are accepted without examination into all colleges and universities that permit certification. The brochure boasts "real personal attention for every boy enrolled."

TRAINING FOR CHARACTER

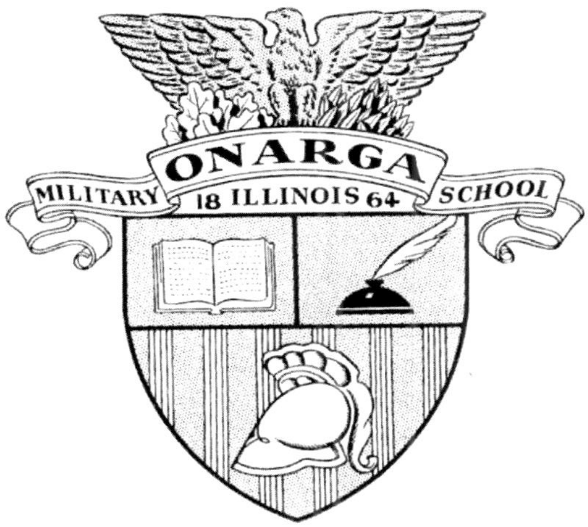

This is the actual coat of arms for the Onarga Military School. The established date reads 1864 because Onarga Military School was founded under the corporate name of Grand Prairie Seminary, which operated as a coeducational institute from 1864 to 1917. Each cadet wore the coat of arms pin on his uniform with pride.

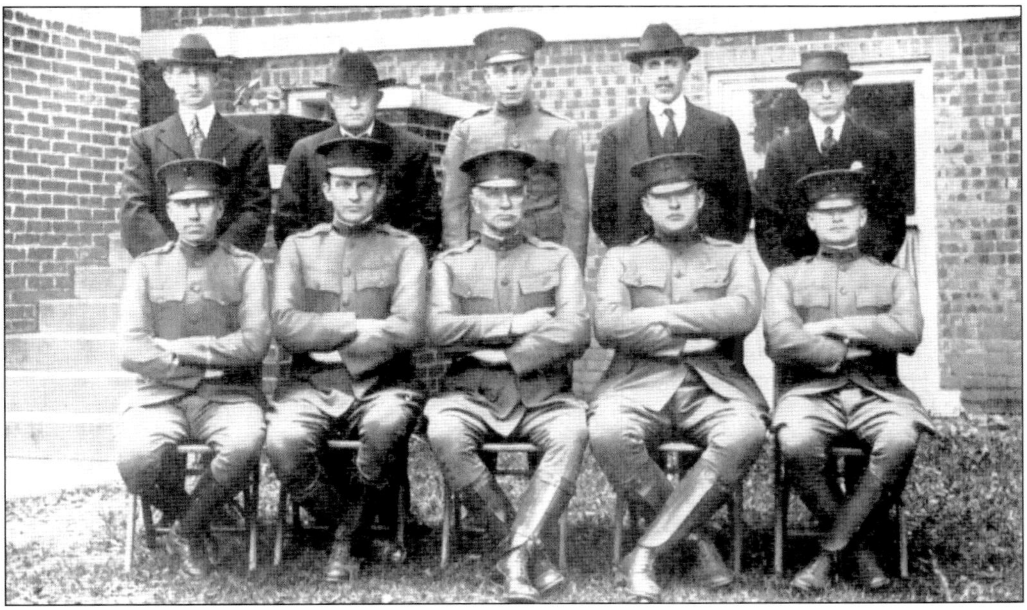

Col. J. E. Bittinger (seated center) was the first superintendent. It was he who leased the Grand Prairie Seminary property in 1919 and changed the name of the institution to Onarga Military School. His sons, Capt. Lyle Bittinger and Maj. Leigh Bittinger, served as principal and commandant. Also pictured are the members of the faculty. Faculty members were chosen based on their proficiency in their respective subjects and their interest in the boys.

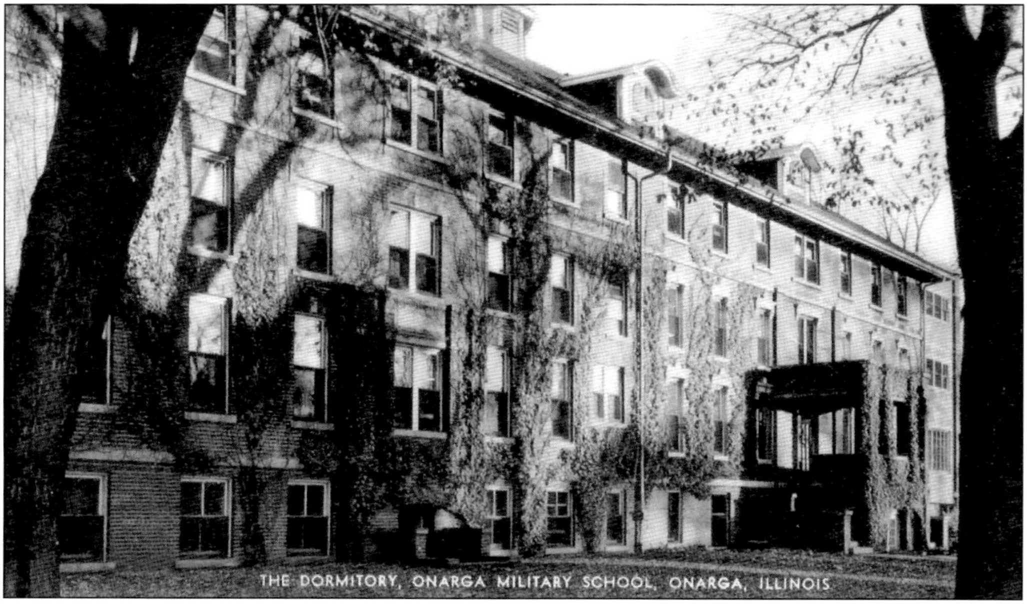

The three-story brick dormitory building could accommodate 100 boys. On the ground floor were the storerooms, kitchen, pantry, and large dining room. The second and third floors of the dormitory were the cadets' quarters. Faculty officers also lived on the second and third floors and had charge of their respective floors. The campus sat on four acres and was beautifully landscaped with large shady trees.

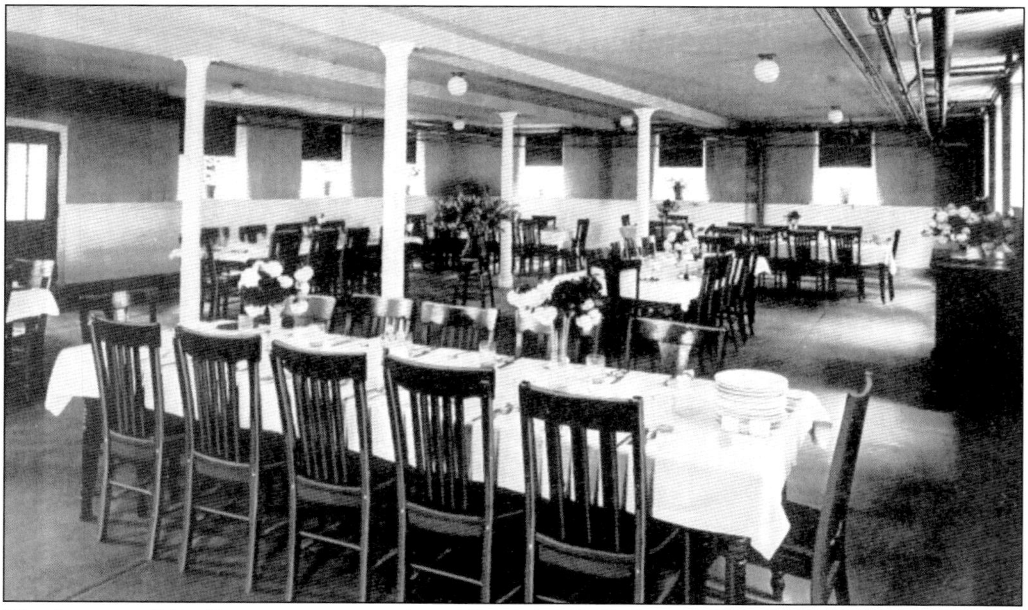

The large, well-lit dining room was where the cadets had their meals. The tables were set with linen tablecloths, and each cadet furnished his own napkins and ring as a part of his table setting. A faculty officer was in charge of each table. The vegetables served were grown in the Onarga Military School gardens and canned in the kitchen. The meats were secured daily from the Chicago packinghouses.

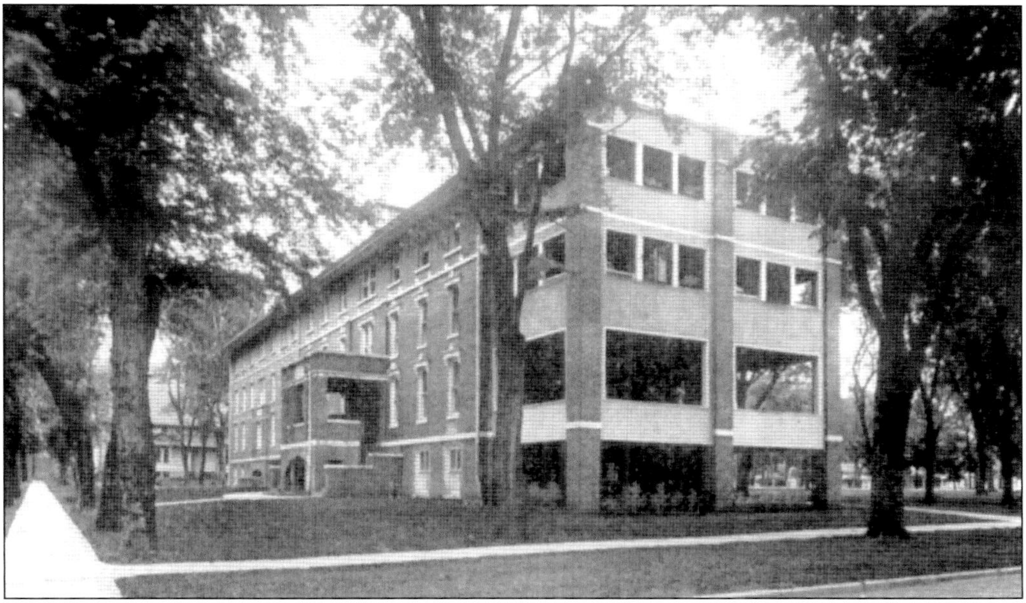

Used in the summer for comfortable sleeping, the sleeping porches were located on the south end of the dormitory. The boys were assigned two to each dormitory room. Rooms were equipped with a bed, dresser, table, chair, and large clothes closet. It was suggested that each cadet bring his own pillow, rugs, and window drapes. The amount of laundry for each boy was limited to 18 pieces per week. All excess laundry was charged accordingly.

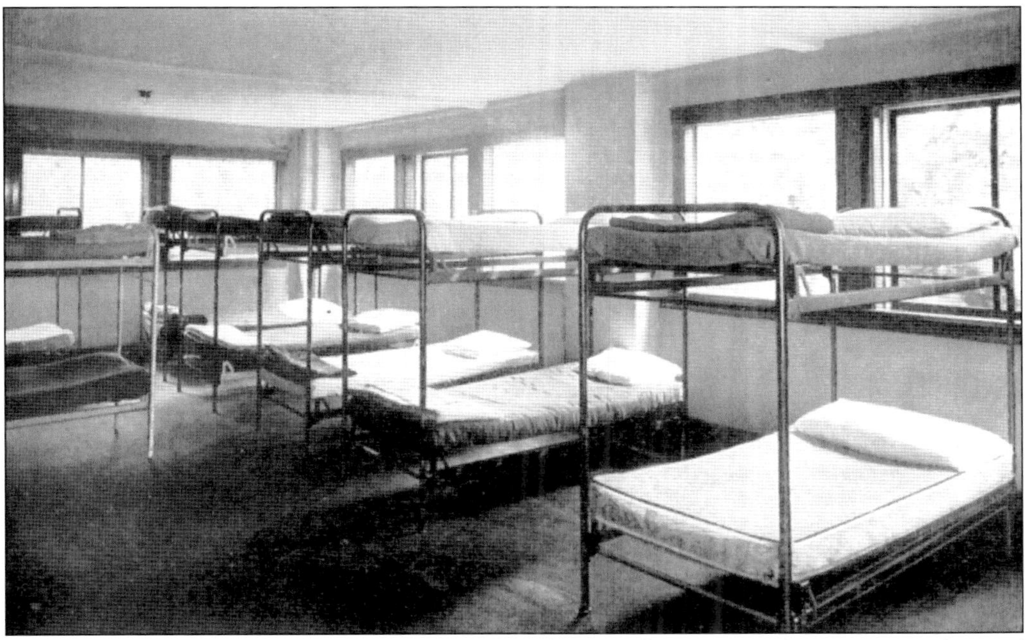

The cadets brought their own wall decorations, such as small pictures and pennants, and a scarf for the dresser. Musical instruments and cameras were permitted, but bicycles, automobiles, or firearms of any kind were prohibited. The Onarga Military School Camera Club was a very popular club for the cadets.

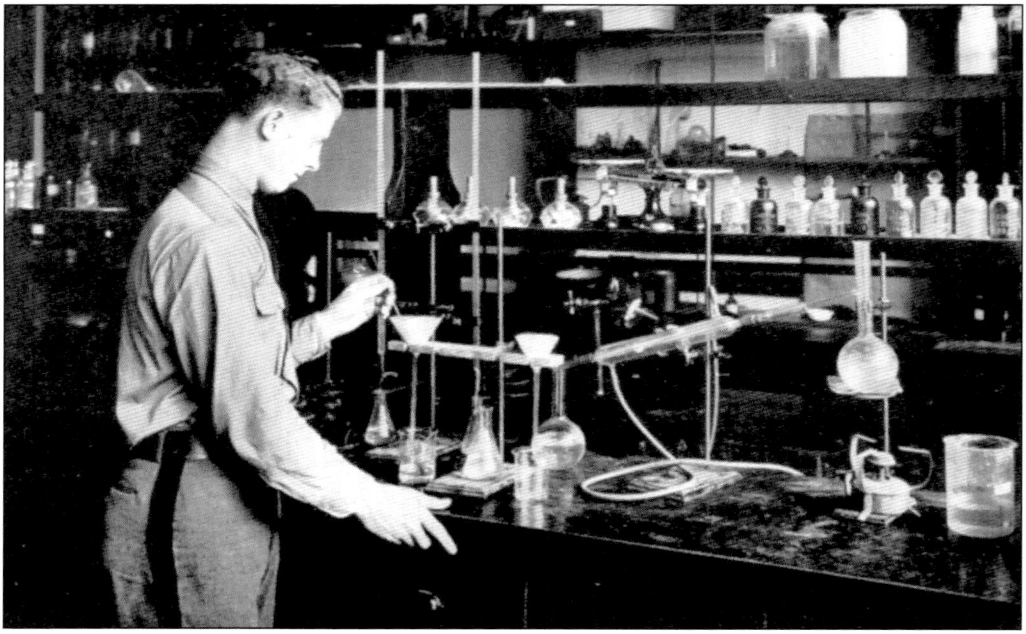

There were no laboratory fees, and schoolbooks were supplied without charge. Students were expected to supply their own notebooks and stationery. In typewriting courses there was a $2 rental fee per month for the typewriter. The school year was divided into four nine-week periods. A progress report to parents was sent at the end of each three weeks.

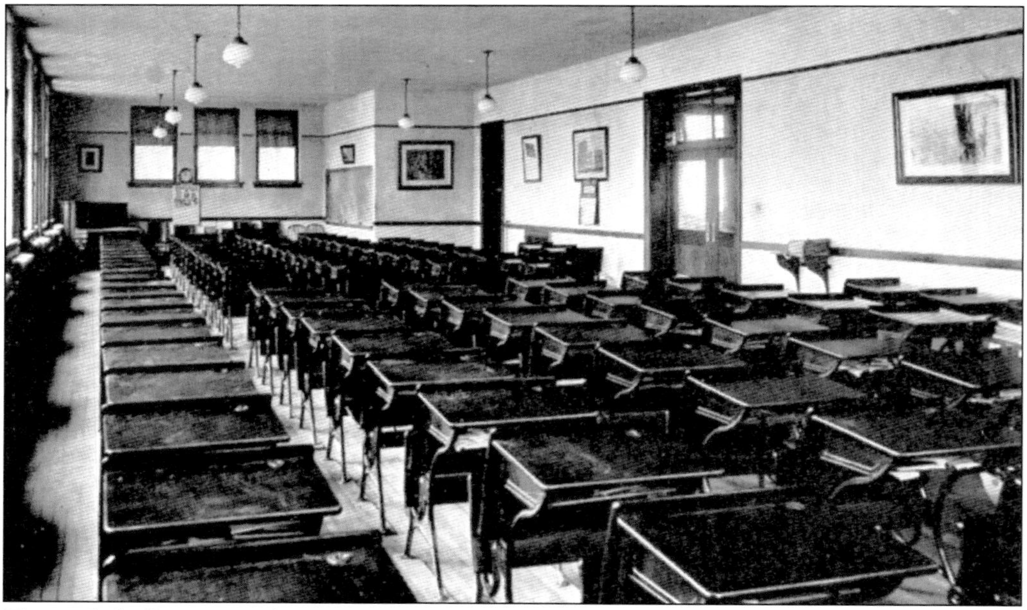

The study hall room was located on the second floor. The discipline was fair but firm. A boy was to do what he was told to do promptly and without question or contradiction. A cadet could be excused from all or part of the evening study hall providing his average in all subjects was above 90 percent. Each student was required to write his parents once a week, the correspondence commonly known as the "Sunday Letter."

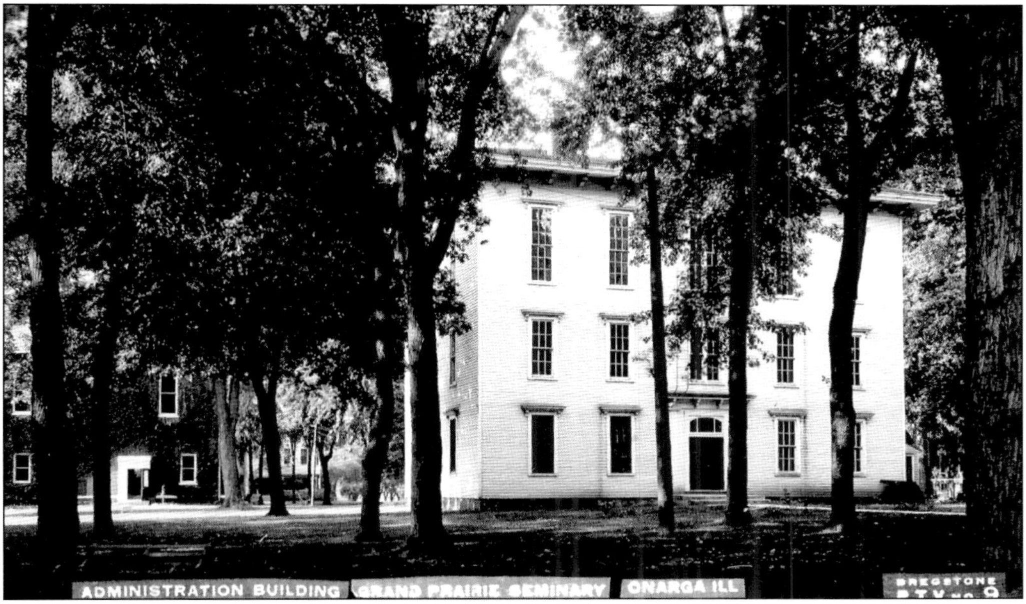

This wooden three-story administration building burned in 1921. It was replaced by the two-story brick structure pictured below. The heating plant, which furnished heat to the administration building, the auditorium, and the dormitory, was located in the administration building. This central plant was entirely fireproof. The new two-story redbrick building was 78 by 48 feet in size. The first floor contained the principal's office and the classrooms while the second floor was recitation rooms, the science laboratory, the study hall, and a fine library. The school brochure stated, "emphasis is placed on development of the physical, intellectual, and Christian character, the embodiment of a useful citizen."

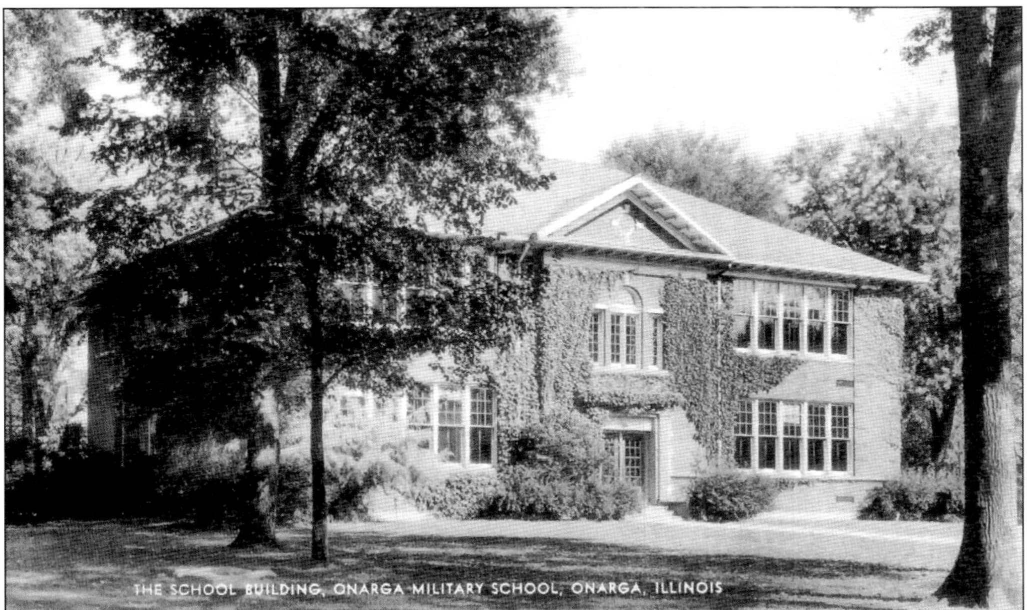

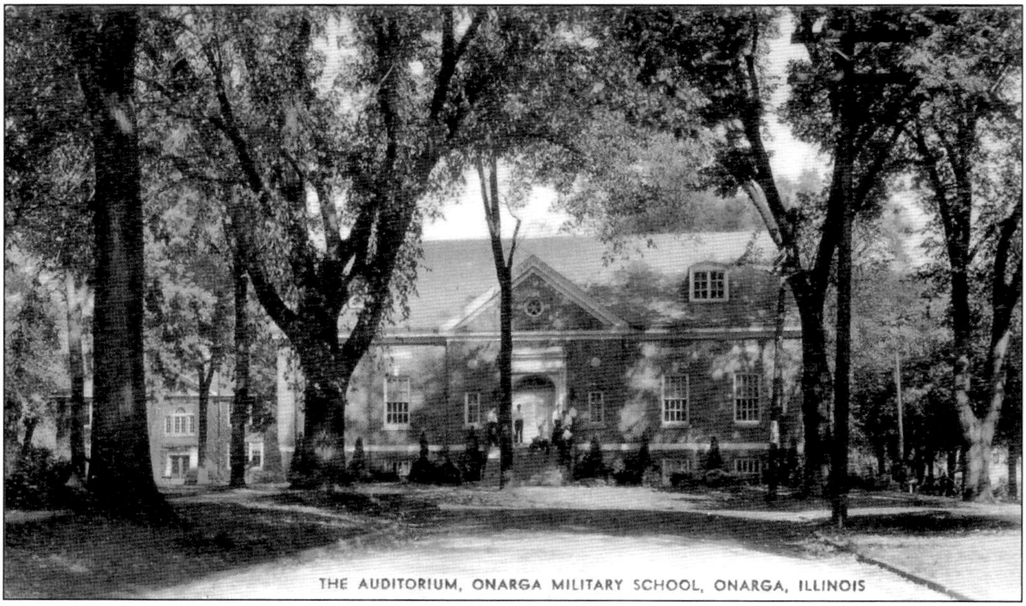

The auditorium burned and was rebuilt in 1933. The new building was a complete recreational center, housing in the lower floor a room with pool tables, two bowling alleys, and an indoor small-bore rifle range. The original auditorium building had been built in 1892 and had a seating capacity of 700.

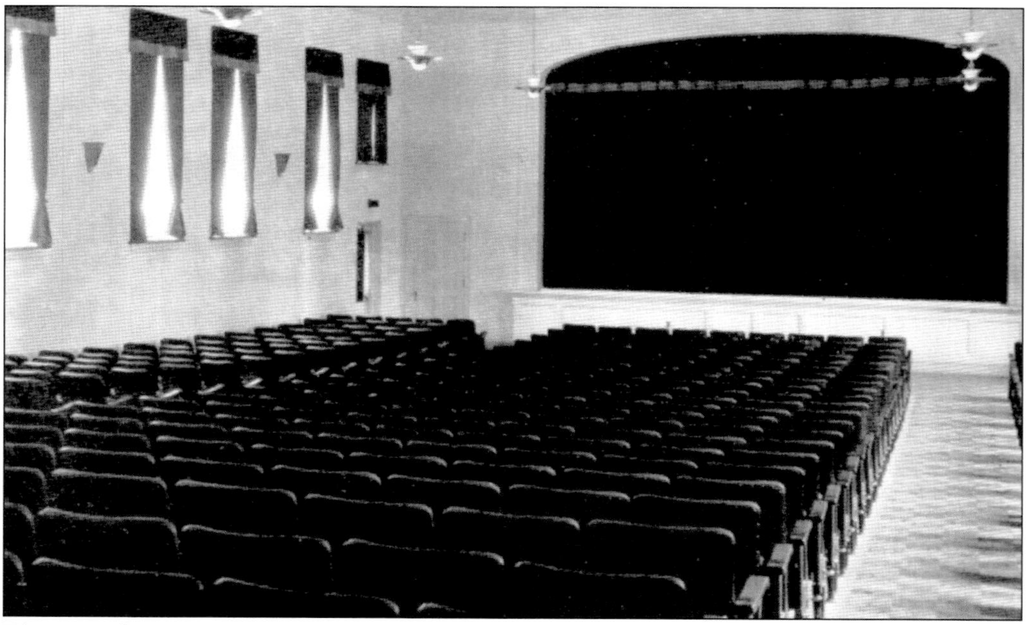

The main floor contained the auditorium room with a seating capacity of 435 people. It was used for stage and motion picture shows, lectures, and recitals. The drama club was organized in 1925, and all plays and productions were performed there. The music department consisted of the Discord Kings, a jazz band, and the Bass Clef Club, which was the cadets' glee club. The cadets also had a full orchestra and marching band.

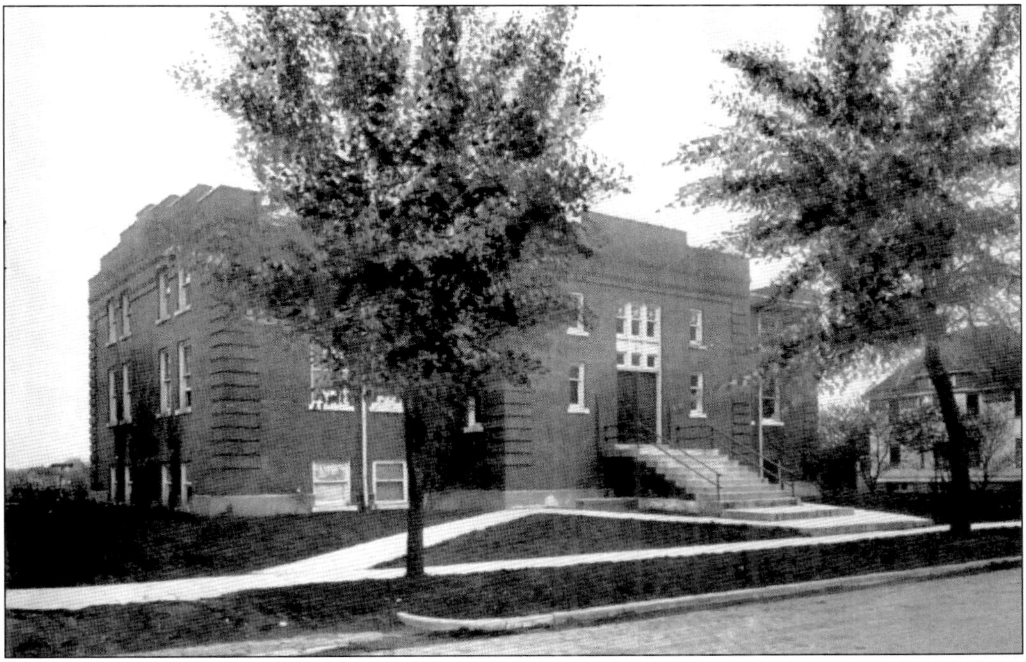

The gymnasium's main floor was 45 by 30 feet. A basketball court and a wrestling room were located in the basement. The gymnasium also housed locker rooms with shower baths. The Onarga Military School played its basketball games at the gymnasium and was a member of the Mid-West Conference. The school colors were gold and purple, and the teams were known as the Yellow Jackets.

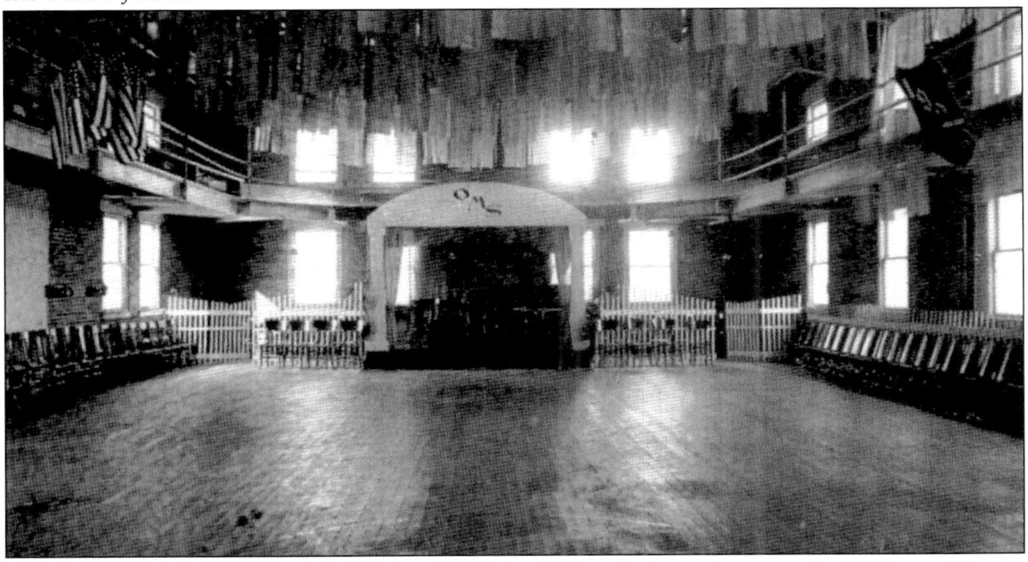

A running track surrounded the floor and was used for indoor track meets. In 1938, an addition and indoor pool were added. Outdoor track meets and football games took place at the athletic field, about two blocks directly south of the gymnasium. The 10-acre field had a football field, baseball diamond, and quarter-mile cinder track. All outdoor athletic contests and all military drills took place at this athletic field.

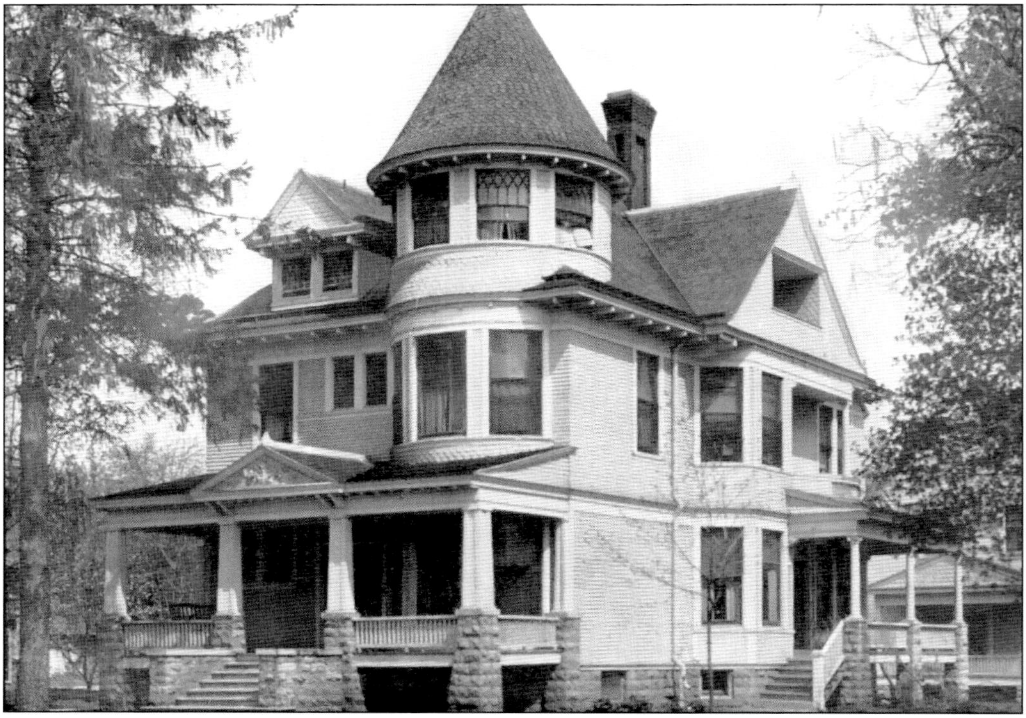

The Rankin house, built in 1892, still stands on the corner of East Lincoln Avenue and North Poplar Street. The house was acquired by Onarga Military School in 1923. It furnished quarters for approximately 25 lower school cadets. The sixth, seventh, and eighth grades were classified as members of the lower school. The upper school encompassed the four years of high school studies.

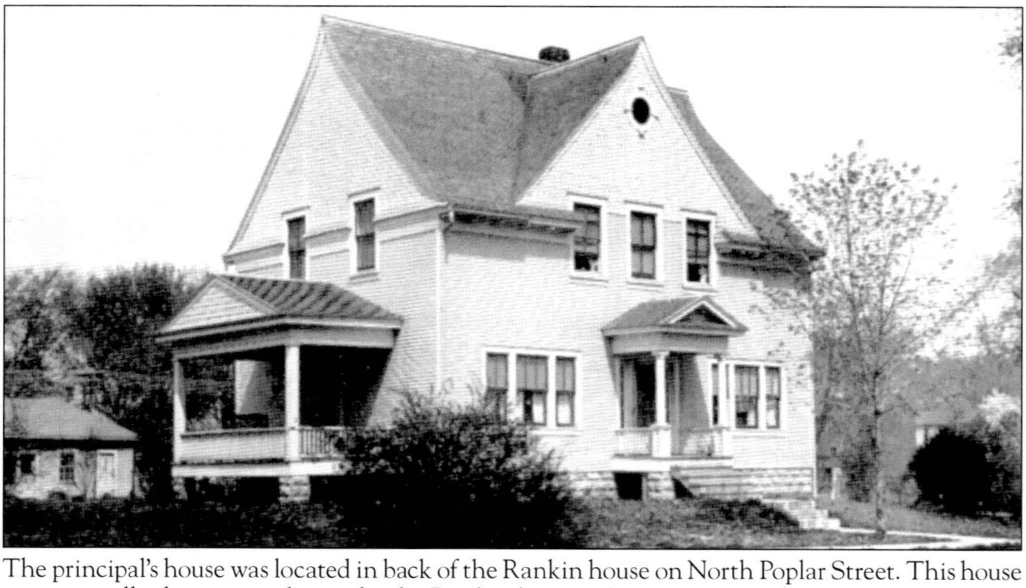

The principal's house was located in back of the Rankin house on North Poplar Street. This house was originally the carriage house for the Rankin home. The infirmary was located directly across the street from the auditorium, south of the campus. The school physician's home was located by the infirmary so he could be available should emergency health issues require his attention.

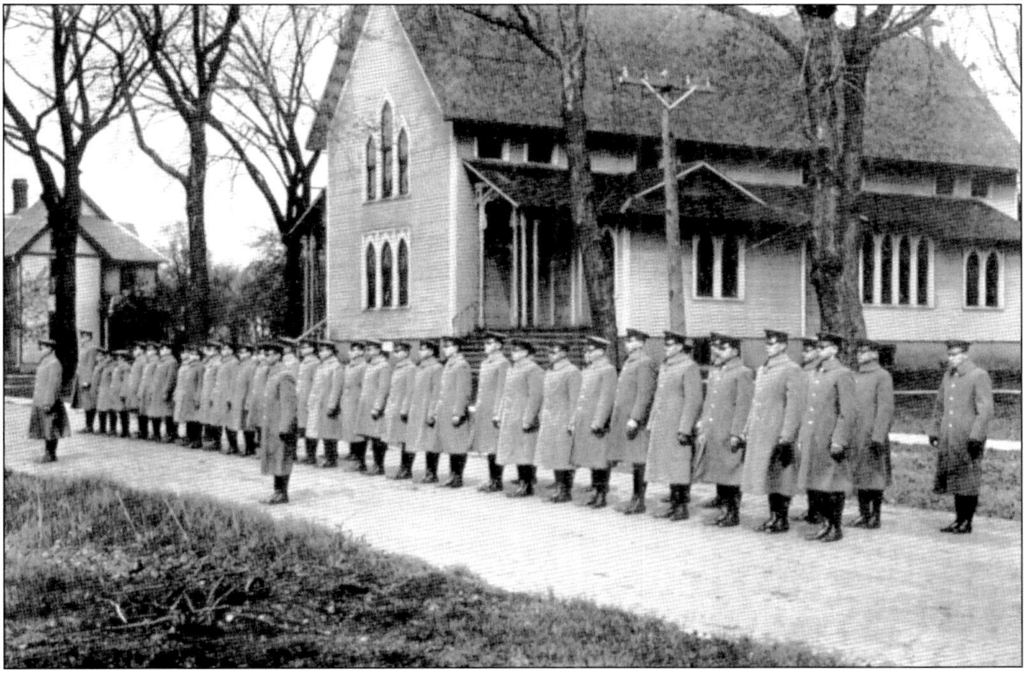

The photograph above was taken in the 1920s behind the old Methodist church. This church was later razed, and a modern brick church was rebuilt. The photograph below was taken in the 1930s on the parade grounds of the school. Military training was varied and was given in infantry drill regulations. These included schooling of the soldier, squad, company, and battalion, together with the ceremonies of battalion parade, inspection, and review. Special attention was given to physical exercises in addition to small-bore rifle firing and theoretical subjects. Onarga Military School was recognized by the State of Illinois by being made a post of the Illinois Guard. All instructors of the school were commissioned therein.

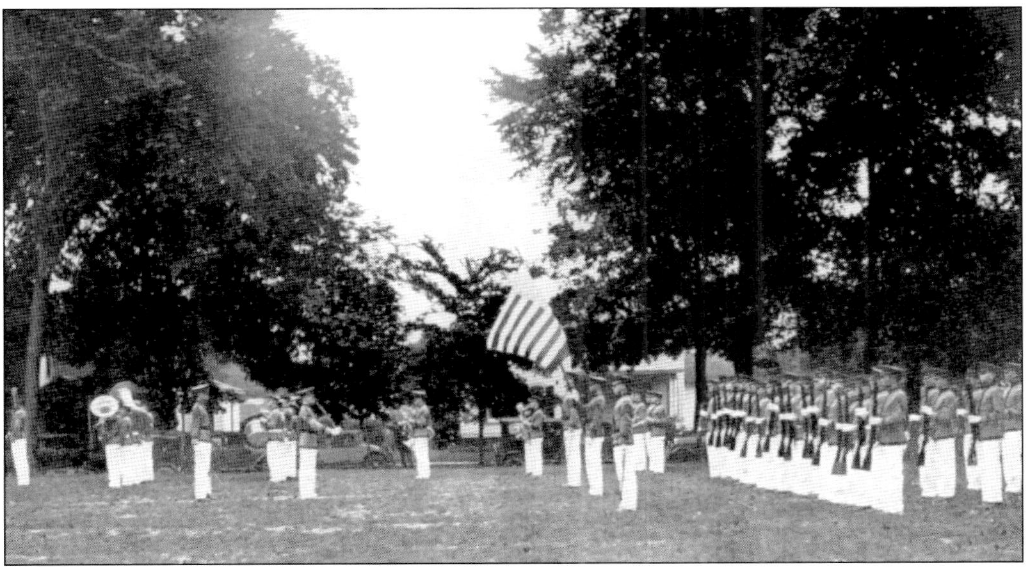

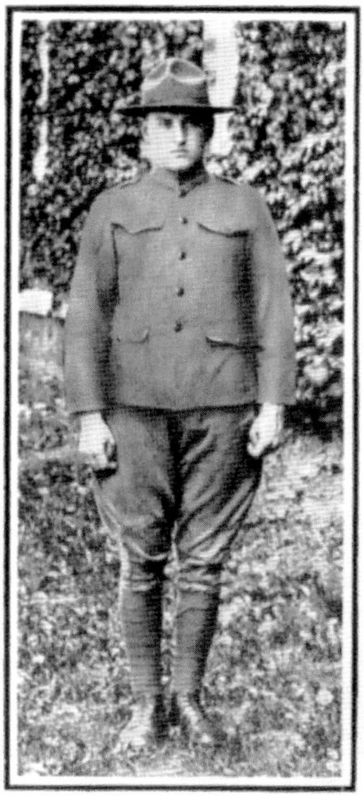

Khaki Uniform

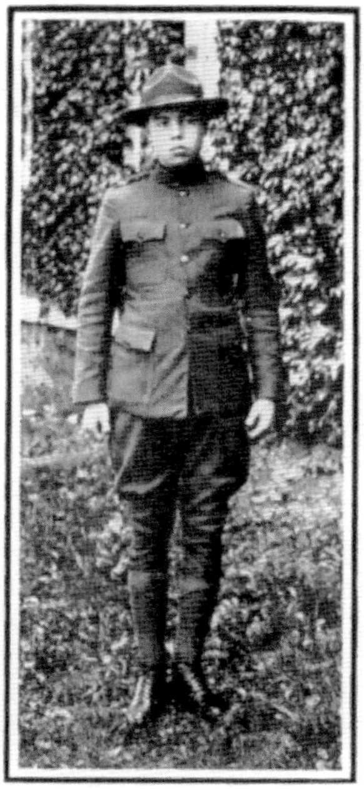

O. D. Wool Service

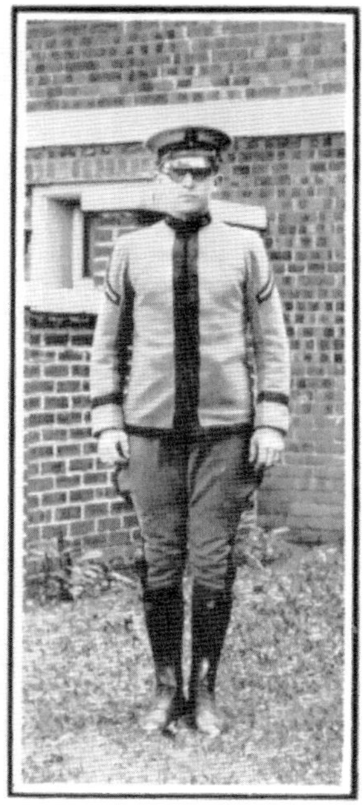

Fatigue Uniform

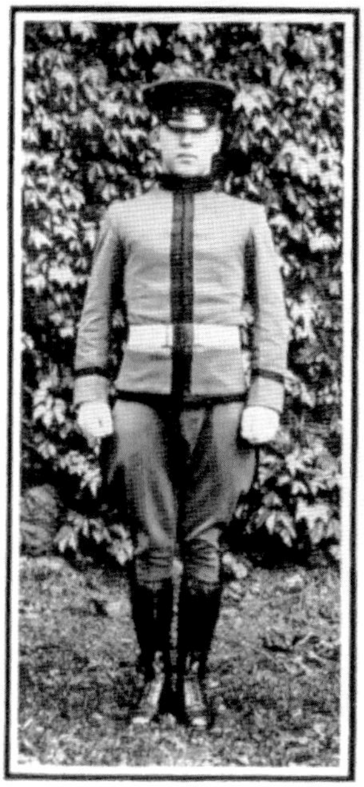

Dress Uniform

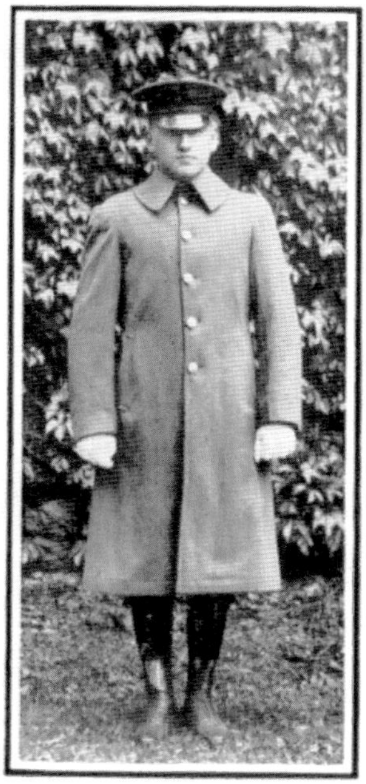

Overcoat

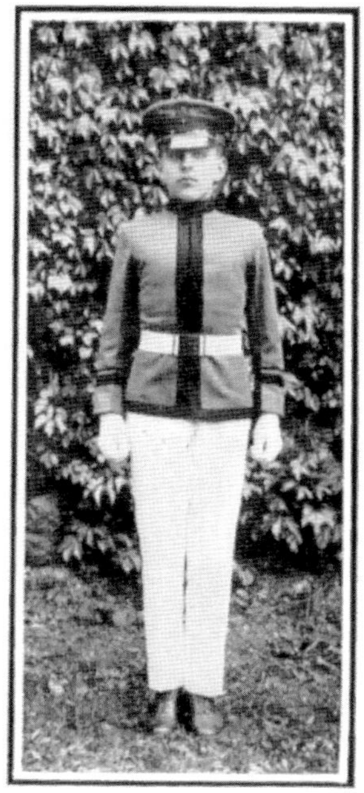

Dress Uniform for Spring

This group of photographs, taken from an old Onarga Military School publication, shows the various uniforms that were worn in the 1920s. Each cadet paid for his own uniforms. The cost for uniforms in the 1930s was $150 yearly. Each cadet also provided his own bed linens, bath items, underclothing, Bible, and two pairs of black shoes.

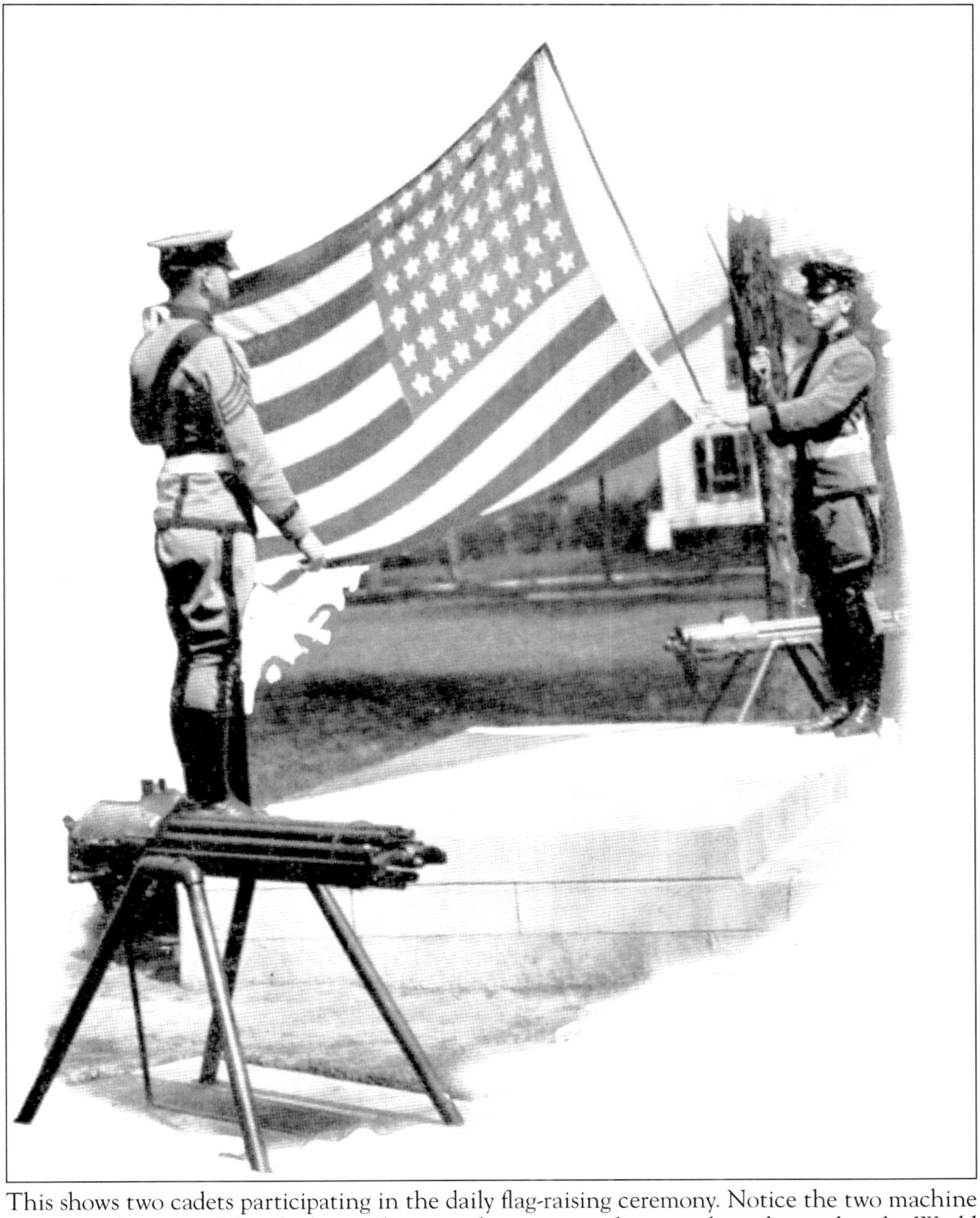

This shows two cadets participating in the daily flag-raising ceremony. Notice the two machine guns on either side of the platform. These are the two guns that were later donated to the World War II scrap metal drive. A strict daily schedule was adhered to: first call at 6:00 a.m.; reveille at 6:25 a.m.; calisthenics at 6:30 a.m.; breakfast at 6:45 a.m.; school from 7:45 to 11:45 a.m.; luncheon at 12:00 p.m.; chapel at 1:00 p.m.; school from 1:20 to 3:00 p.m.; military drill (three periods per week) from 3:05 to 4:00 p.m.; athletics and recreation from 4:00 to 5:45 p.m.; recall from play at 5:45 p.m.; dinner at 6:00 p.m.; study period from 7:00 to 8:45 p.m.; call to quarters at 8:45 p.m.; tattoo at 9:15 p.m.; and taps at 9:45 p.m.

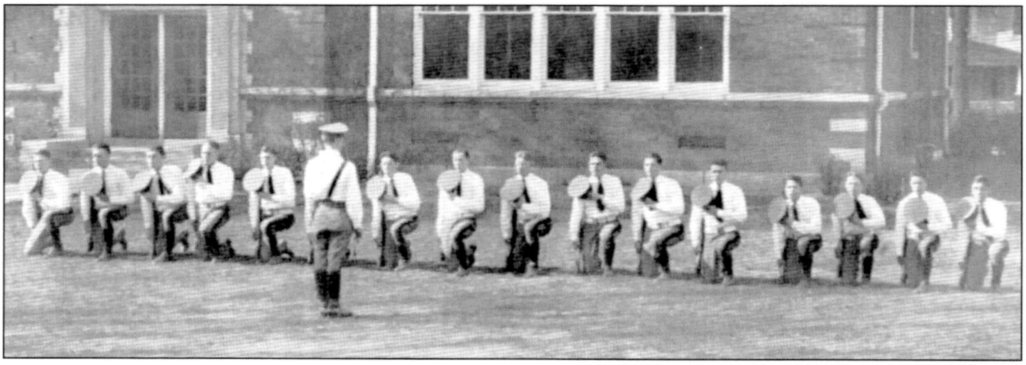

Every spring a crack company of cadets was formed. The company shown here is from the 1930s. The group was composed of those cadets who had shown themselves most adept at the required military drills. It was a distinct honor to be selected for the crack company, and the members were entitled to wear the crack company bar. The school's stated philosophy was that military work did not encroach upon regular school duties in any way. It was simply another one of the means used to bring about the realization of the school's purpose—the development of good character. The prep school band from the 1930s is shown below. Tuition did not include private music instruction. The music department was exceptionally fine and was maintained for every branch of music. Private weekly lessons were given for a small fee.

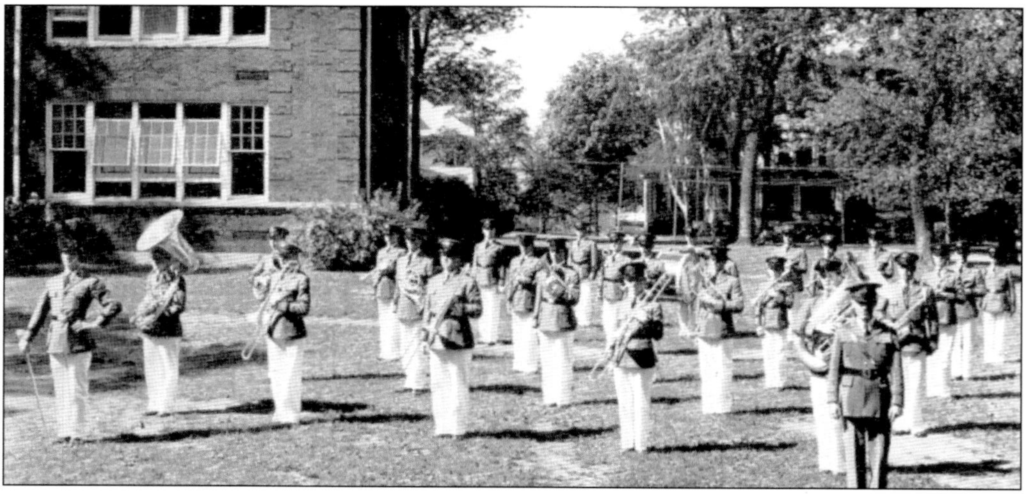

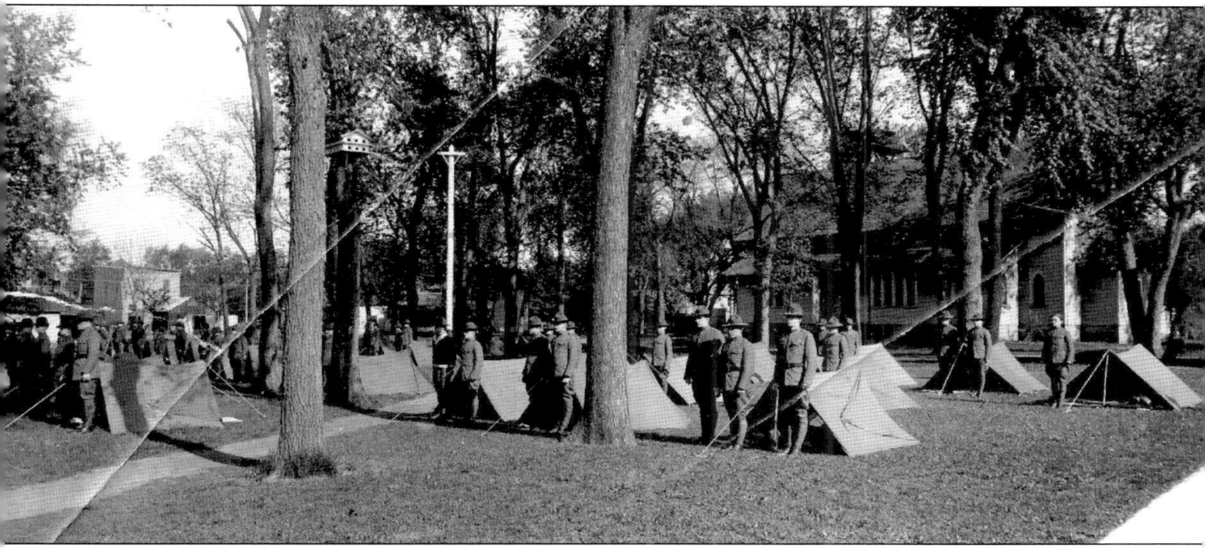

This picture shows some of the activities held during the Onarga Military School Dad's Day celebration weekend held in the fall. The photograph is from the mid-1920s. Dad's Day weekend was a very special celebration giving the cadets the opportunity to show off their military and academic skills for their fathers. The cadets are shown on the campus grounds in their olive drab wool service uniforms ready for inspection and a night in the field. Notice the old wooden Methodist church in the background.

Alma Mater

I

In the township of Onarga
Stands our dear old school,
We are jealous of its record
And its Golden Rule.
It's spirit ever has been valiant,
It's teachers always true;
Here we stand with heads uncovered,
Looking up to you.

II

In our conduct we'll be upright,
Loyal let us be,
Never giving up or failing,
Thinking e'er of thee.
Truth and light shall be our watchword,
Conquer and Prevail;
Hail to thee! Our Alma Mater
O. M. S., All hail.

James S. McAnulty, '22

The poem "Alma Mater" was written by James S. McAnulty, class of 1922. The enrollment at Onarga Military School was then 80 cadets. By 1941, the registration was 126 cadets. In 1953, Col. Lyle Bittinger retired after 34 years as superintendent and Col. L. E. Adams was employed. The philosophy of the Onarga Military School was stated this way: "We take vital personal interest in each boy. Careful attention is given to the cultivation of gentlemanly manners and conduct. We appeal to the best that is in the boy—to his sense of honor and manhood, and, by precept and example, strive to inculcate in him a desire for that courtesy and grace which are the marks of a gentleman." That was an Onarga Military School cadet.

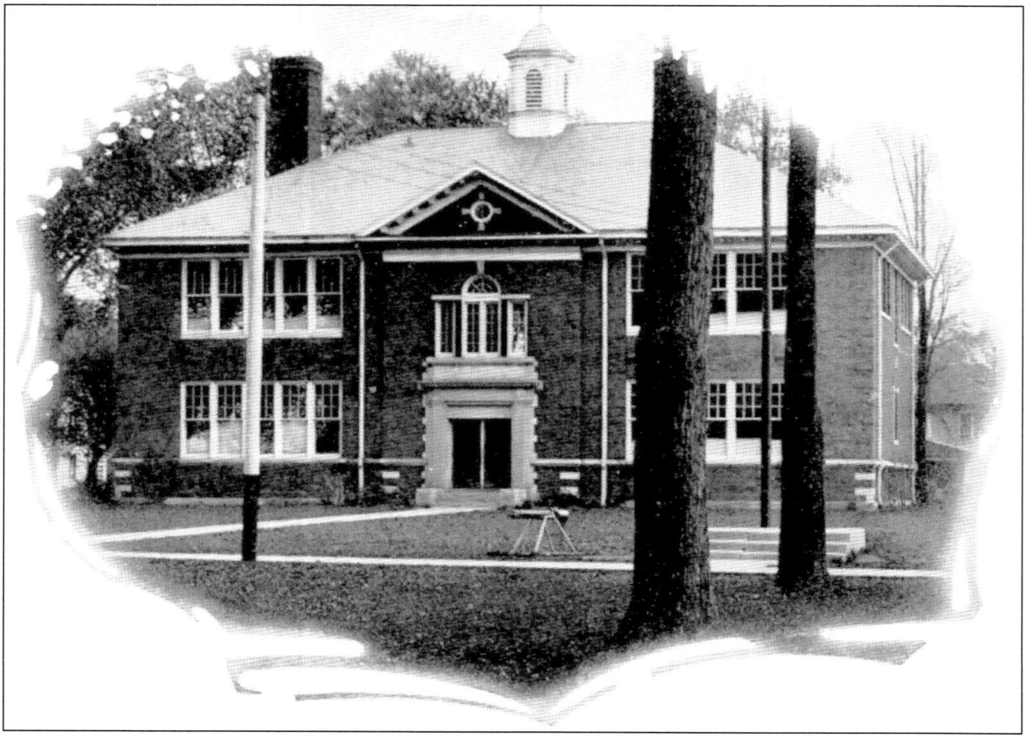

Three

Pinkerton's Larch Farm and Timothy Webster

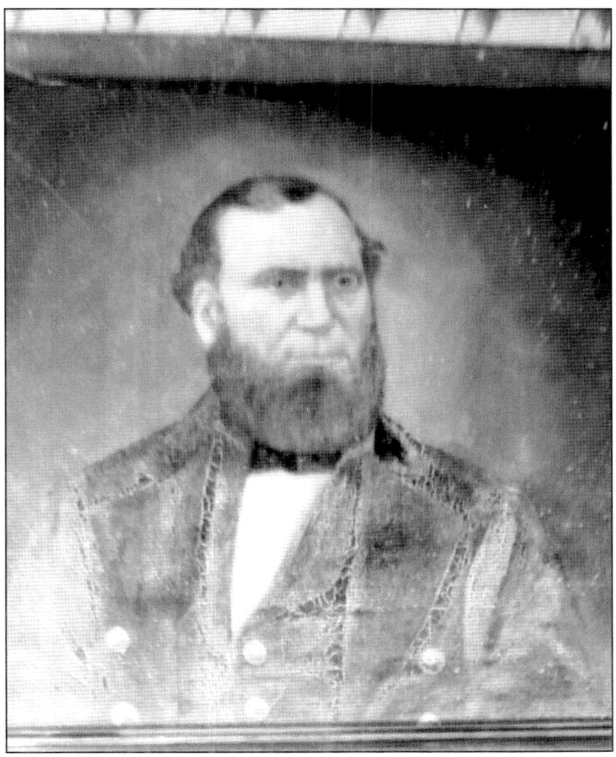

Allan Pinkerton was born in Scotland, the son of a Glasgow police sergeant. He settled in Chicago and in 1846 became the city's first detective. In 1850, he opened his own detective agency, the forerunner of the world-renowned Pinkerton Detective Agency. In 1861, Pinkerton was called upon to protect president-elect Abraham Lincoln from assassins believed to be planning to assassinate the president as he travelled through Baltimore to Washington, D.C. Shortly after the start of the Civil War, Pinkerton was instrumental in founding the United States Secret Service and was appointed by the federal government as its chief.

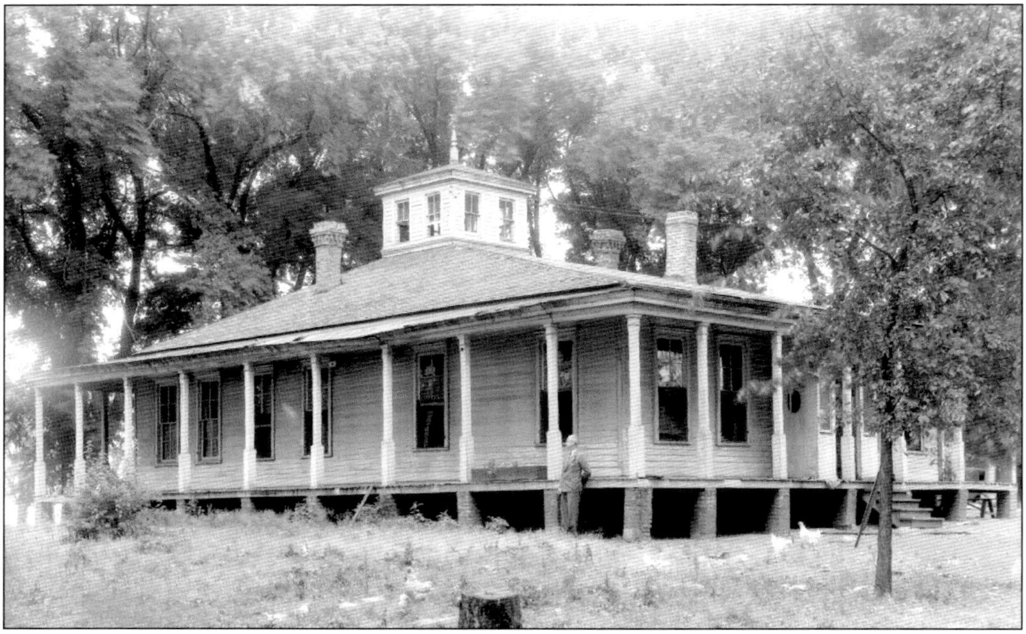

In 1864, Allan Pinkerton purchased a tract of land about one mile north of Onarga on the main line of the Illinois Central Railroad. Shown above, the home he built—called the Larches or the Larch Farm because of the thousands of Larch trees that Pinkerton imported from Scotland and planted on the property—was completed in 1880. The original square building had a veranda on all four sides. Directly above the small room in the center of the attic was a cupola, which had a short flagpole on top. The structure had six rooms, three on each side of a wide hall that ran the entire length of the building. One of the many outbuildings on the grounds of Pinkerton's Larch Farm was the wine house, called the Snuggery. Shown below, it was built partially underground and was connected with the villa by an underground passage. The sloping walls of the ceiling were covered with portraits of heroic Scots attired in kilts.

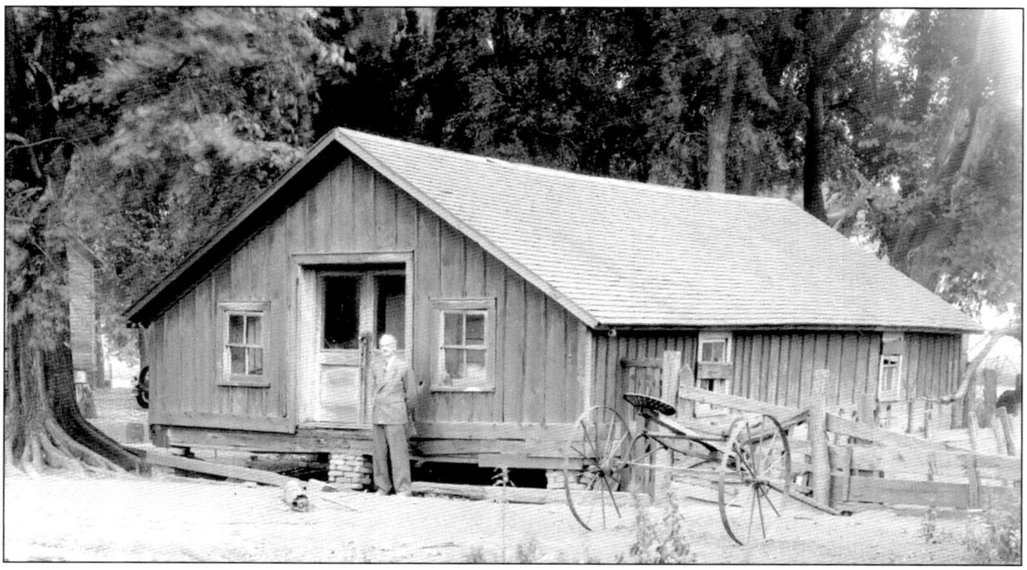

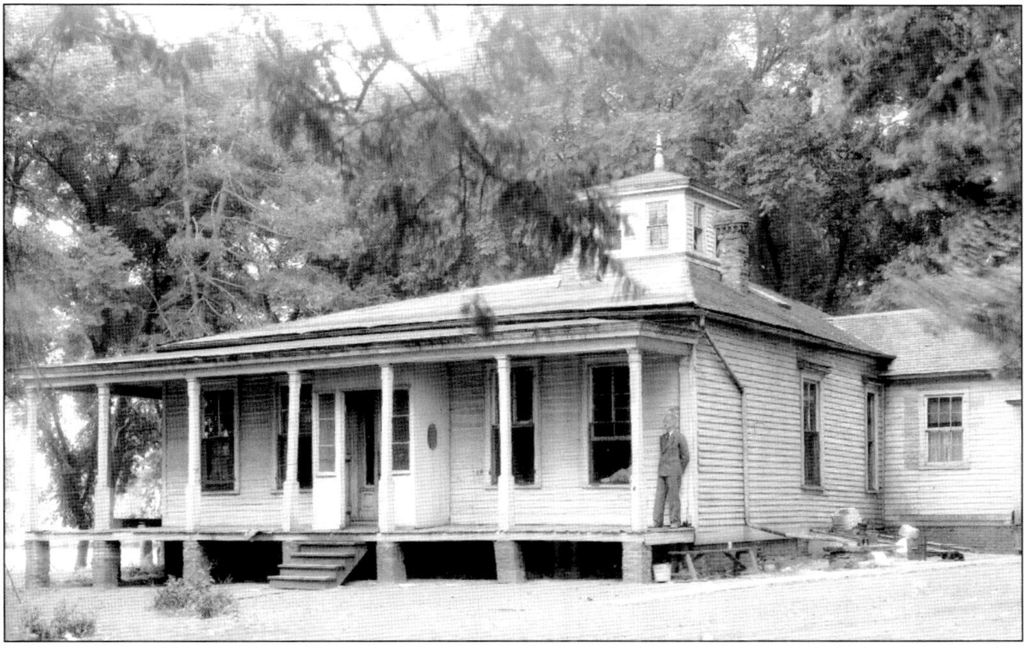

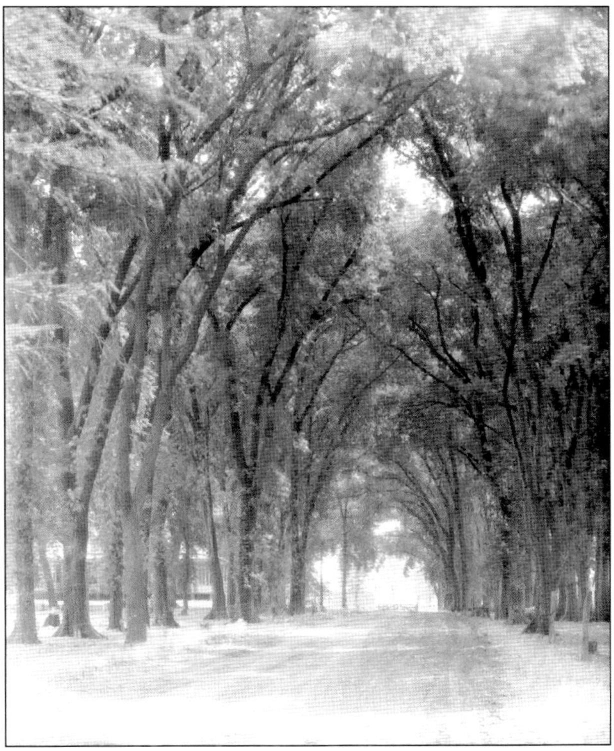

The main building at the Larch Farm, which Pinkerton affectionately called the villa, became one of the most beautiful showplaces of the day. It was a comfortable, although not elaborately built home. In decorating the home and landscaping the property, he spared no expense. The villa was never used as a family home but was the scene of many a high carnival when he went there with his cronies for days of relaxation. Leaders in sports, the stage, writers of note, and painters of national reputation would gather as Pinkerton's guests. Approaching from the west, the long lane from the road to the villa was lined with hundreds of larch trees.

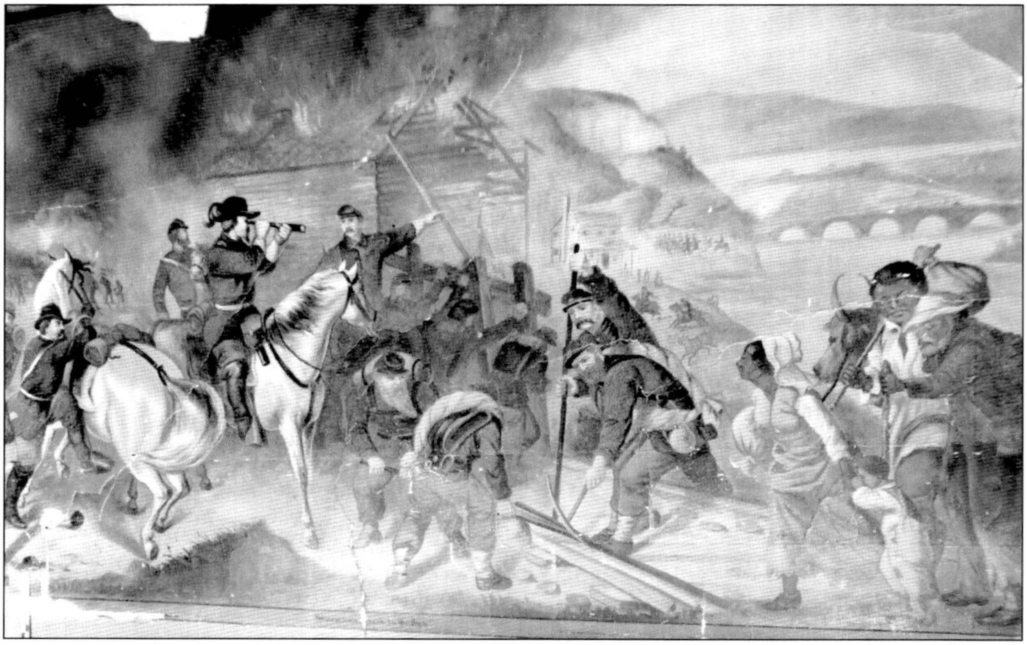

The interior of Allan Pinkerton's Larch Farm villa was lavishly furnished, and murals covered the walls. Along each side of a wide hall that ran the entire length of the main building were paintings of battle scenes and officers of the Civil War, the work having been done by F. W. Seyer in 1882. The two murals shown here are titled "Sherman's March to the Sea" and "Gen. McClellan and Staff."

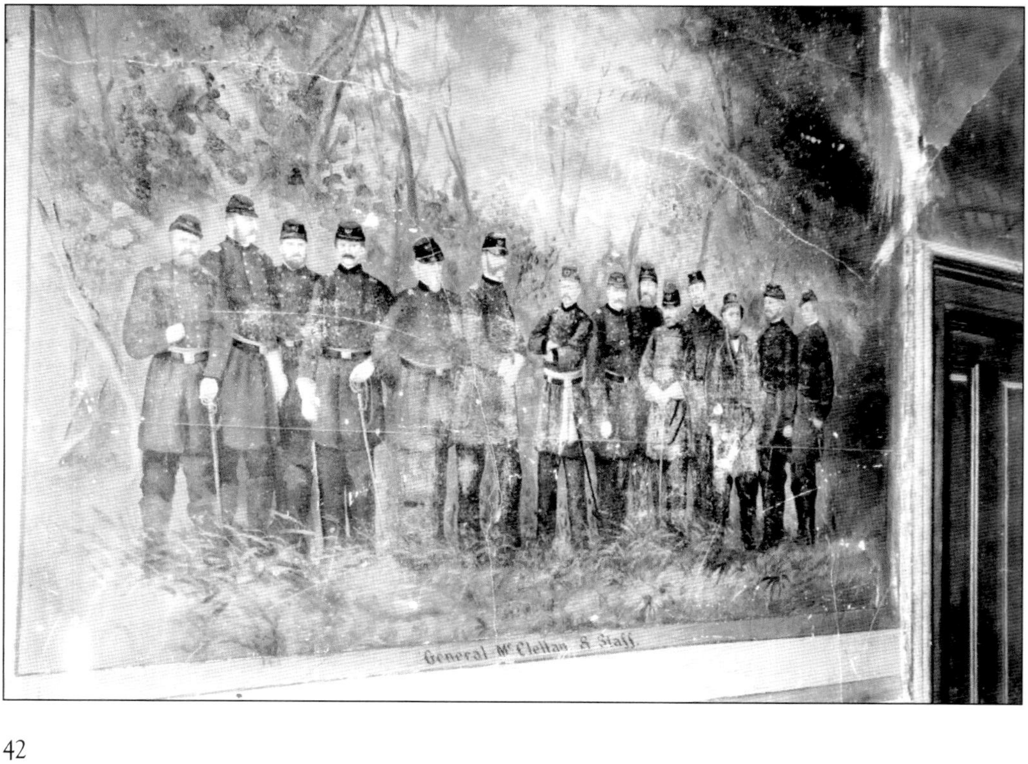

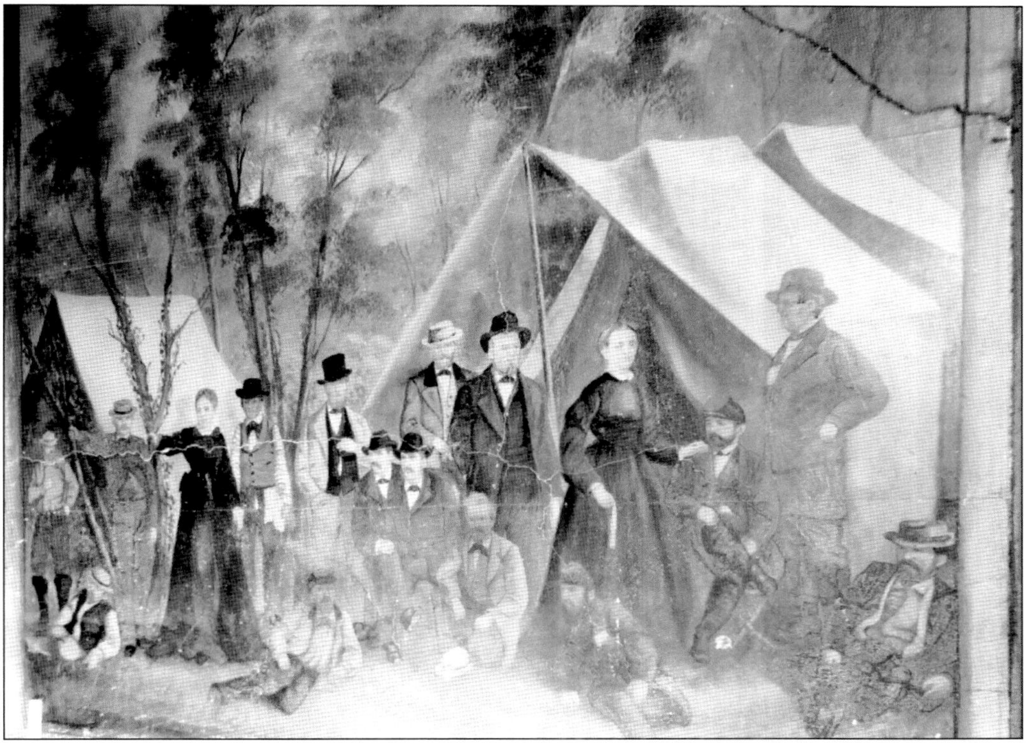

This mural is titled "The Secret Service." The detective agency that Pinkerton formed at the start of the Civil War was the forerunner of the Secret Service. Pinkerton developed several investigative techniques that are still used today. Among them are shadowing (surveillance of a suspect) and assuming a role (undercover work). At the time of Pinkerton's death in 1884, he was working on a system that would centralize all criminal identification records. During the latter years of Pinkerton's life, he wrote at least 10 books. Probably the best known of these books was *The Spy of the Rebellion*, published in 1883, one year before his death. Pinkerton did not physically write the books attributed to him, but dictated the text to an assistant who, after editing and getting Pinkerton's approval, wrote the actual text to be submitted to a publisher.

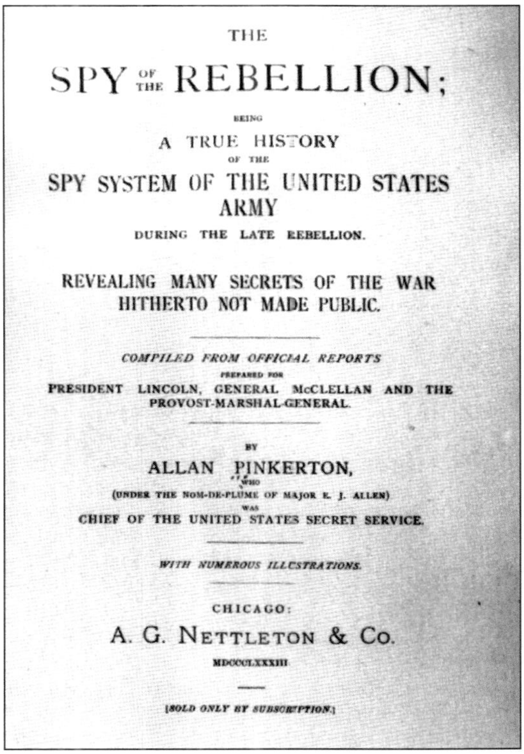

THE

SPY OF THE REBELLION;

BEING

A TRUE HISTORY

OF THE

SPY SYSTEM OF THE UNITED STATES ARMY

DURING THE LATE REBELLION.

REVEALING MANY SECRETS OF THE WAR HITHERTO NOT MADE PUBLIC.

COMPILED FROM OFFICIAL REPORTS

PREPARED FOR

PRESIDENT LINCOLN, GENERAL McCLELLAN AND THE PROVOST-MARSHAL-GENERAL.

BY

ALLAN PINKERTON,

WHO

(UNDER THE NOM-DE-PLUME OF MAJOR E. J. ALLEN)

WAS

CHIEF OF THE UNITED STATES SECRET SERVICE.

WITH NUMEROUS ILLUSTRATIONS.

CHICAGO:

A. G. NETTLETON & Co.

MDCCCLXXXIII

(SOLD ONLY BY SUBSCRIPTION.)

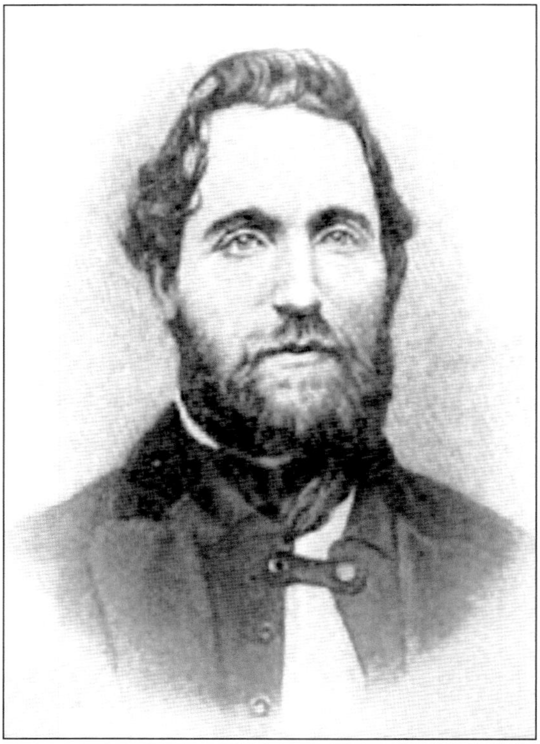

Timothy Webster was Allan Pinkerton's spy of the rebellion and most famous agent in the Civil War. It was Webster who had uncovered the 1861 plot to assassinate Pres. Abraham Lincoln. In 1858, Pinkerton suggested that Webster move his family closer to the Chicago office and suggested that Onarga, a small rural town, would be ideal. Webster moved his family to a farm west of Onarga where he could easily commute to the Chicago office via the Illinois Central Railroad. In 1862, while on a mission to Richmond, Virginia, Webster's identity was revealed by two other agents. He was arrested, tried, and hung on April 29, 1862. In 1871, Pinkerton sent agents to locate Webster's body and return it to Onarga for burial. He shares a double tombstone in the Onarga cemetery with his son, Timothy Webster Jr., who was also killed in the Civil War.

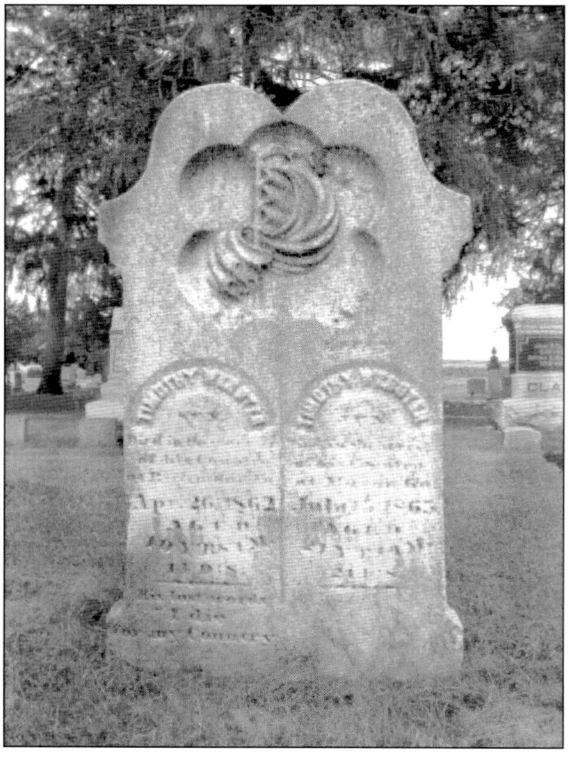

Four

School Days

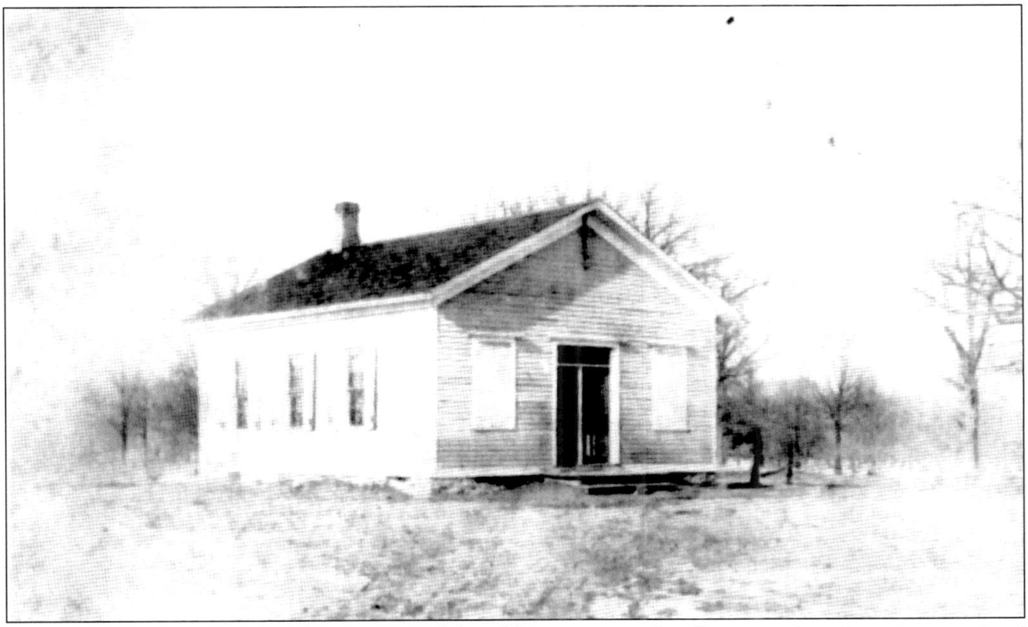

Many people have wonderful memories of the old one-room schoolhouses, the education received there, the teachers, and the friendships. Such rural schools, 20 in all, made up Onarga Unit District No. 1. The photograph above is of the Davis School located southeast of Onarga. Other schools in Onarga Unit District No. 1 were Longview, Grove, Ridgeville, Parker, Hames, Brown, Farley, Brooks, Grob, Oak Grove, Ramsey, Strezey, West, Hitchcock, Ward, Prairie Chapel, Hale, Holz, and Del Rey. The children who lived too far away to walk often rode a pony or brought a sulky or horse-drawn kid hack.

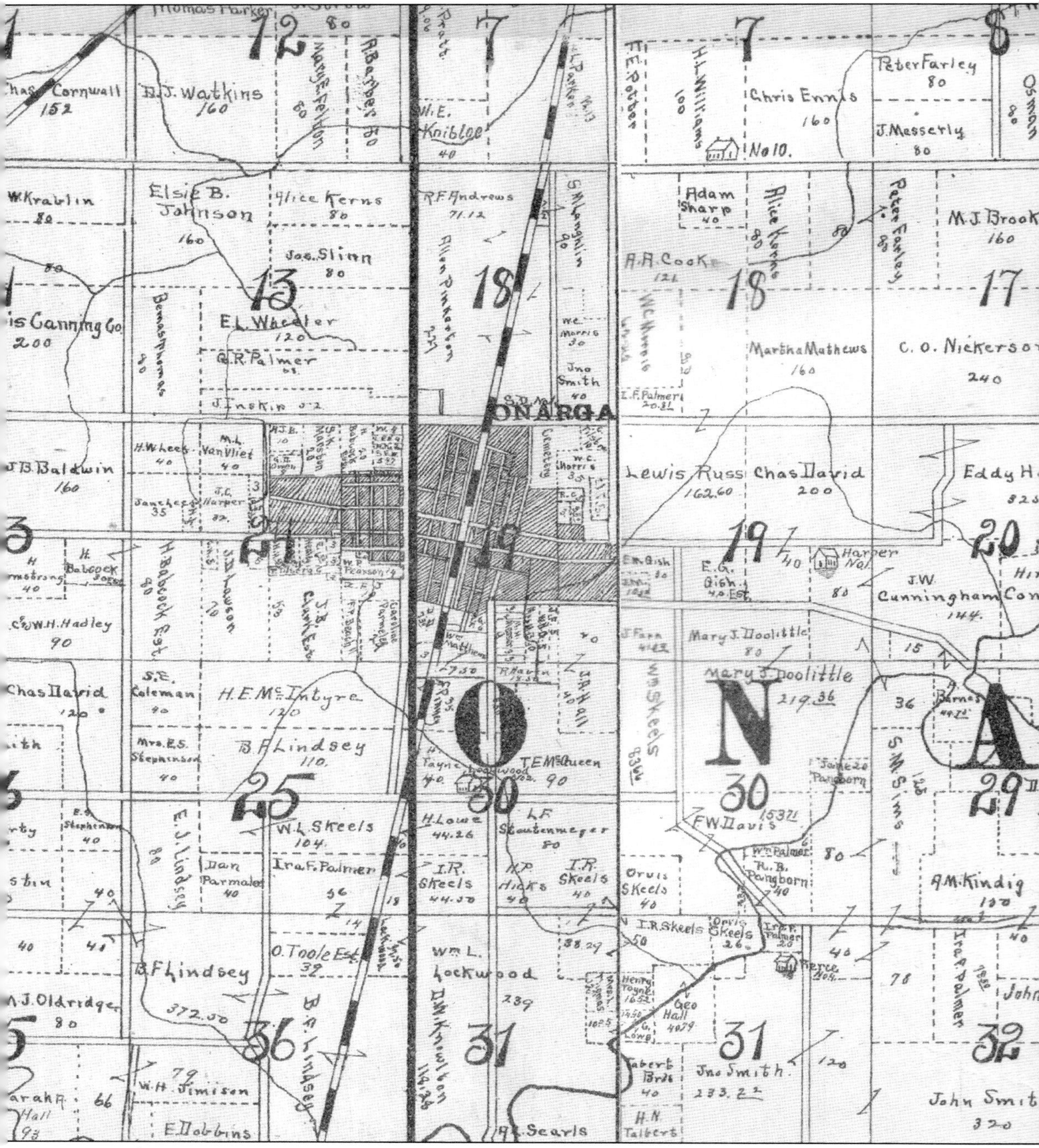

Teaching in a one-room schoolhouse required planning. General exercises, agriculture, nature study, current events, and sanitation may have started the day as well as learning a song and memory selections. Lessons included reading, writing, spelling, arithmetic, history, geography, and natural sciences. Teachers also taught sewing and cooking. A teacher would have to be sure she was spending enough time with each of her classes. The older students helped the younger children. This not only helped the teacher be more efficient, but it also reinforced the lessons

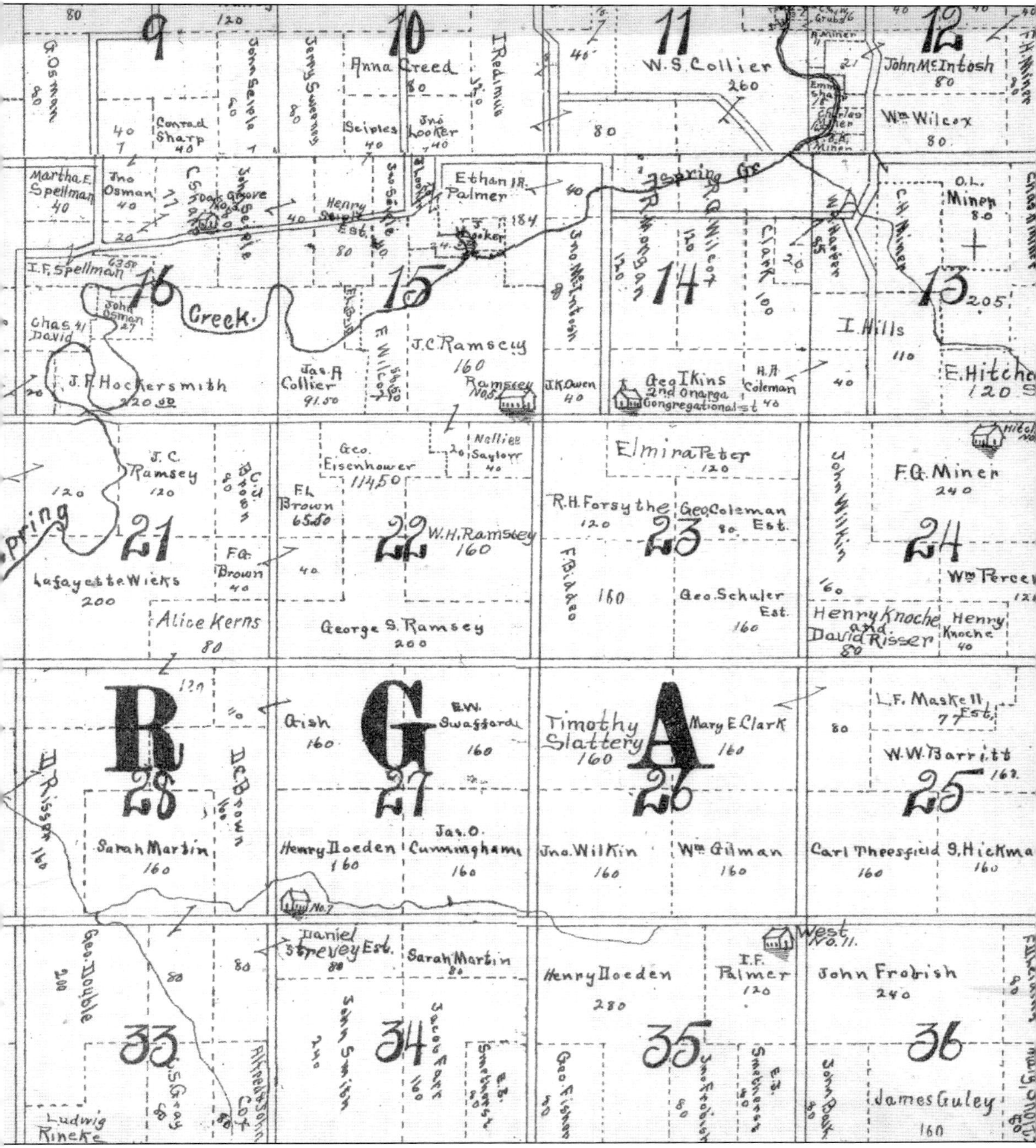

that the older students had already learned, and it gave younger students one-on-one attention. Sometimes a teacher would prepare a stew or soup for lunch. She took care of her students like they were her own children—always concerned with their health and welfare. This plat map from the 1920s shows the location of all country schools in existence at the time. They are marked by the small schoolhouse building symbols.

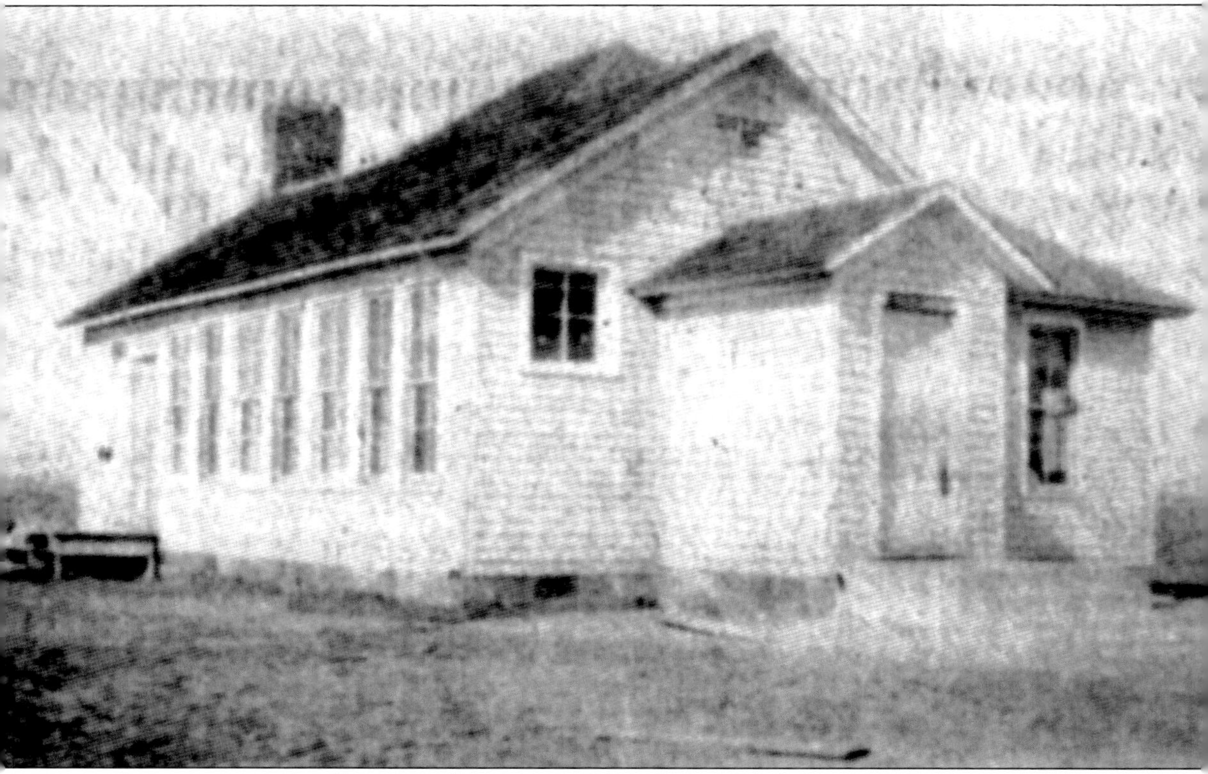

The one-room schoolhouse, such as Prairie Chapel pictured above, served as a center of rural town activities, a place where families gathered. Learning was not isolated, but a part of the little country community. There were boxed lunches and socials. These socials helped the school raise money for books or other necessary supplies. At the end of the year, students would present a program for the community. These programs included plays and recitations of poems. Other special events included spelling bees and arithmetic matches. Christmas was a very special time. Sheets were draped against the back wall of the room with *Merry Christmas* painted on them and decorated with tinsel. Homemade ornaments were used to decorate the tree. Students would build a stage and place it in the front of the classroom so everyone could see, even the little ones. Music was a very important part of the Christmas program. And, if there was enough money that year, candy was ordered from a mail-order catalog for the children.

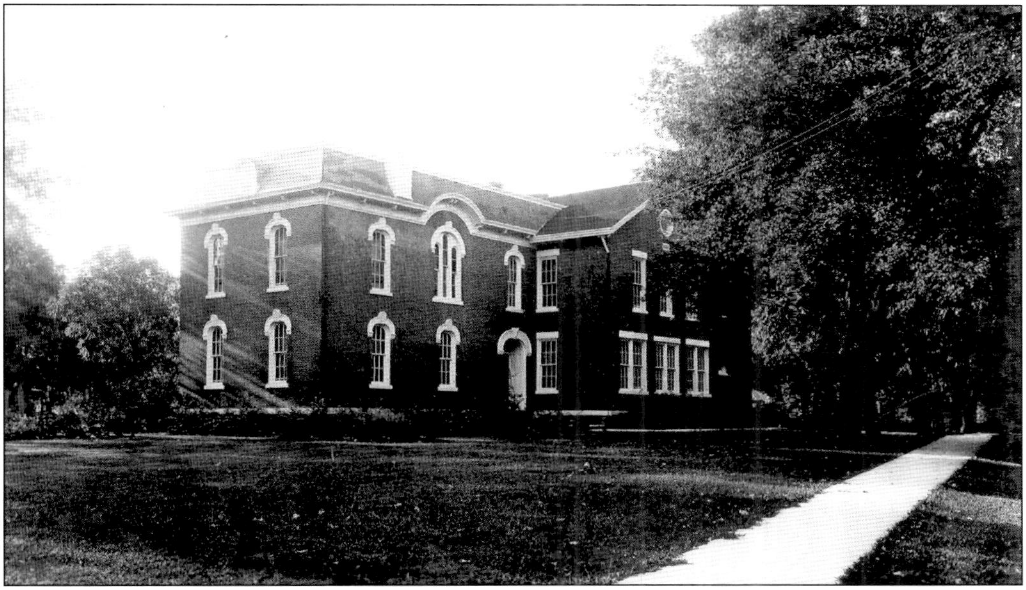

The first village school was a brick schoolhouse built in 1867. In 1872, F. P. Beach was contracted to build an addition to the north. It was 25 feet by 40 feet and two stories high with a mansard roof, which was the fashion in the day. The completed cost was $4,189.92, and the addition had a seating capacity of 275. It was at this time that the principal's room was arranged upstairs. In 1898, an addition was added to the south. After this addition, the 1867 cornerstone, which faced the south, was moved to the west side of the building, thus changing the direction that the building faced. This addition cost $3,575. A gymnasium was added on the south and the floors were rebuilt in 1939.

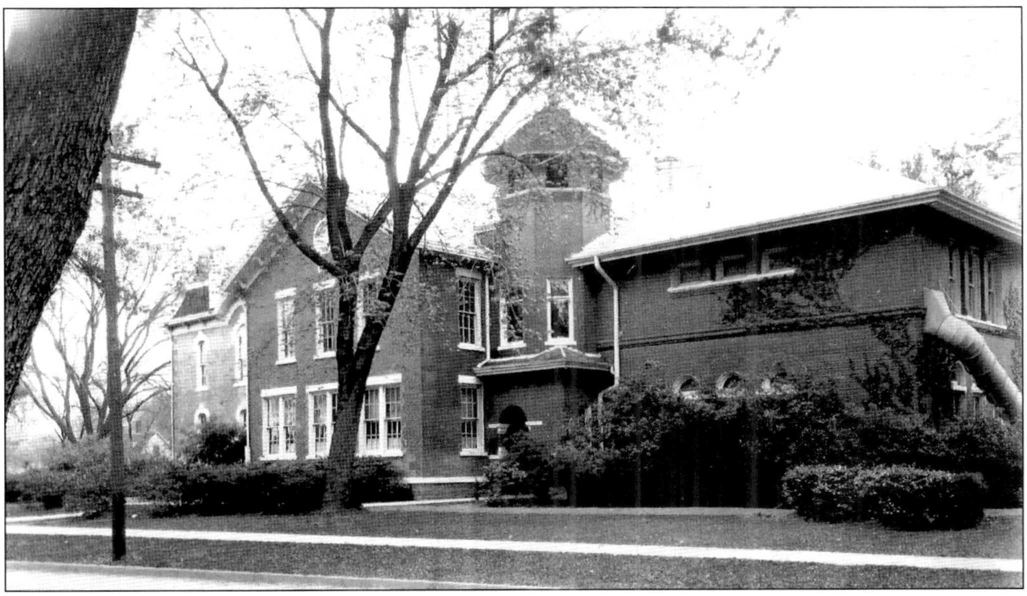

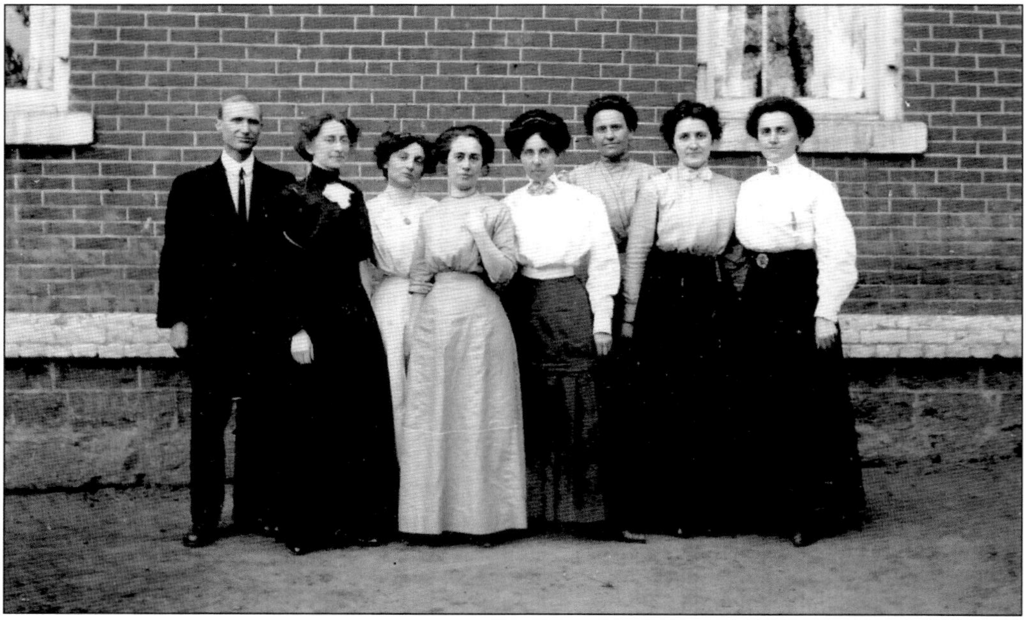

Both of these photographs were taken in front of the public school building. Above, the public school teachers for 1911–1912 were Professor LeMarr; Miss Jennings, high school teacher; Miss Marganthales, first grade; Miss Graham, second and third grades; Miss Foster, third and fourth grades; Miss Cook, fifth and sixth grades; and Miss Rush, seventh and eighth grades. The photograph below was taken in 1941 and shows the grade school rhythm band.

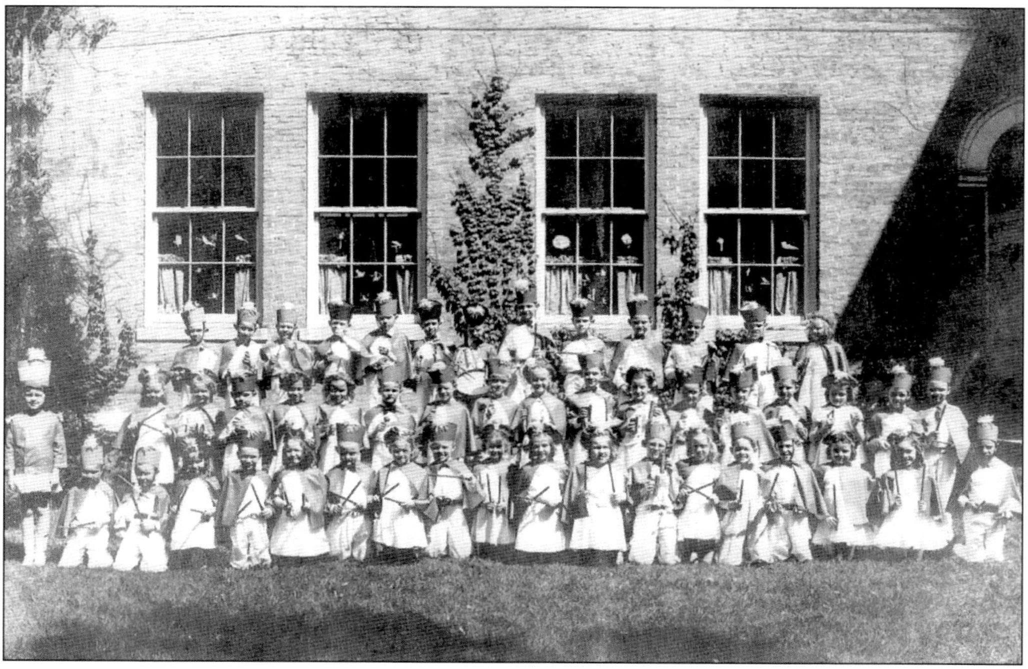

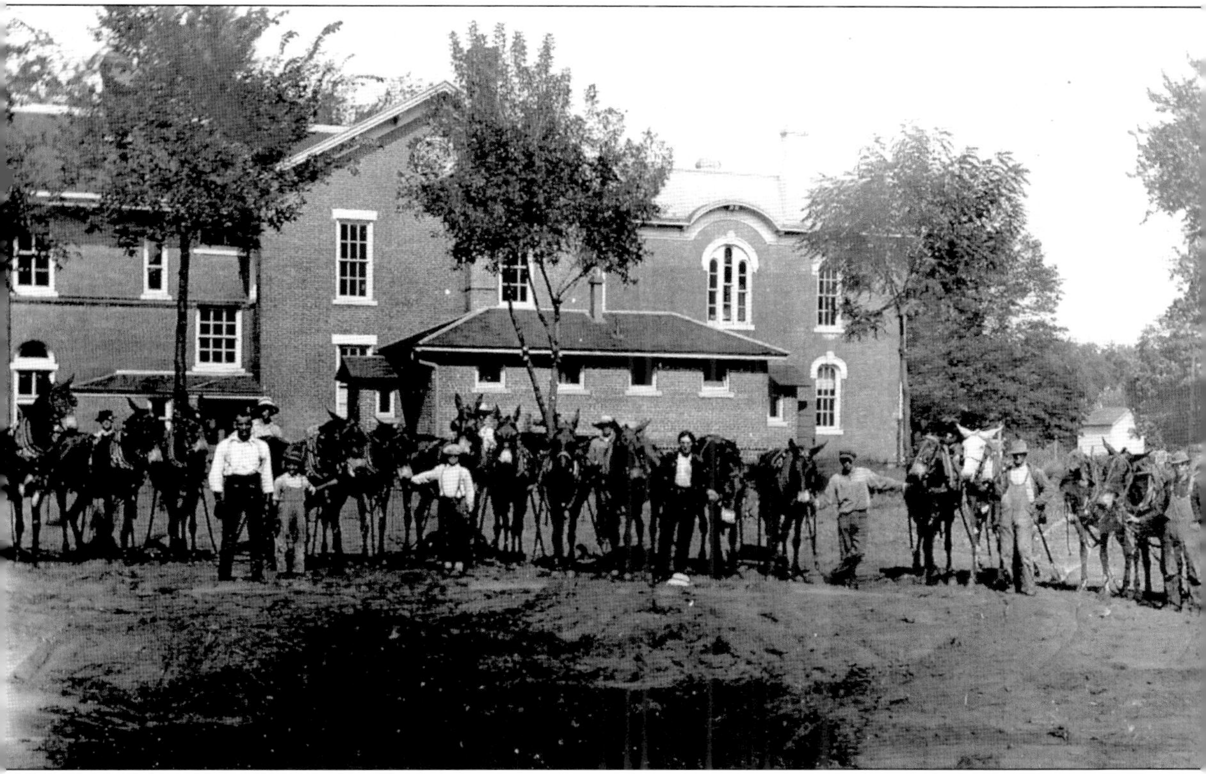

Frank Wallace, or "Old Wallie" as he was known, began his duties as janitor and custodian of the Onarga Grade School on August 1, 1910. Not only was he a faithful servant to the property, he was just as watchful over the teachers and students, caring for their comfort and health. In August 1931, Wallace, a big man, quick of movement and hardworking, made a beauty spot out of a barren waste of blowing sand and sandburrs. The old Freeman house, along with two other homes that sat at the southeast corner of the grade school lot, facing south, were razed, and Wallace fixed up that corner of the school grounds into a miniature park, bringing the entire block into the grade school grounds. This photograph shows the mules and workers who leveled the ground and rid the area of sandburrs . . . for just a little while.

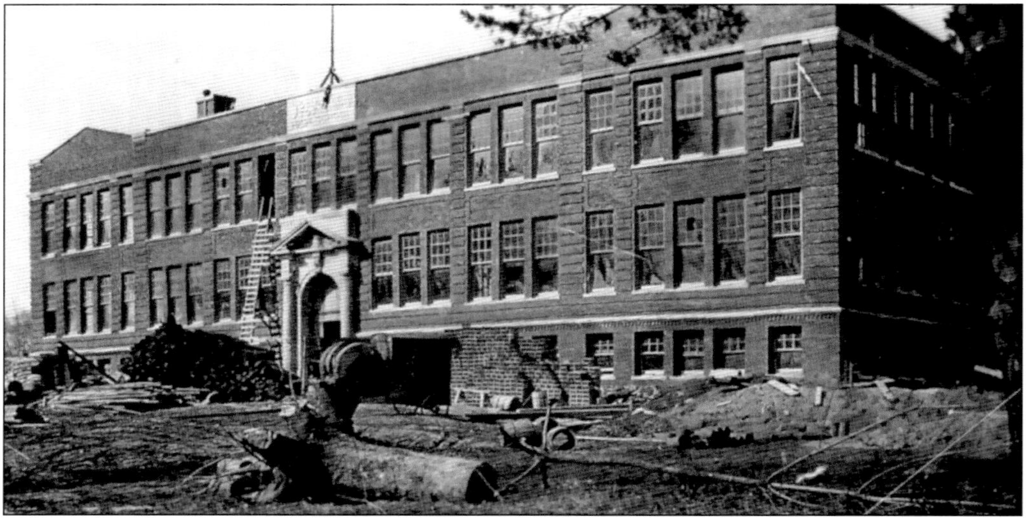

In 1880, a two-year high school department was offered. The first Onarga High School graduation was held in May 1880, with five graduates—all girls! It was apparent to the board of education and parents that a four-year program would be necessary to prepare students for college, the world of business, and everyday life. In 1901, the Onarga High School was fully accredited by the University of Illinois. Due to the increase in student population, a new building was much needed. In 1916, there were deep and serious discussions about a new building with the latest and most modern designs. Construction was awarded to Schmidt Brothers Construction Company of Chicago, which brought a "small army" of workmen to erect the building.

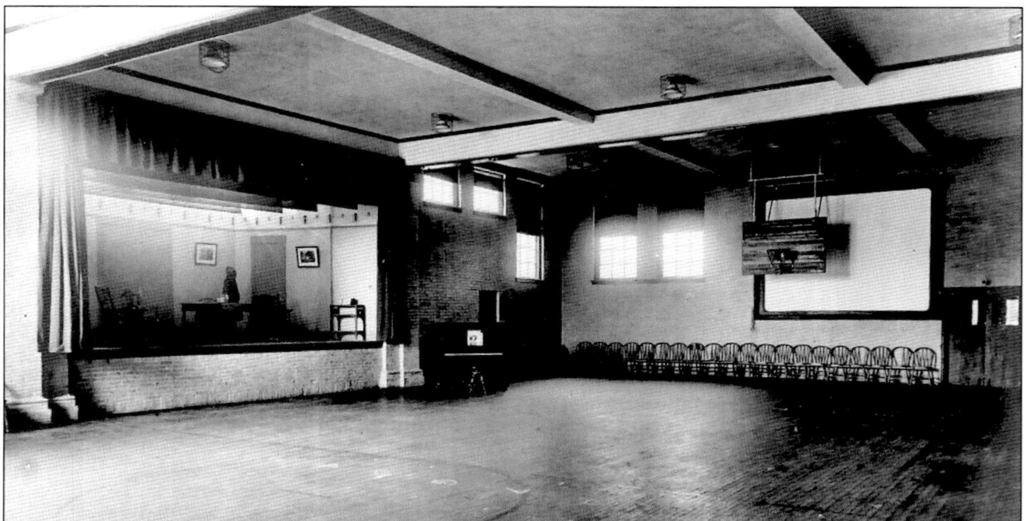

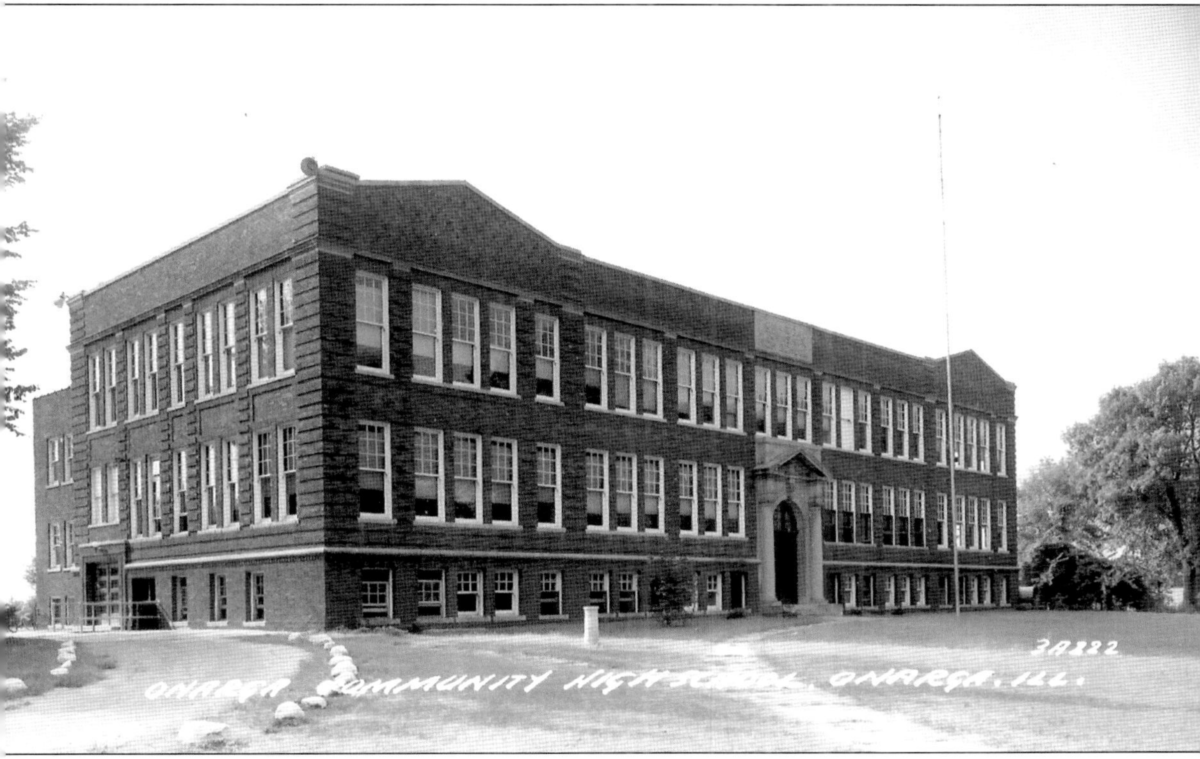

The Onarga High School sat on five acres of land. There were about 45 rooms, including a large study hall, a gymnasium with a stage, recitation rooms, laboratories, bookkeeping and typing rooms, several domestic science rooms, manual training rooms, offices, restrooms, and locker rooms. Every room was lit by electricity. The high school had a central heating system and a clock system to keep everyone on schedule. There were nine teachers, including the superintendent, at the new building. School began on September 3, 1917, in the new building. There was an enrollment of 105 students that year. As the years progressed, new activities were added to the curriculum; music and drama were instituted, providing the students and public with plays, contests, and concerts. Each decade for Onarga High School had students meeting new and different teachers who inspired and encouraged the best efforts from their charges. Many Onarga students continued their educations at various colleges and universities.

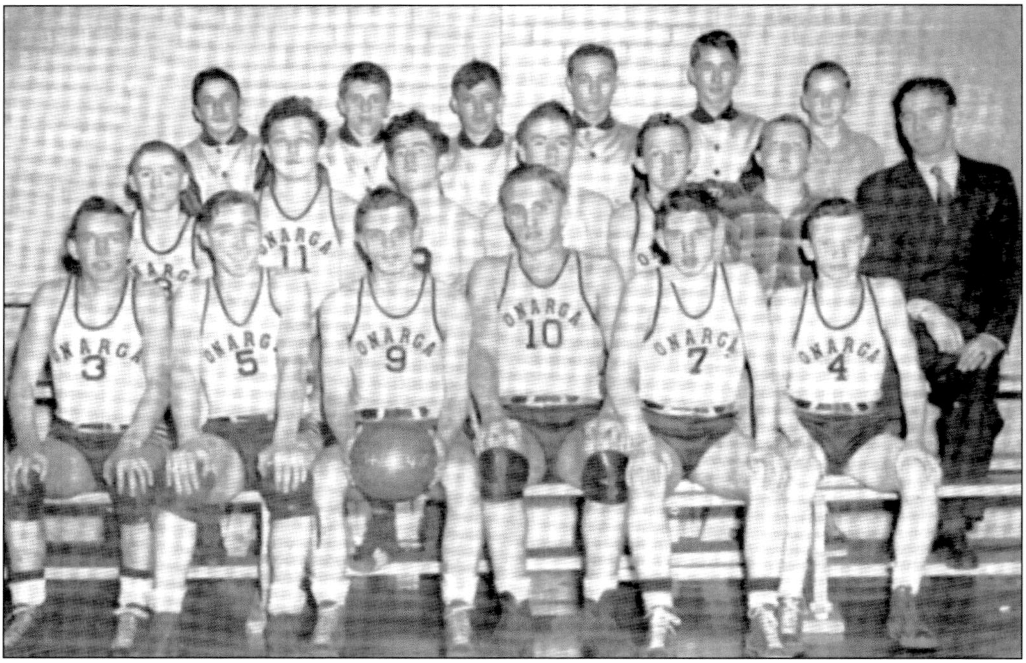

In the beginning, athletics for boys was only moderately stressed. Sports needed to be consistent with good health and schoolwork. For girls, athletics was for the purpose of "school recreation and amusement." As time passed, athletics became increasingly competitive and important, especially for the male students and much later for the girls. The boys competed for positions on the football, basketball, baseball, and track teams, hoping to help set new records of wins for Onarga High School. The athletic department was always a source of pride for Onarga. There were many outstanding winning teams in the history of Onarga High School.

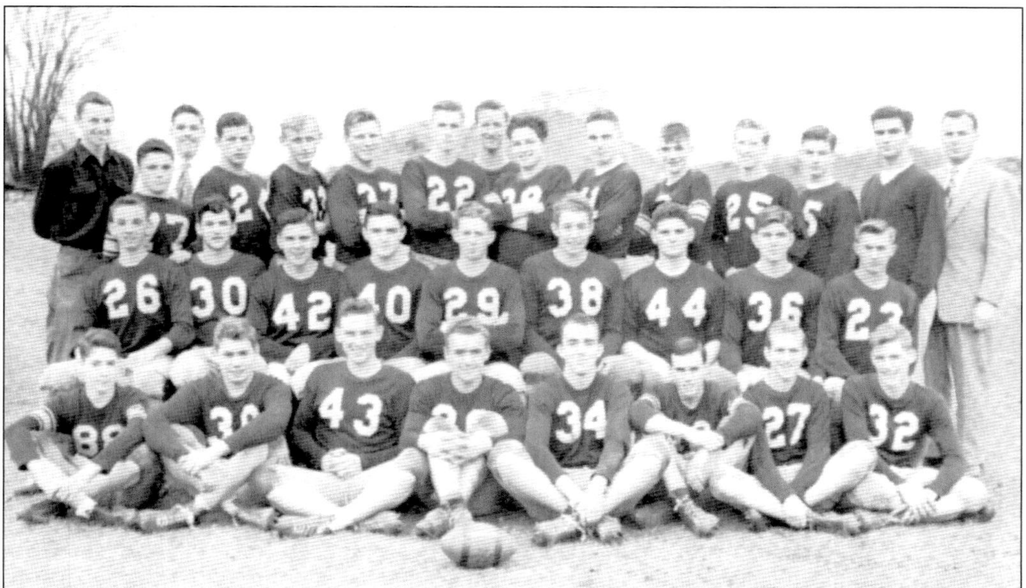

Five

Religion and Repose

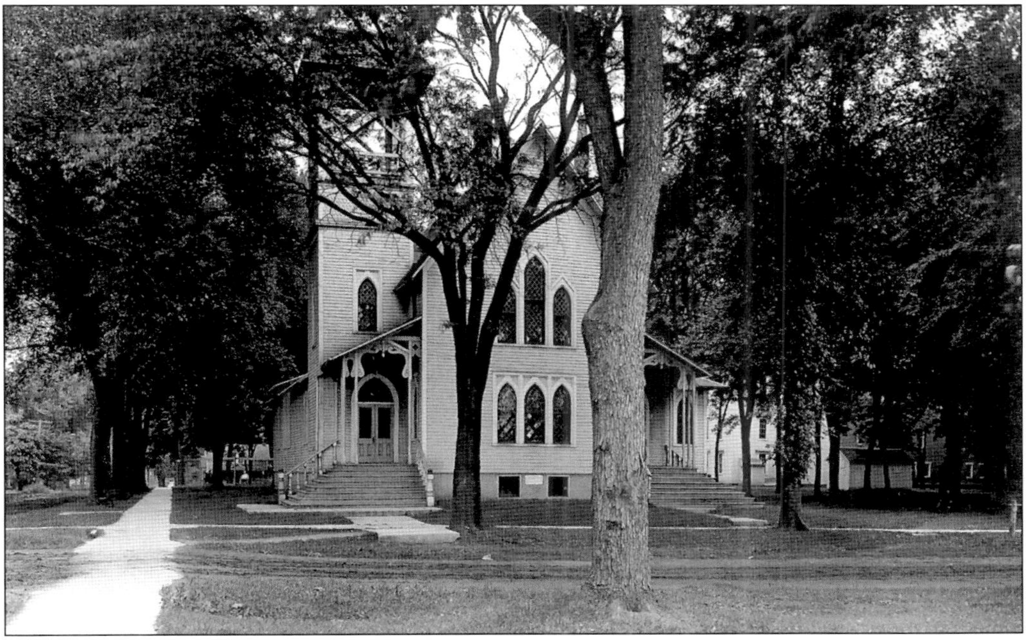

In the settling of the prairie, it was the Methodist preacher with his horse and saddlebags who first brought the gospel to the men, women, and children in the town of Onarga. Reverend Springer, in the year 1834, was the earliest preacher on Spring Creek and the first Methodist preacher located in Iroquois County. The above church was the second Methodist church to be built in Onarga and was located on the northwest corner of the Seminary Block. Built in 1881, this was a beautiful church with a tall bell tower with a four-sided steeple tapering to a point, standing high above the trees.

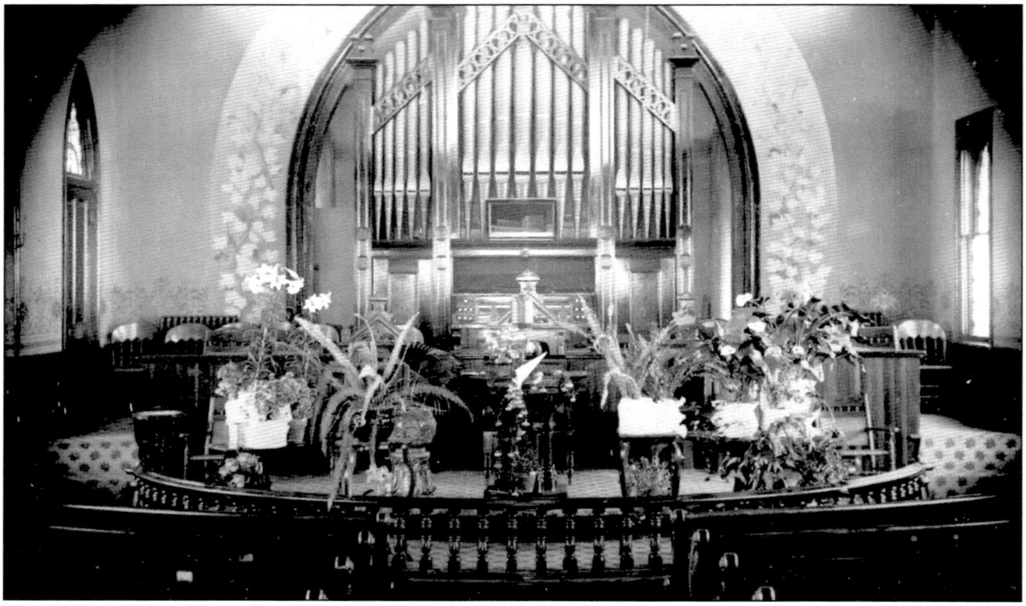

This *c.* 1881 photograph depicts the interior of the Methodist church. A large pipe organ stood under the round stained-glass window. There was seating capacity for 500 persons, and each seat was supplied with a comfortable cushion. The pulpit was in front of the choir loft surrounded by a beautiful railing. Three walnut chairs, upholstered with fine plush, and a solid walnut desk comprised the pulpit furniture. This church served the Methodist people of Onarga and the surrounding county for 44 years.

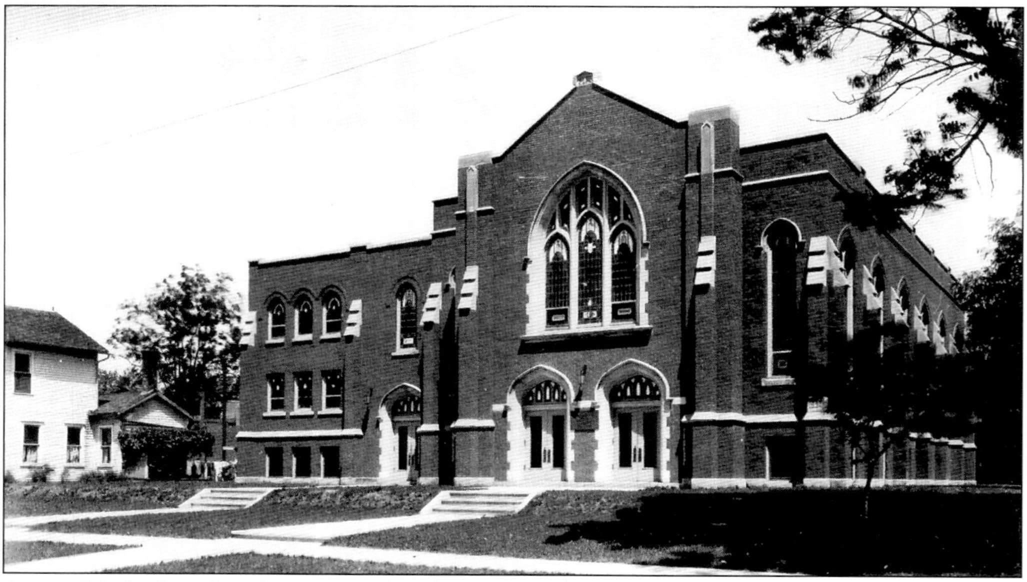

A new Methodist church was completed in 1924. The large redbrick church building occupied the corner lot located at 109 East Seminary Avenue, just across the street and west of the Onarga Military School. It was dedicated in June 1925. The church was erected at a cost of $67,000. The interior of the church was built in the Akron style with beautiful oak woodwork, solid oak doors, and the church's pride and joy, a magnificent Eastlake-style pipe organ.

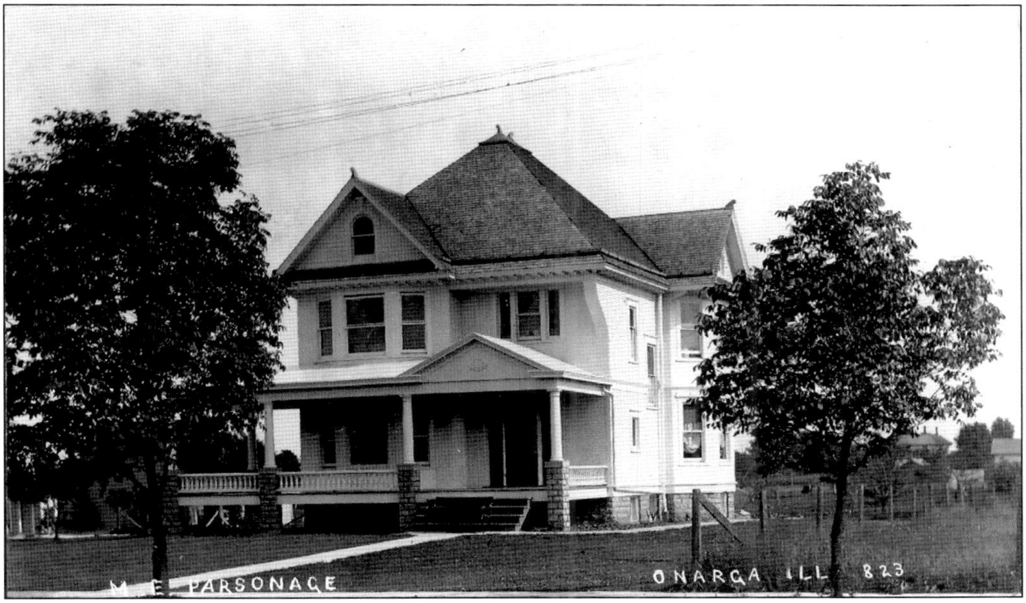

On November 8, 1903, the minister and family moved into the brand-new parsonage on East Lincoln Avenue. His words at that time were, "It is a thing of beauty and we hope it will be a joy forever. From garret to basement it is modern in every respect with all the up-to-date appliances for heating, lighting and making life comfortable and pleasant."

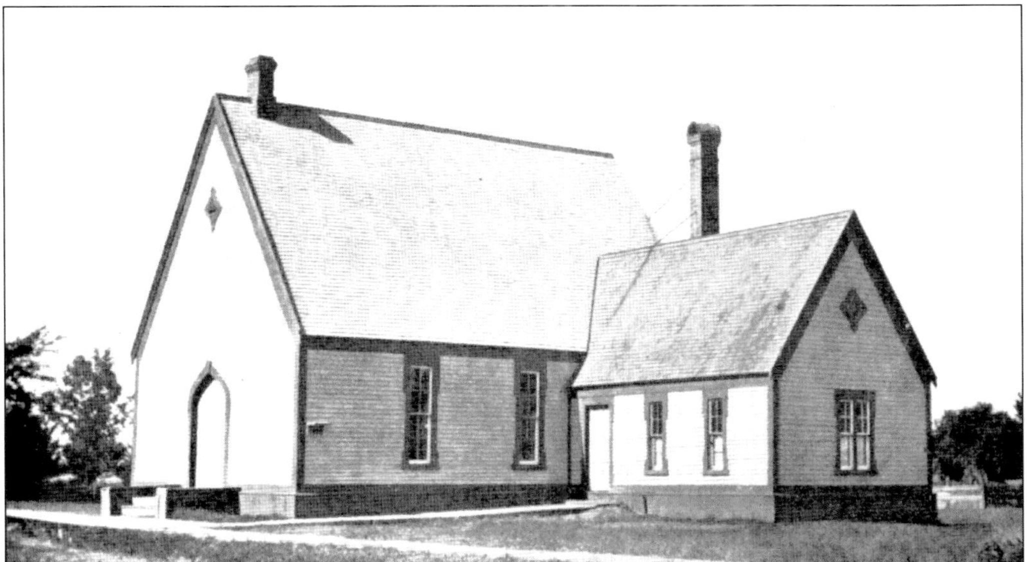

The first Presbyterian minister, Reverend Tayler, arrived in Onarga in 1856 and began to hold meetings in schoolhouses and the depot buildings. With a membership of 14, the Onarga Presbyterian Church was formally organized under the Presbytery of Peoria on March 3, 1857. The organizing elders were C. C. Wells, W. P. Pierson, and Darius Mathews. The first church building, completed in 1859, was this Gothic structure, built at a cost of $1,850. This first church stood at the corner of Wilson and Maple Streets.

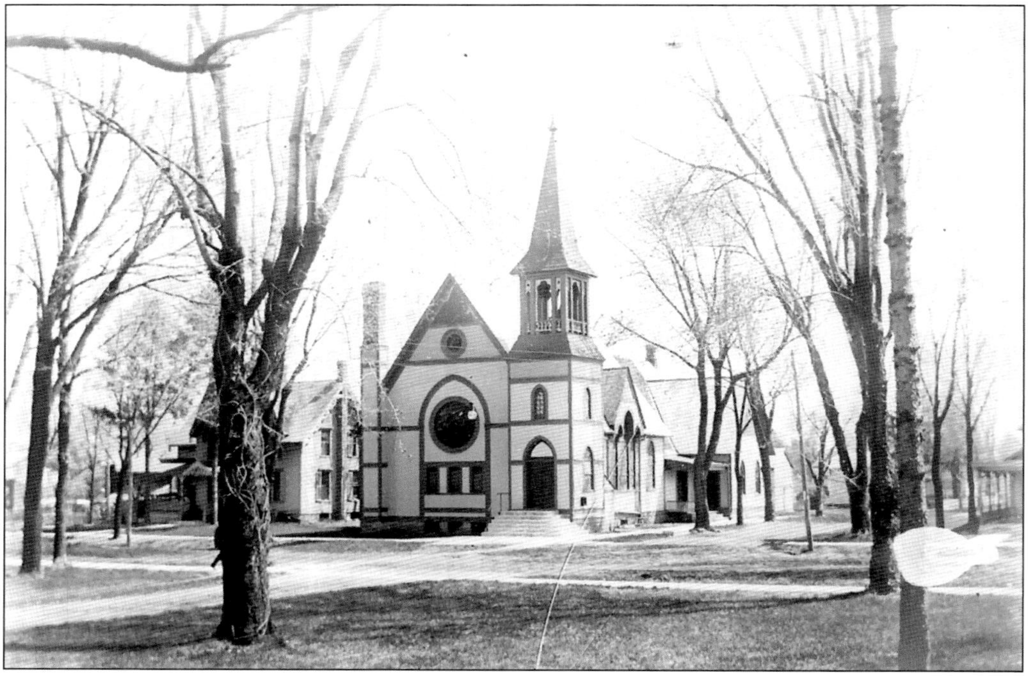

By 1880, church membership had risen to 125 and Sunday school attendance was 100. The church above was built in 1881 at a cost of about $4,500 and was located at the corner of Seminary and Maple Streets, north of where the original church had stood. This church was remodeled extensively in 1904 and 1905. A new pipe organ was installed in 1905 and was dedicated with a performance by nationally renowned organist Clarence Eddy on May 7, 1905. Unfortunately, the church and all its contents were destroyed by fire that same month. Rebuilt on the same site as the previous church, the last building, shown below, was occupied by the Presbyterians until they disbanded in the early 1970s and is now the home of the Onarga Christian Church.

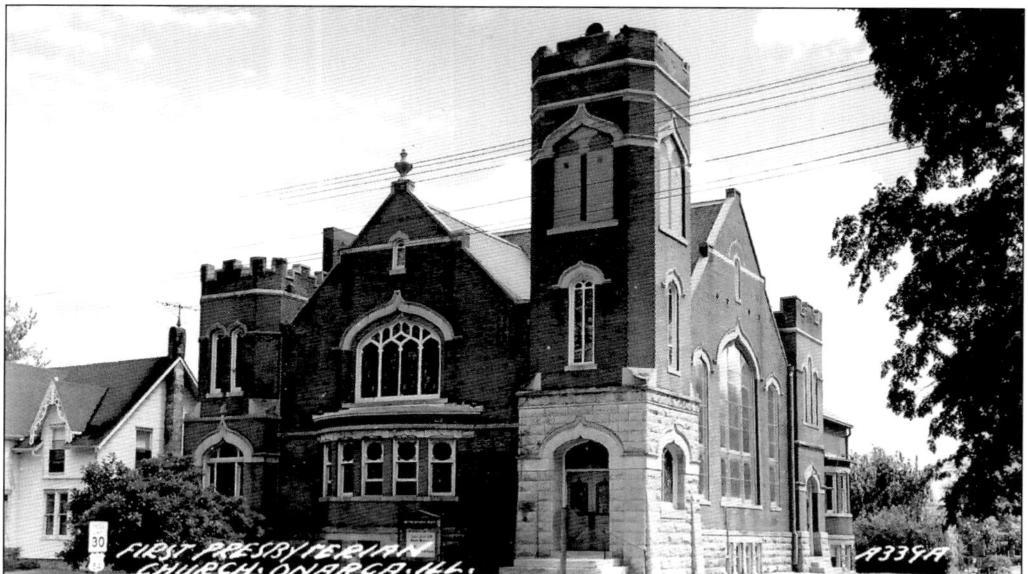

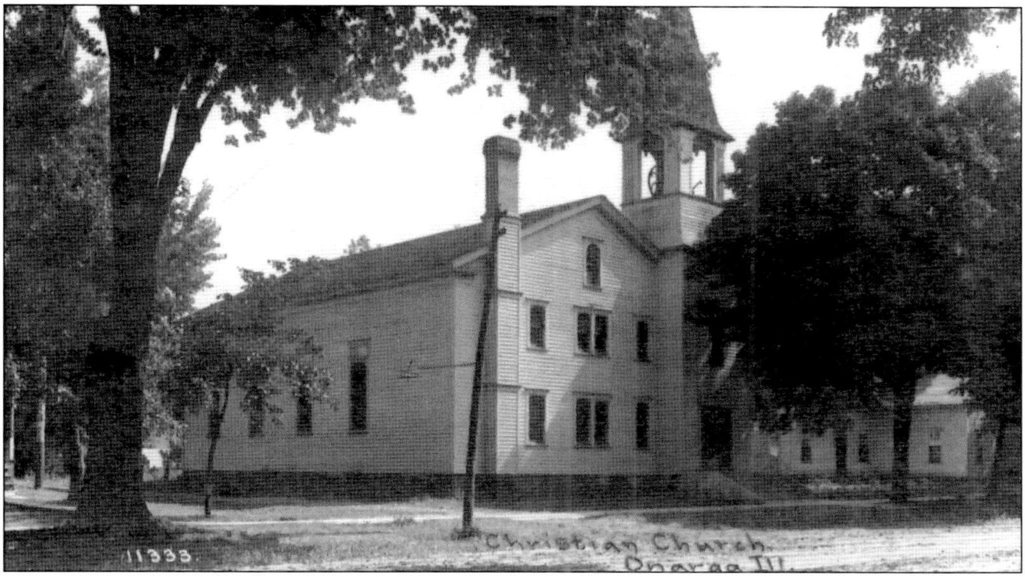

The Onarga First Congregational Church was one of 20 churches organized under the direction of the Illinois Home Missionary Association, Rev. Adam Lowry Rankin, and Rev. Lemuel Foster, who became the first pastor of the Onarga church. The church was organized on December 9, 1858, and held meetings for the first two months in the Onarga Methodist Church. In 1860, it acquired the property shown here. The church struggled with a small membership but was still in existence in 1879.

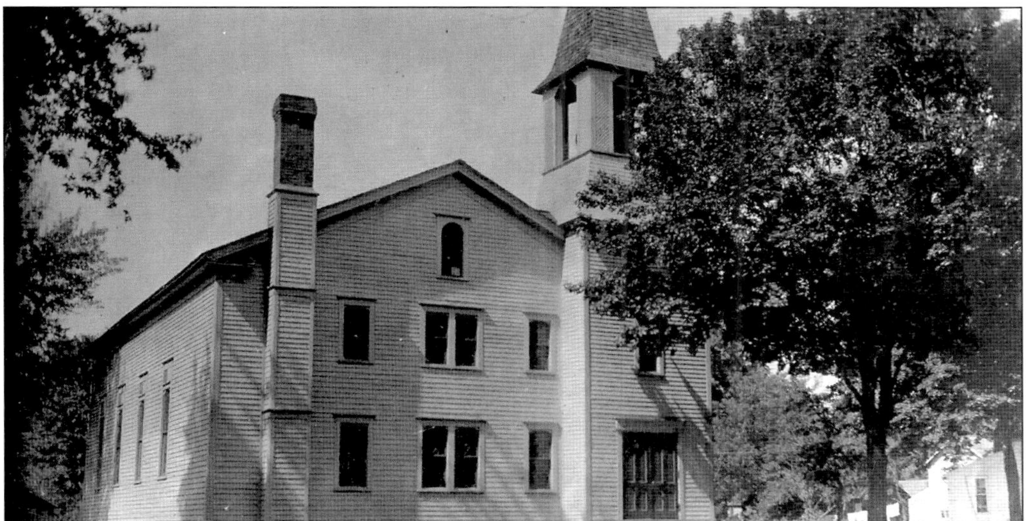

The Spring Creek Church of Christ began east of town in February 1877 and met for 10 years in one of the schoolhouses that sat at the intersection of 1100 East and 1500 North Road. The young church became the Onarga Christian Church when it moved to Onarga in 1887, occupying the church building pictured here in the 500 block of West Seminary Avenue that had been vacated by the Congregationalists. This church was extensively remodeled in 1928. The congregation remained in this building until 1976, when it moved to its current home at the corner of Seminary Avenue and Maple Street.

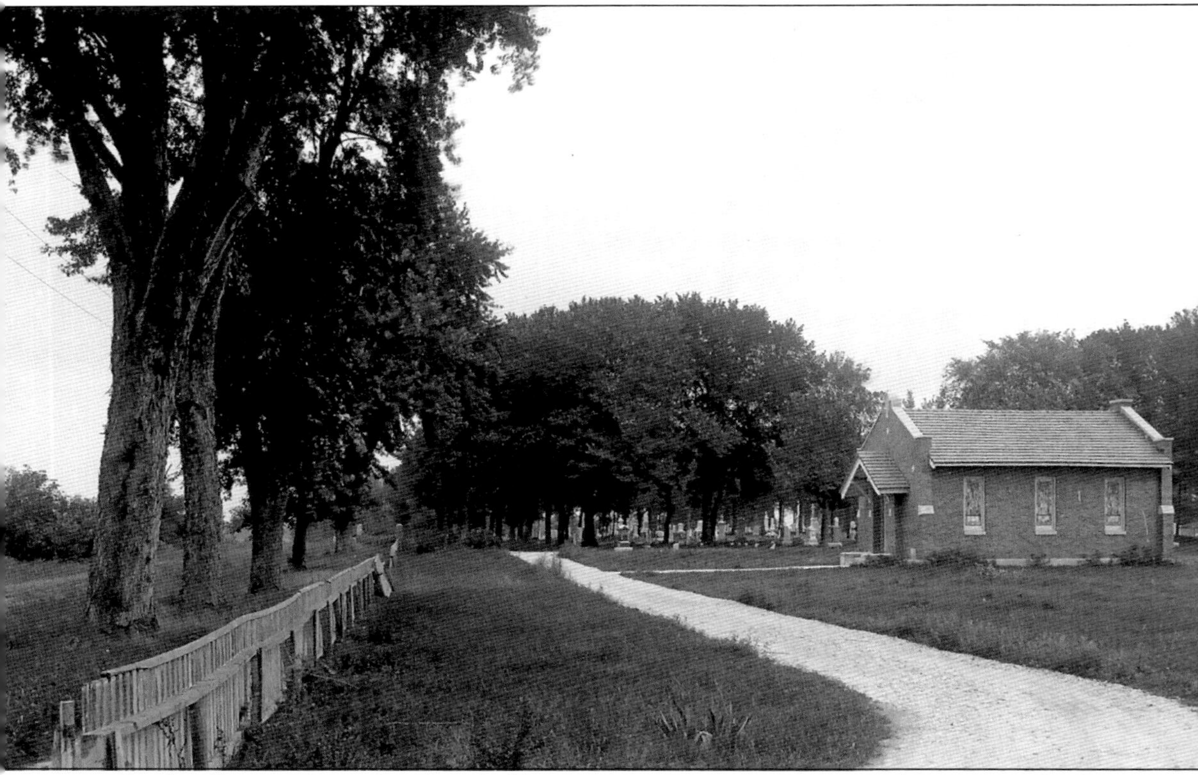

The first Episcopalian Church to hold services in Onarga was organized in 1858 with about 25 members. The exact location of this first church building—erected in 1867—is not known. By 1880, the church was no longer holding services. In 1913, Linda M. Groh Johnson of California donated funds to the cemetery association to erect a chapel in memory of Andrew Groh. The nondenominational chapel built to Groh's memory was to be used for funeral services as needed. Local contractor Gleason Thorne built the chapel at a cost of $2,568. During the early 1950s and 1960s, the cemetery chapel became home to the small but faithful congregation of St. Faith's Episcopalian Church. At that time the chapel was furnished with an old reed organ that required manual pumping. Concerned with the stamina of the organist, who was pregnant at the time, Dr. Francis Mexson rigged the instrument with a vacuum cleaner motor to create an "electric" organ. St. Faith's disbanded in the late 1960s. The cemetery chapel is still maintained and continues to be used for funeral and memorial services.

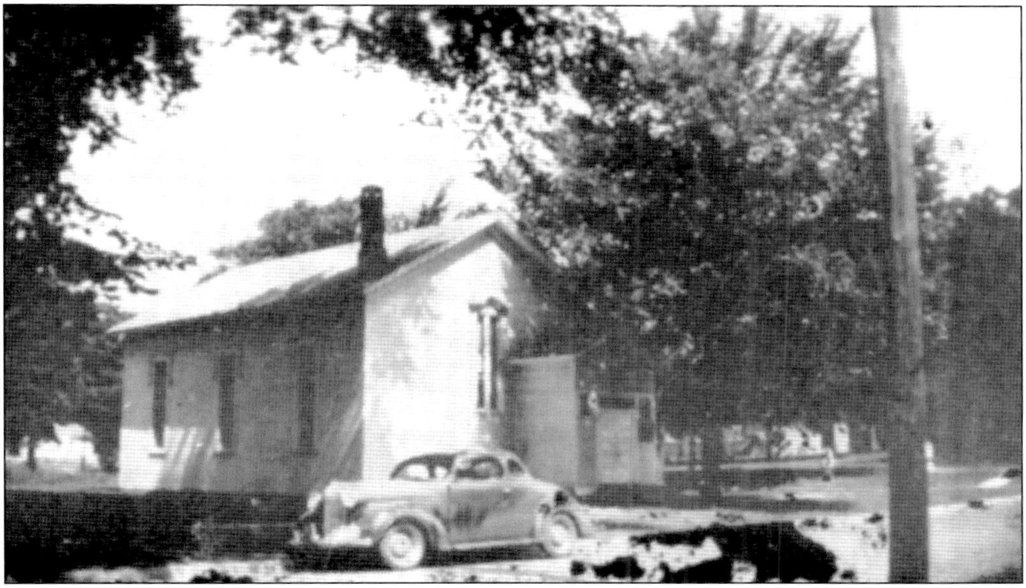

The Pilgrim Holiness Church sat on lot 1, block 20, at the corner of Walnut Street and Seminary Avenue, and was originally built by the Congregational Church. The church was built in the spring of 1866 and was 29 feet by 42 feet, and 18 feet high. The church was built in the utilitarian style with clapboard siding and double wooden church doors to the front.

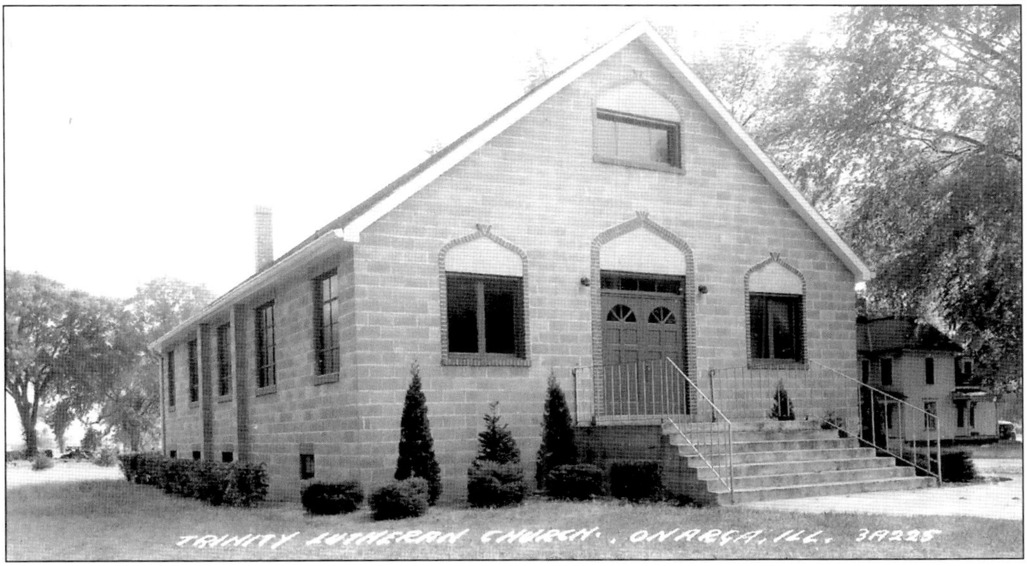

On March 9, 1947, Pastor C. Haller began regular services at the International Order of Odd Fellows hall in Onarga. On June 4, 1947, the Trinity Evangelical Lutheran Church of Onarga was organized with 11 charter members. A building site on West Seminary Avenue was chosen and purchased for $900. On July 11, 1948, the groundbreaking ceremony was held after morning worship, and eight days later, the construction began. A special cornerstone-laying ceremony was held on September 5. On January 11, 1949, the divine service was held in the basement of the new church building, and on December 18, 1949, the first service was held in the new church auditorium.

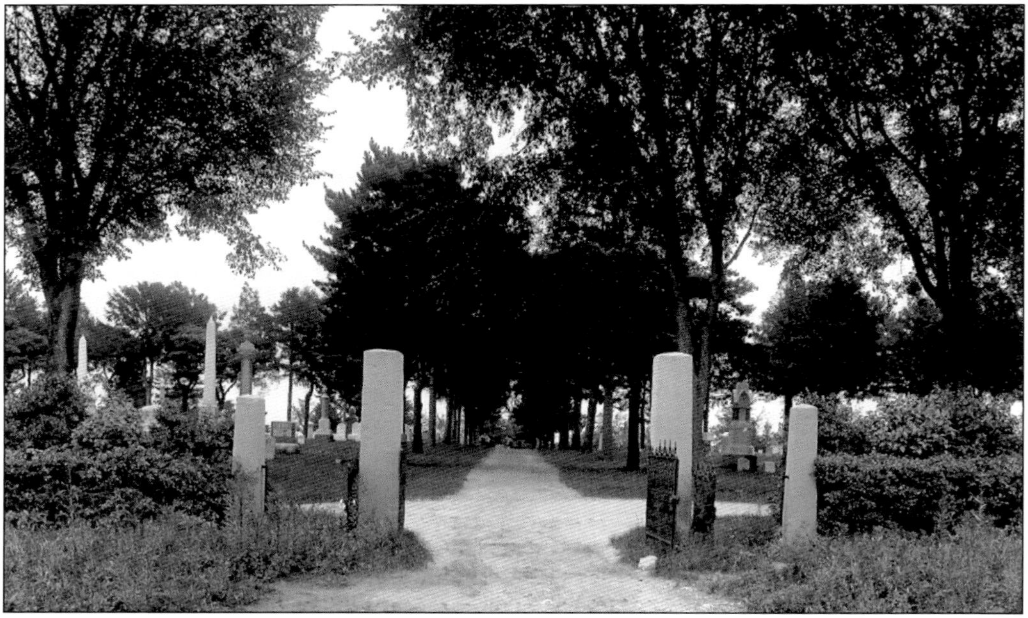

The Onarga Cemetery Association was organized in March 1858 when 36 persons subscribed $5 each toward a cemetery fund. In the summer of 1858, a tract of land was purchased and laid into blocks, lots, walks, and driveways. In 1867, the grounds were ornamented by shade trees, a reception vault was constructed at an expense of $350, and a fine substantial gateway with iron gates was put up, at a cost of $175. In 1877, five acres were purchased on the south at an expense of $550. H. W. Beckwith described the cemetery as "a beautiful knoll, rising gently from all sides to the summit near the center, the soil is sand, and naturally well-drained. There is a fine growth of elms along the main driveways and a variety of evergreens along the walks."

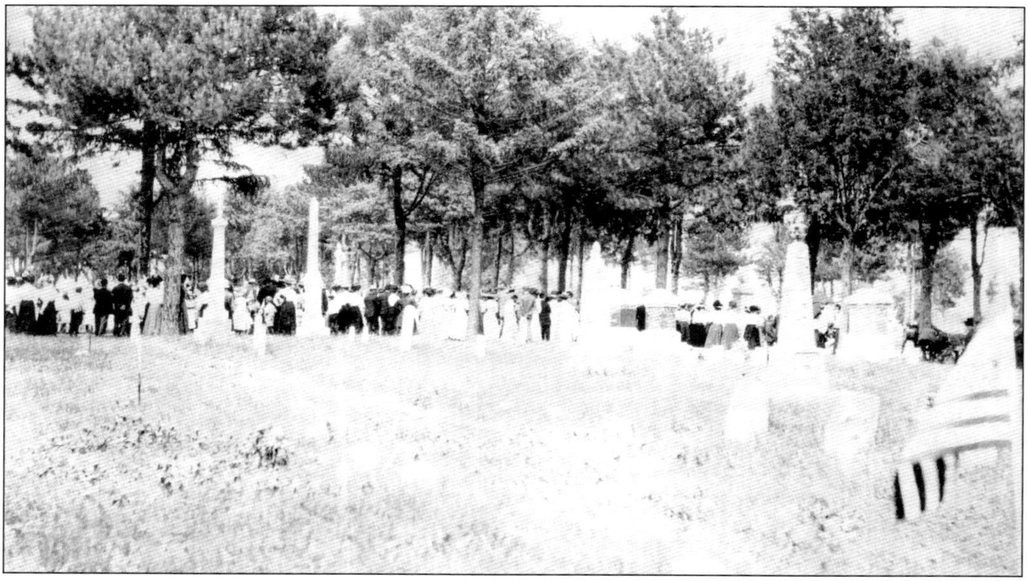

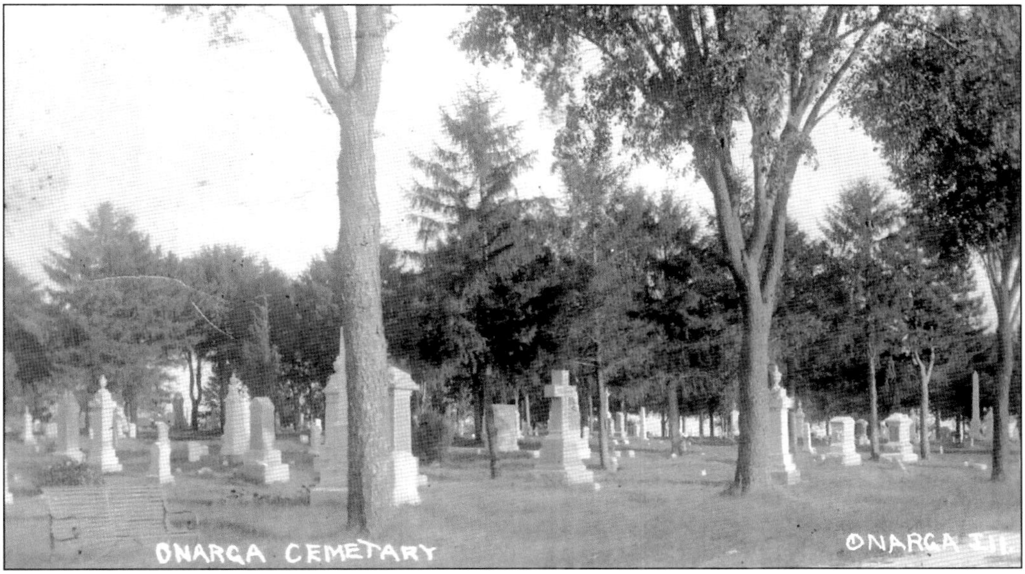

In the 1860s, many graves from farm and roadside burial grounds were transferred to the Onarga Cemetery. One such burial ground was the Pangborn Cemetery, located on the edge of the timber on a high bluff east of Spring Creek on what is now the Ikins farm. In addition to the Pangborn, there were at least three other cemeteries existing in the area at the time—the Frame and Jefferson Cemeteries, both east of Spring Creek, and the Lehigh Cemetery at Del Rey. Of these, only the Lehigh Cemetery was still accepting burials after the 1860s.

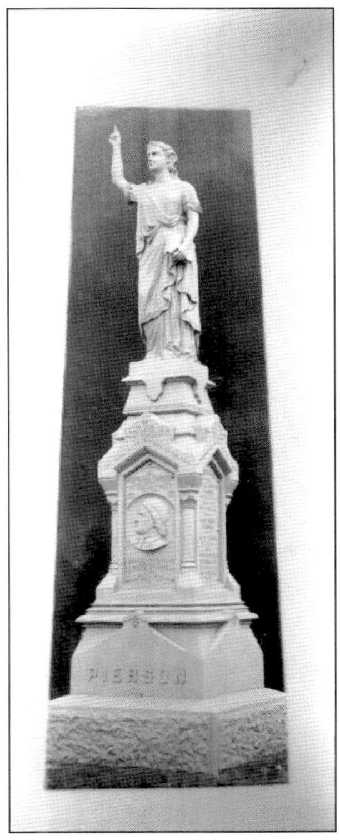

This is the original picture of William Pierson's grave marker, one of the most notable in the Onarga Cemetery. The marker was made by the Chicago Bronze Company. The monument is engraved on three sides with Pierson's genealogy. Among Pierson's ancestors were Rev. Abraham Pierson Sr., a cofounder of the city of Newark, New Jersey, and Rev. Abraham Pierson Jr., rector and first president of Yale College. Dr. Edward H. Parker's poem "Life's Race" is engraved on the fourth side.

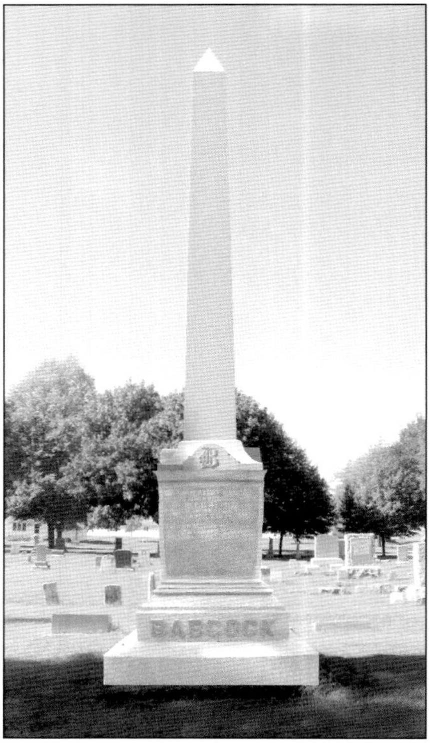

The Onarga Township Cemetery has many beautiful and impressive stones. The stone on the left, which is in the shape of an obelisk, was erected for Dr. William A. Babcock. Dr. Babcock was a Civil War surgeon, and Onarga's GAR post was named in his honor. For many years, Decoration Day and Memorial Day ceremonies were held at Dr. Babcock's stone. The beautiful stone below was erected for M. T. Amerman, who was not only Onarga's undertaker and embalmer but also ran a successful grocery store.

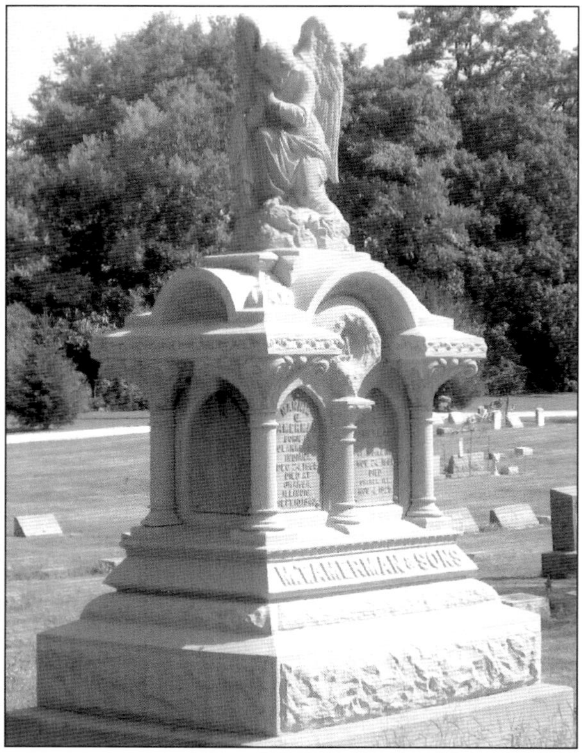

Six

Disasters, Natural and Otherwise

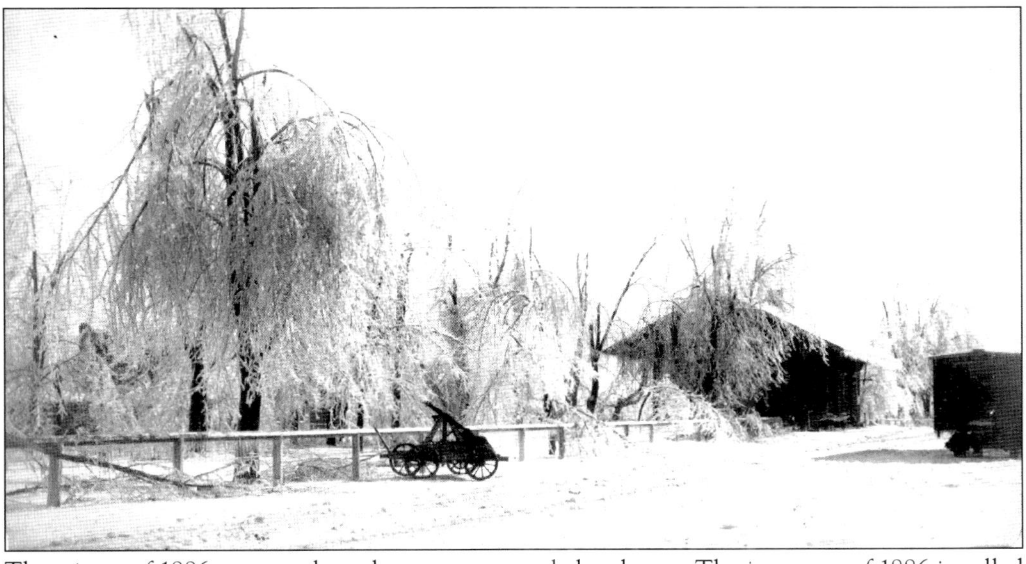

The winter of 1886 came early and was an extremely harsh one. The ice storm of 1886 is called the "ice storm of the century." The trees were completely and heavily coated with ice, from the ground to the tips of the smallest twigs. Not only were the upper sides of the limbs sheeted with ice, but all along the undersides were millions of tiny icicles an inch or two in length. The weight of all this was immense, and all through the day, crashing of falling branches could be heard. This photograph shows Onarga's depot and the devastation that the "ice storm of the century" caused.

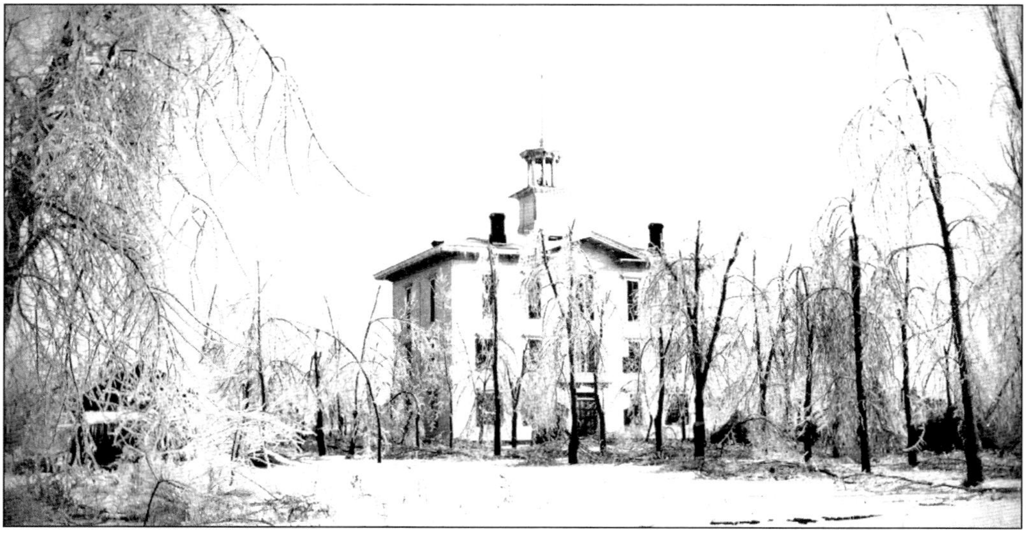

The sidewalks were as slippery as greased glass. There was no school, with the officials deciding that the children would be better off at their homes. Several extra hands were kept busy clearing away the debris. It took many years before the shade and ornamental trees could recover their beauty from the devastating ice storm of 1886. These photographs show the Ladies Seminary Building and the Onarga Cemetery.

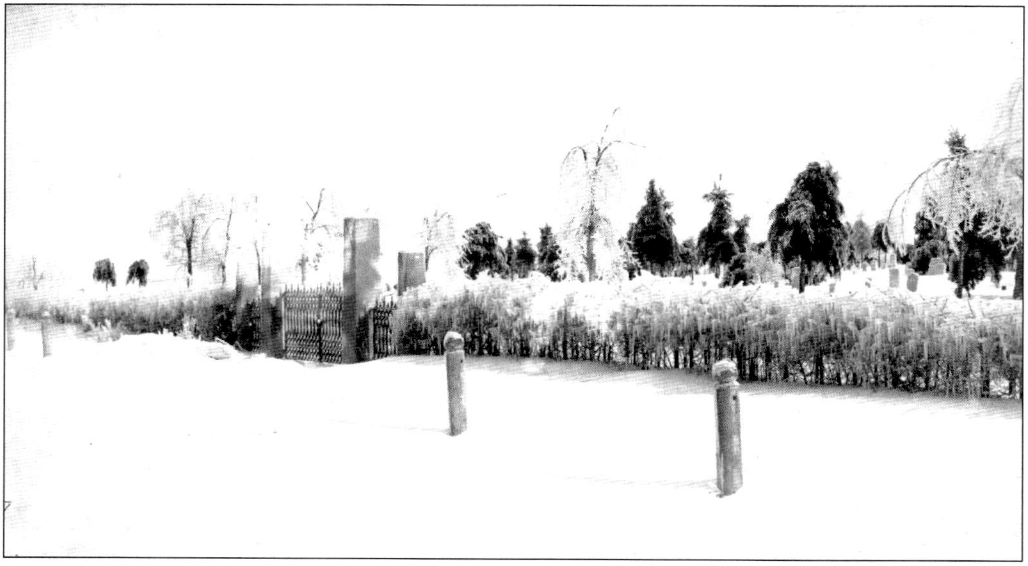

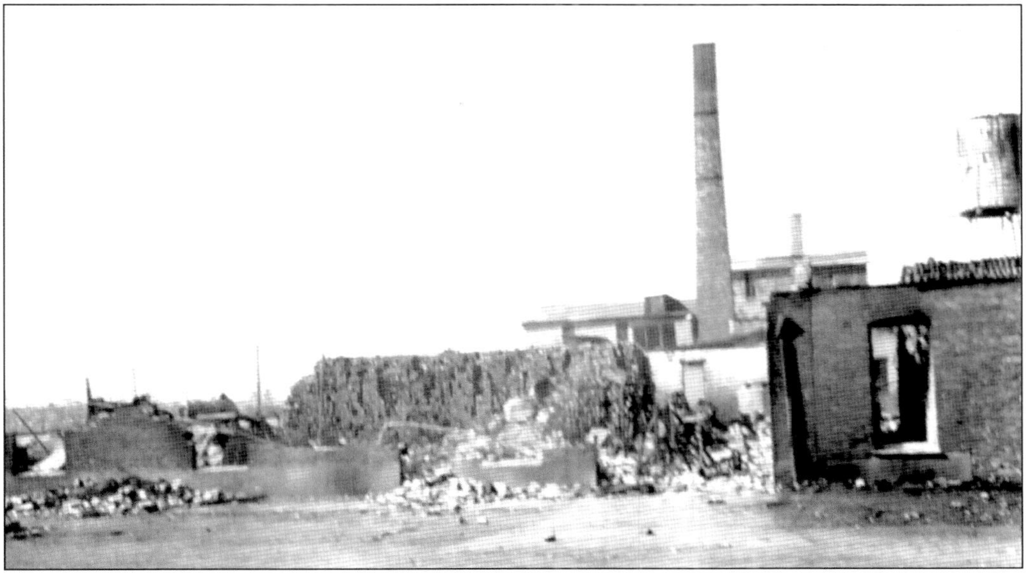

The Onarga Canning Company plant was destroyed by fire on Thursday, August 25, 1949. The plant was a roaring mass of flames when the fire company arrived to battle the blaze. The fire had apparently broken out near the smokestack or over the cooking rooms. There were second stories over both of these places. It is possible that the fire had started earlier in the day and became evident only after breaking through the roof. A south wind carried the flames from the point where they were first discovered across the entire roof area to the north. All the building north of the stack was in flames in a matter of minutes.

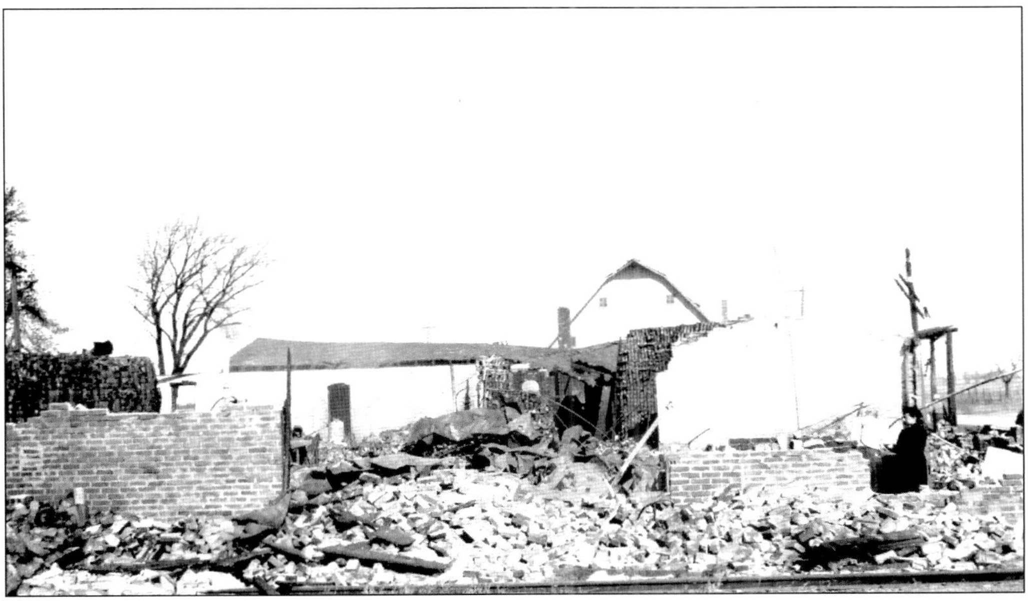

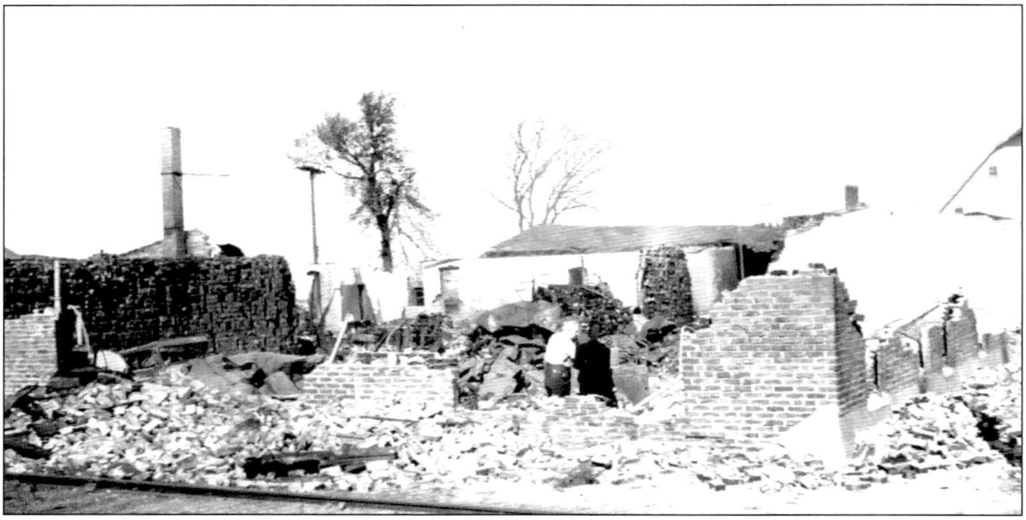

The fight against the flames in the main portion of the factory was futile. The fire could not be confined to any one area. Determination of how much of the canning factory could be salvaged took many days. Estimates of damage varied from $400,000 to $1 million. The fire was brought under control about four hours after it was discovered. Firemen remained on duty all night to keep the flames under control. Chief Clarence Talbert directed the company of firemen for the first time since taking over as chief. Later that evening, he was heard to say that he felt like a new doctor that just lost his first case. A fellow fireman remarked that he could be proud that he saved more than the foundation—he had two chimneys to his credit!

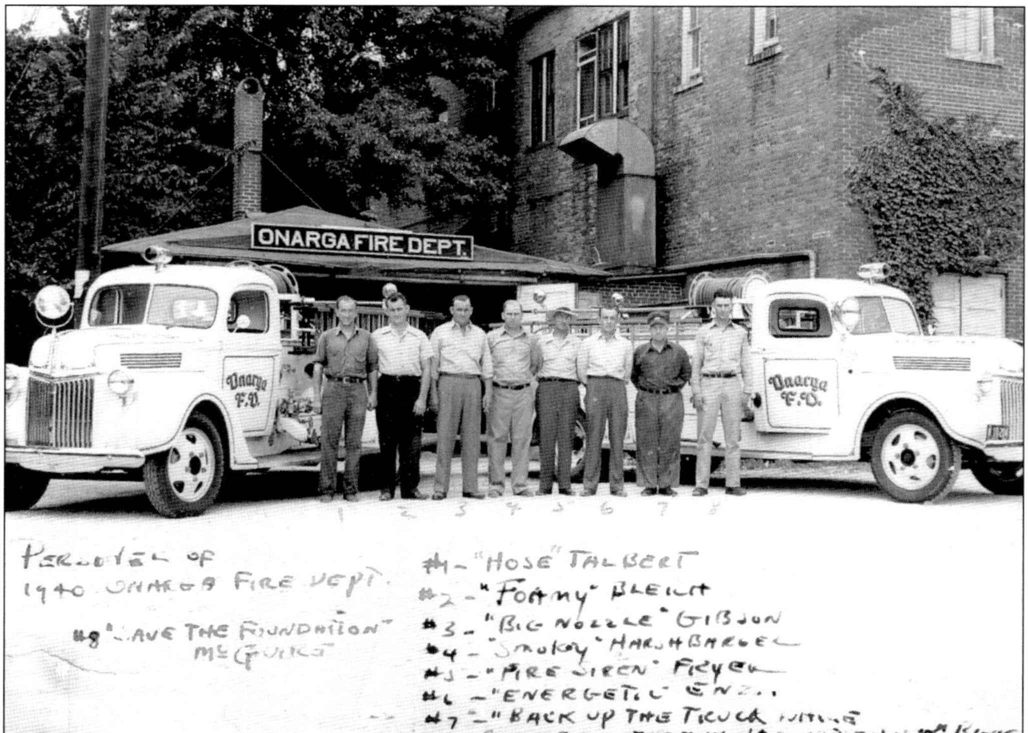

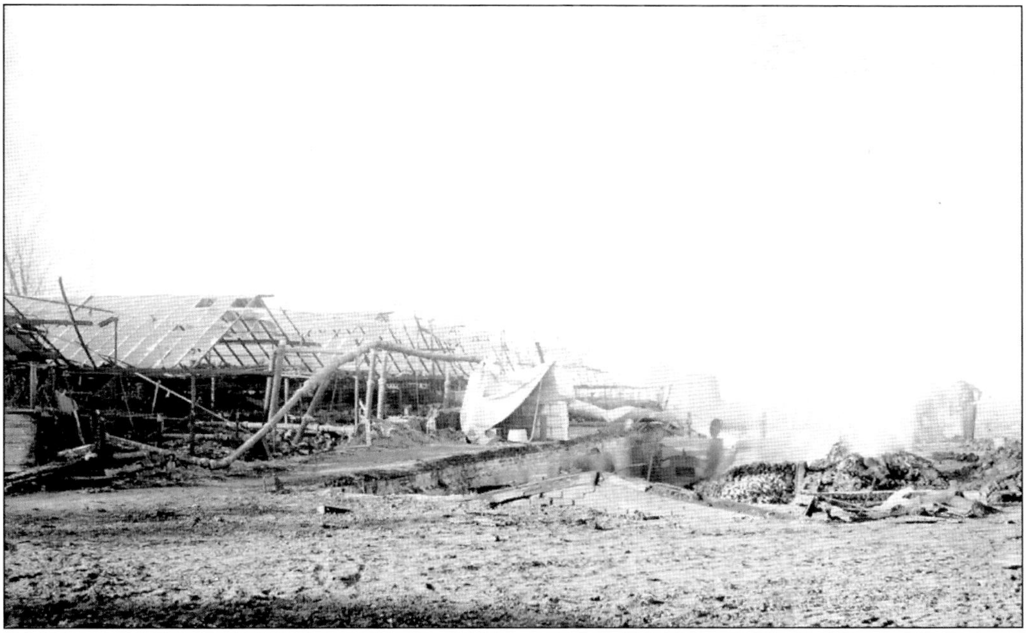

Onarga has had its share of fires as well as other disasters. The photograph above depicts the Onarga Greenhouse fire on Sunday, December 31, 1911. This fire caused total devastation of the greenhouses. The photograph below is of the C. D. Risser home, which was located on East Lincoln Avenue. The photograph shows the home, which was totally destroyed in this winter fire, still burning. In the forefront of the photograph are pillows, tables, and Oriental rugs that had been dragged into the yard for safe-keeping. The grand Wheeler Home can be seen in the distance.

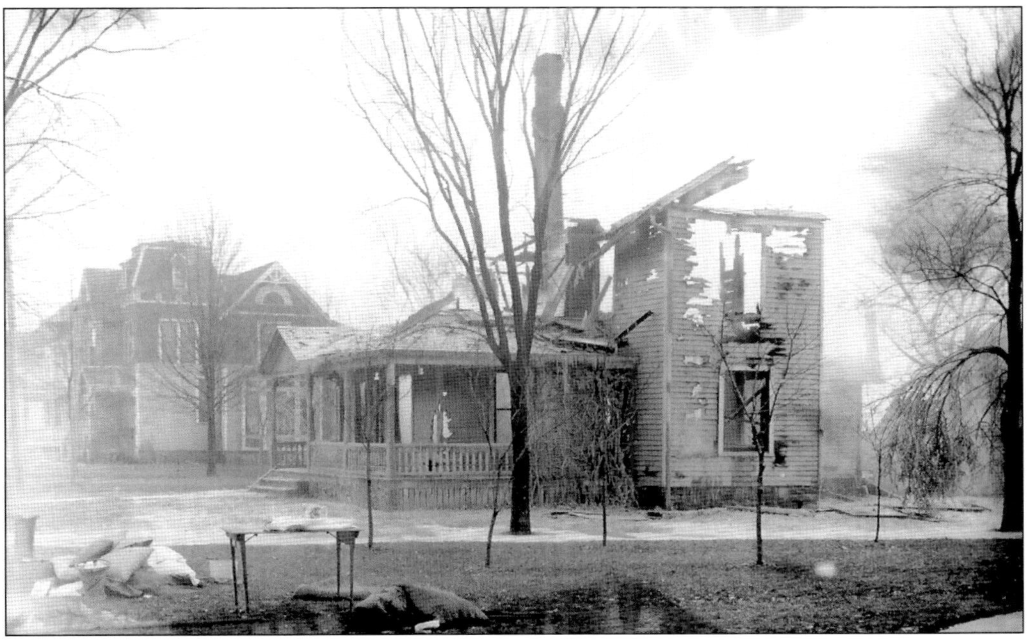

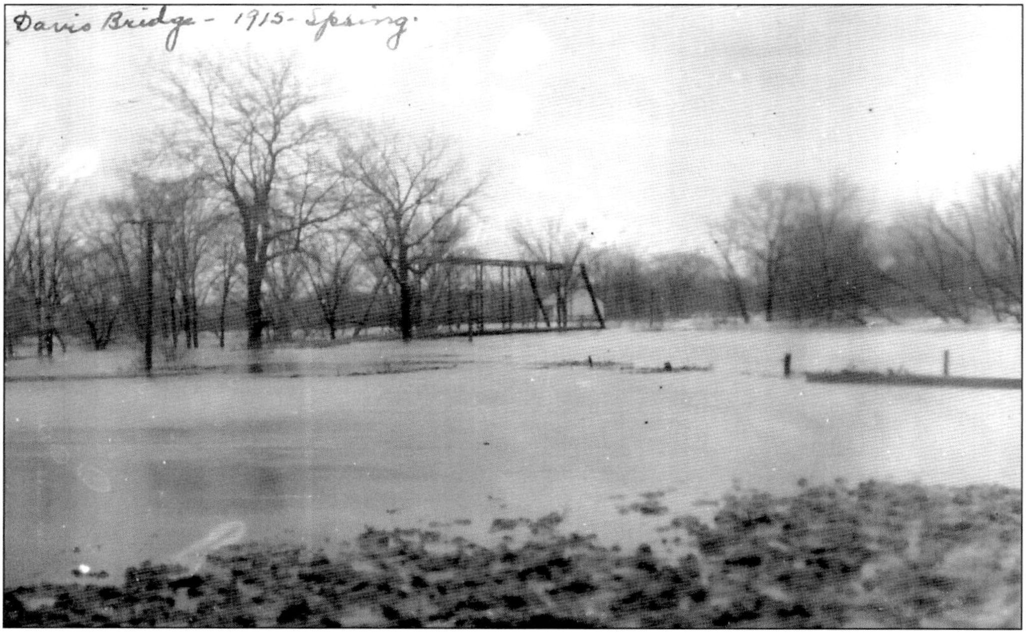

Almost every spring, when thawing from the long icy winter commenced, Spring Creek overflowed and flooded the surrounding area. The subject of the above picture is the Davis Bridge, which was located southeast of Onarga. The steel bridge was heavily traveled and eventually fell in the creek. This photograph was taken in the spring of 1915.

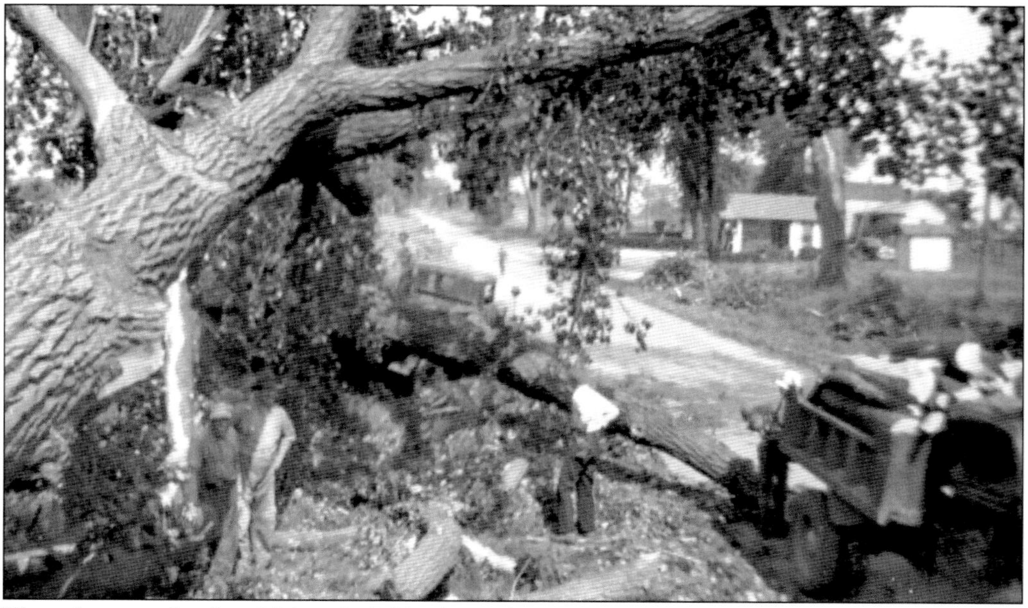

This photograph, dated May 6, 1938, shows large trees that were downed in a windstorm. McFadden's Gas Station, in the 800 block of West Seminary Avenue, is on the upper right-hand side of this photograph. A truck was crushed by the tree branches. From the piles of downed branches along the road, this storm must have caused immense damage to Onarga, or at least lots of cleanup.

Plain in its pioneer style of architecture, the seminary building burned on Tuesday, April 19, 1921. Many mourned the loss of this beautiful building because of the many hallowed memories. It was presumed that the fire must have originated from electric light wires and, although the full pressure of the waterworks system was on, the long string of hose necessary to reach the fire, approximately 500 feet, proved unsuccessful.

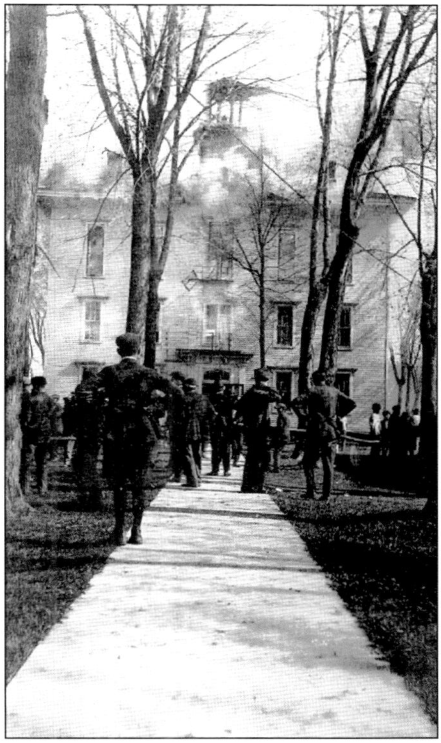

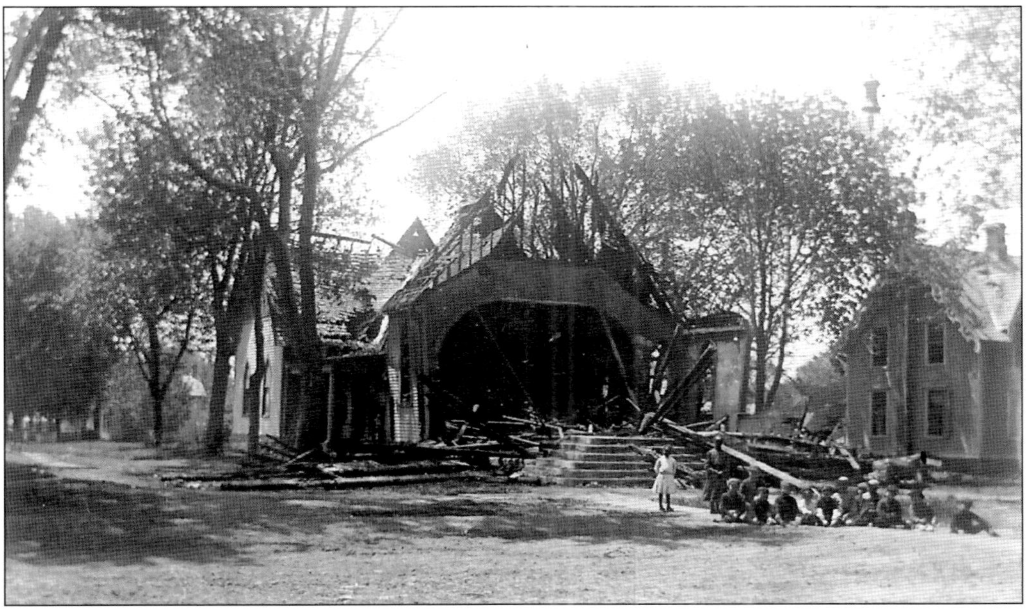

Around midnight, May 22, 1905, Robert Sutton, Onarga's night watchman, fired three shots into the air to signal that the alarm be sounded. The Presbyterian church was on fire. The timing of the fire was especially devastating since the church, built in 1881, had recently completed $1,000 of interior renovations and paid $3,000 for a new pipe organ that had been dedicated only two weeks earlier. The church and its contents were smoldering ruins.

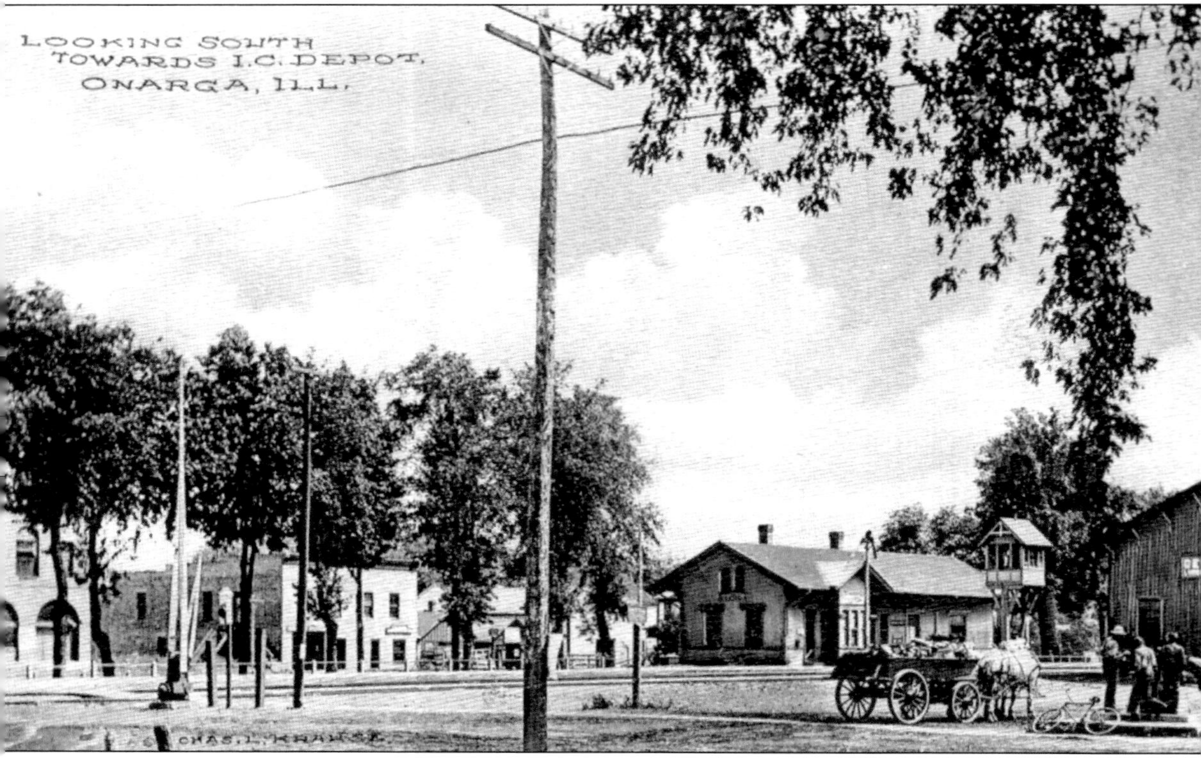

Shortly after 10:00 a.m. on July 31, 1939, the Onarga community was the scene of a typical, old-time Jesse James–style daylight train robbery. Two heavy-set bandits, both dressed in the garb of train men (light blue overalls and jackets, blue striped white caps, and red handkerchiefs), staged a daring holdup of the mail car on the local, southbound Illinois Central Railroad passenger train No. 31. The bandits were after the $56,513 government cash payroll for airmen at Chanute Field, Rantoul. A plea of guilty and full confession of the daylight Wild West train holdup at Onarga came from Arthur Tracy of Chicago and his partner, John Waldon. On that morning, residents of Onarga observed the two men loitering about town, sitting in the park. Earlier that day, they had eaten their breakfast at Duncan's Restaurant, and Albert Kanosky stated they had been in his tavern. However, when the train left the station, the men disappeared. After wrestling with the Illinois Central mail clerks, their plot was foiled.

Seven

All in a Day's Work

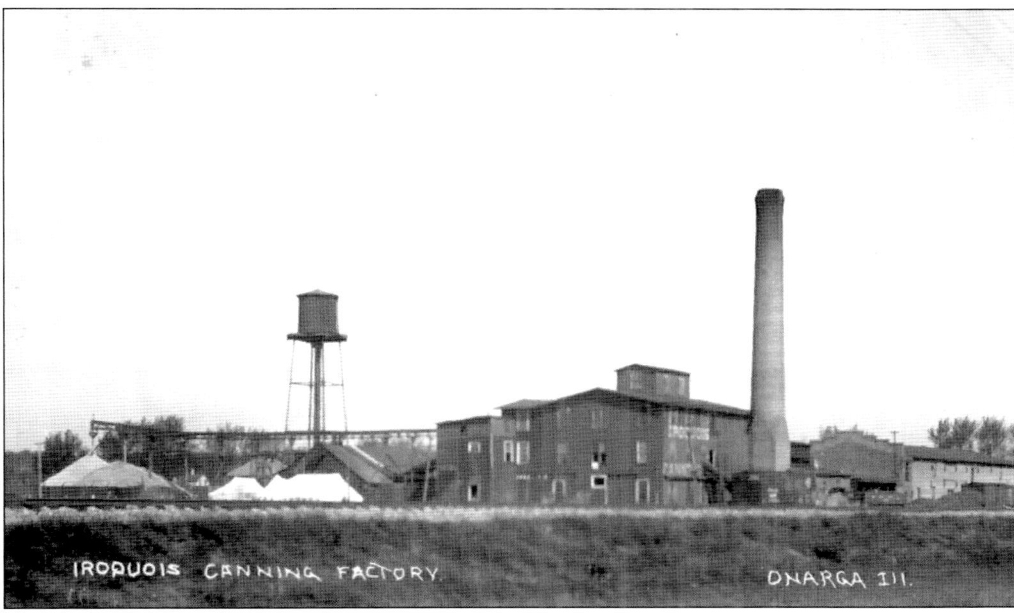

The Iroquois Canning Corporation was established in the late 1800s. It was a thriving business that employed over 400 people, farmed approximately 4,000 acres, and contracted with farmers to raise sweet corn. The mules used in farming this acreage were housed in the large barns on Pinkerton's Larch Farm. The Rissers founded the canning company, but on April 14, 1909, L. J. Risser died in New York. In 1918, Frank Carrington acquired the factory from Annabelle Risser. At the time of the fire, August 25, 1949, it was owned by Jack Brunwasser and Dr. Karl A. Meyer also had an interest in it.

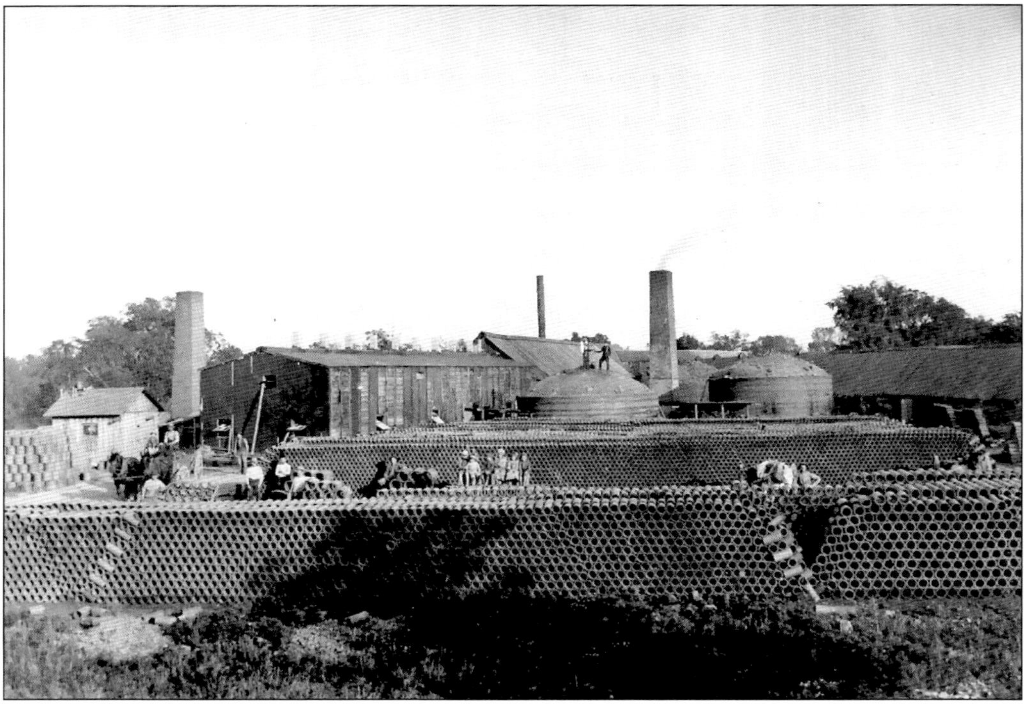

Another factory of this era was the tile factory located approximately one and a half miles east of Onarga, where the Woodland slab crosses Spring Creek. This factory manufactured clay drainage tile, which was used to drain the farmland of the area, making it much more productive. In addition to the drainage tile, drainage ditches were also dug to help convert wet, marshy ground into very productive farmland. The picture below is believed to have been taken west of Onarga, where a large number of yoked oxen are pulling an excavating device.

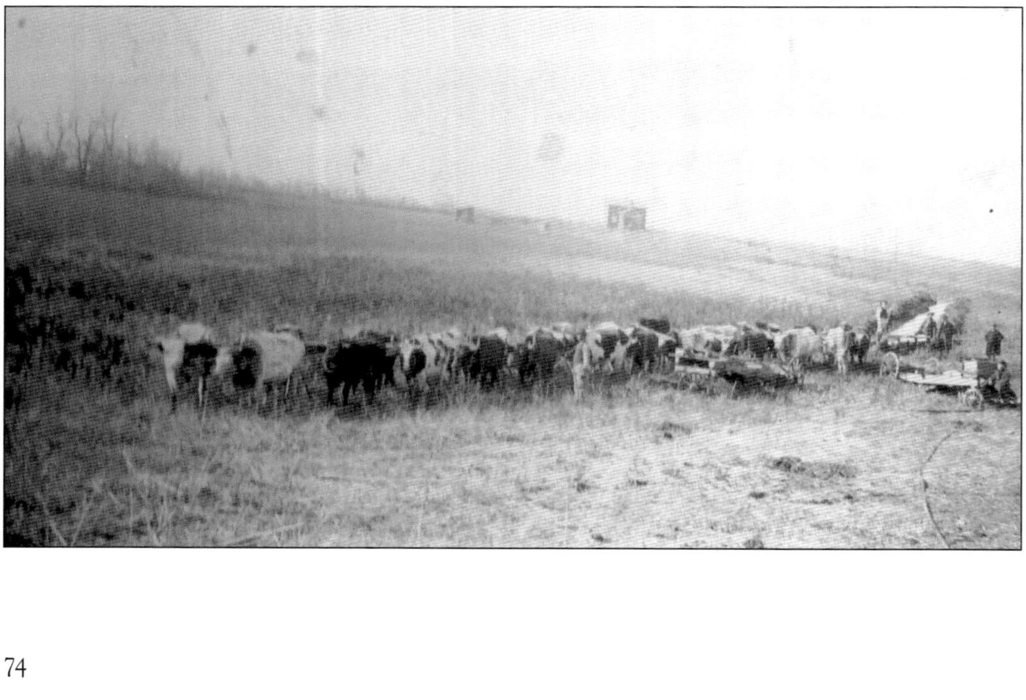

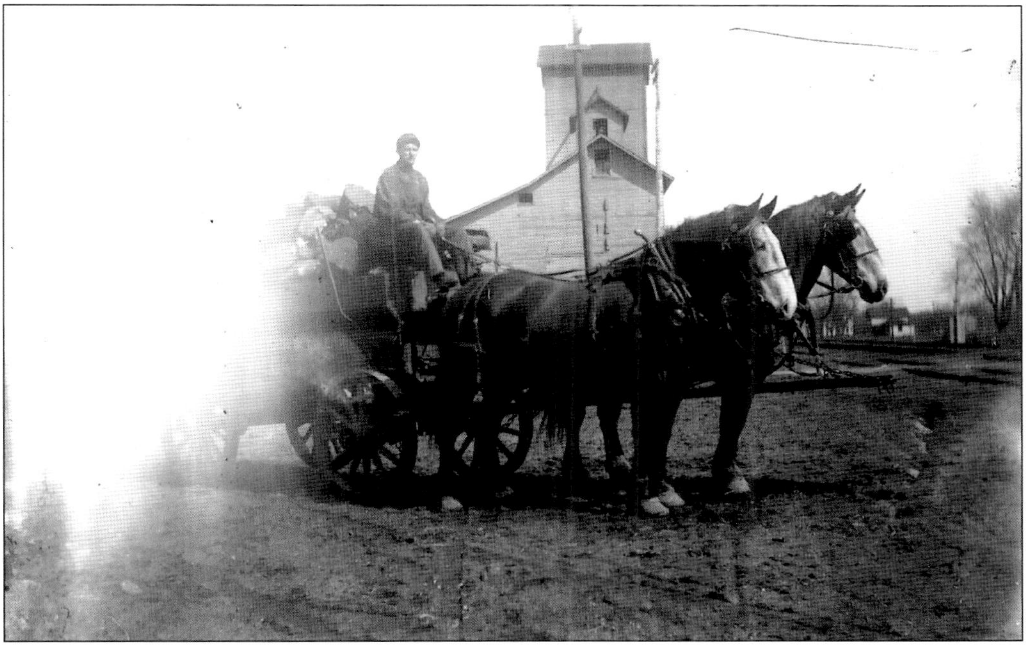

During this time, horsepower was used to deliver many kinds of products. Residences and businesses were heated with coal. The coal bins for the businesses on Chestnut Street were housed below the raised sidewalks in the front of the stores, making it much easier to unload the coal wagons. Note the large chunks of coal on this wagon pictured in front of the old elevator on the north end of Chestnut Street. During the summer, when coal was not needed, the draymen would deliver hay to the local residents. Remember, at this time, instead of a garage attached to the house, residences would have a barn in the backyard to house a horse and buggy, and of course these horses had to eat.

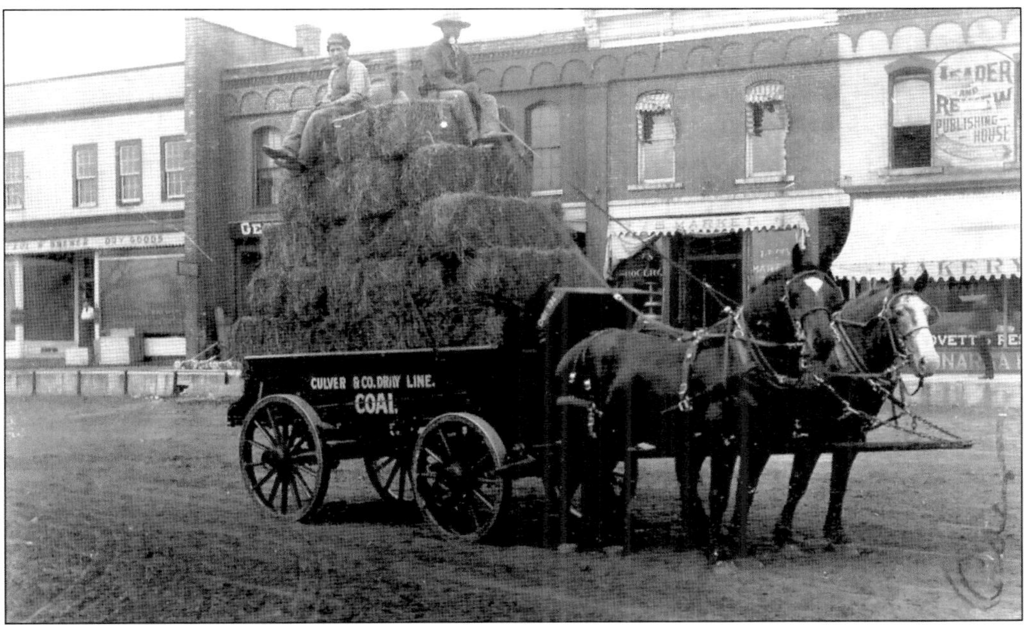

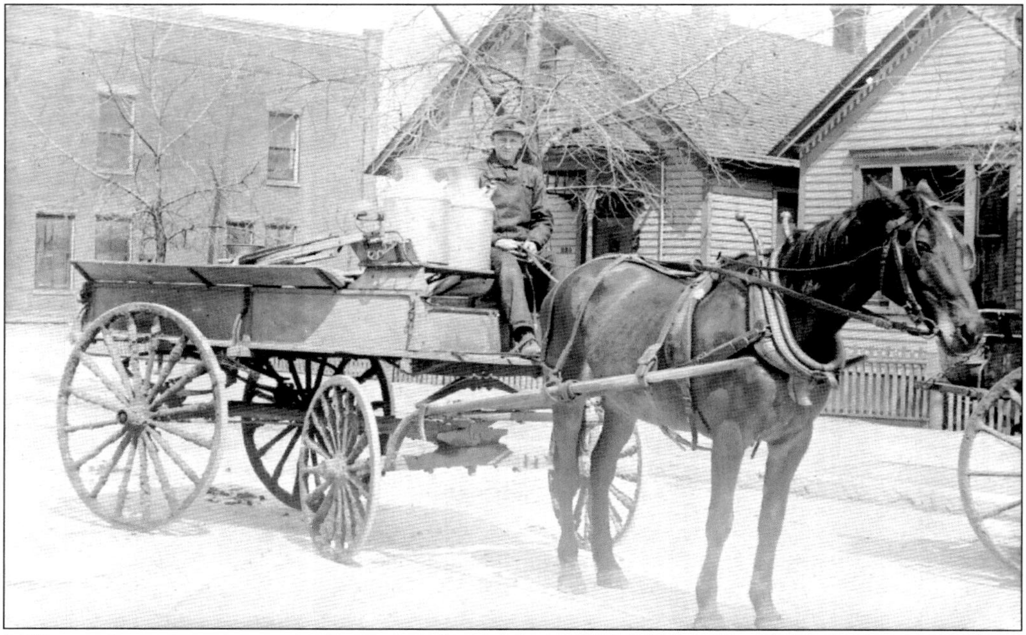

Milk was brought to town in large metal containers and delivered to the cream station where it would be separated and resold. Pictured above is a farmer delivering his two large milk cans to town. During the summer, this milk, along with other produce, would need to be cooled to prevent spoilage. Before electrical refrigeration was common, this cooling was done in iceboxes. The ice was delivered by the iceman. Below is the Amerman Ice Wagon making its rounds.

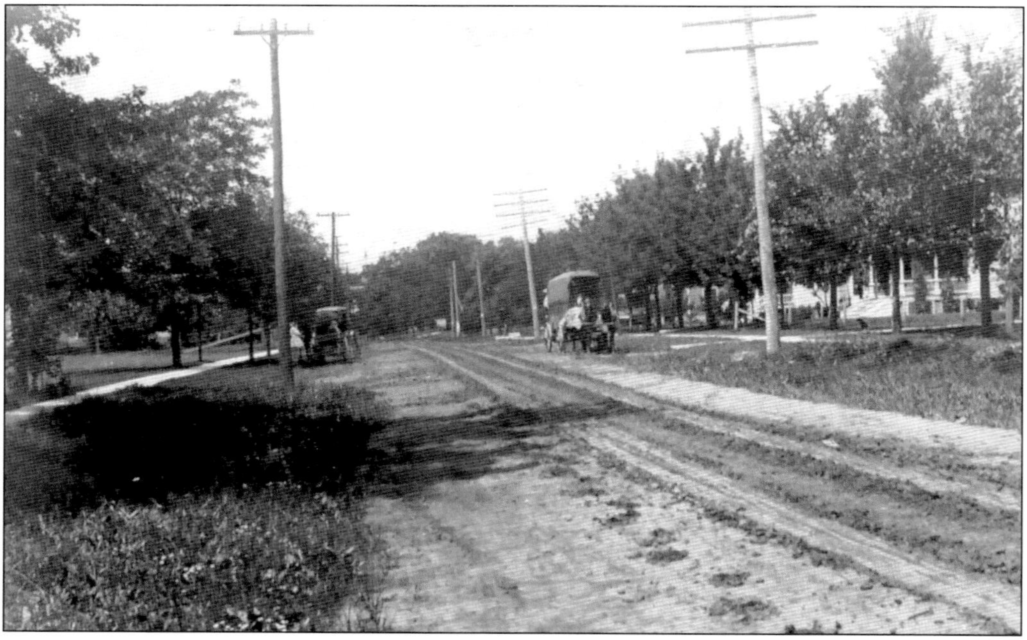

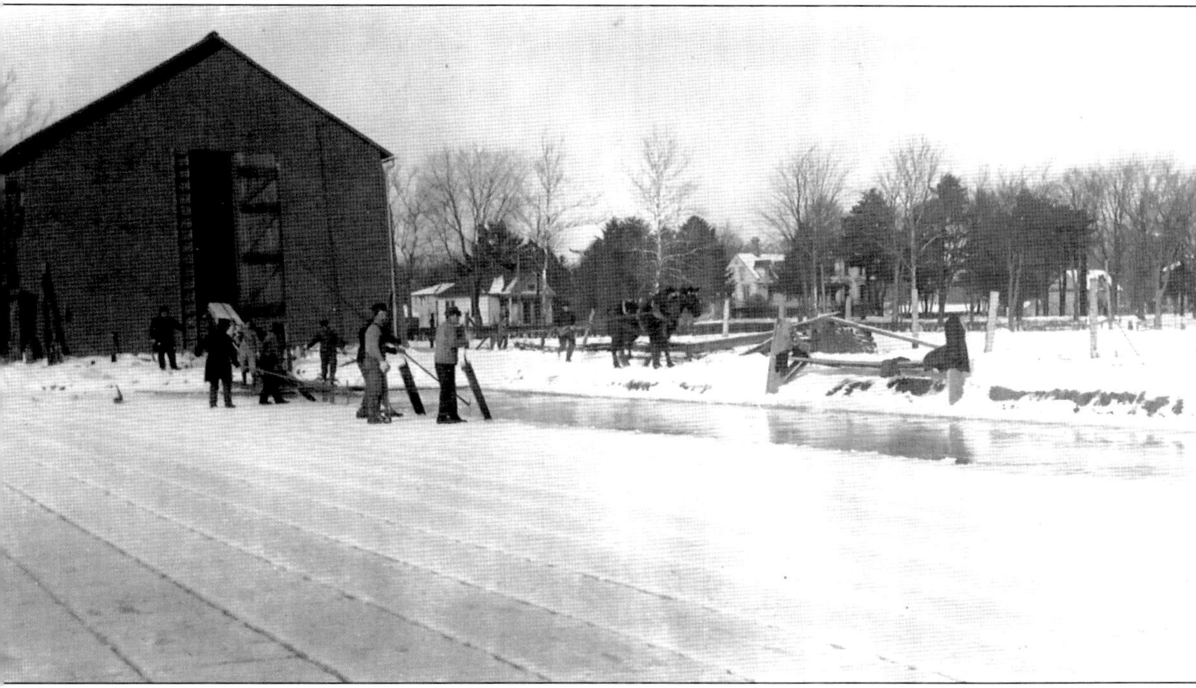

This is the Onarga Ice Pond and House, listed on this 1910 postcard as "One of the Great Wonders of Onarga." Harvesting ice required specialized equipment and tools. In addition to the horse-drawn ice scorers and ice plows, a variety of hand tools were used, including axes, saws, tongs, breaking bars, picks, pikes, and sleds. Note the scores made in the ice and the workers using the saws. The blocks of harvested ice were stored in an icehouse and insulated with straw or sawdust. The icehouses were made of wood with double walls. The space between the walls was filled with sawdust for insulation. The Onarga Ice Pond and House were located on South Evergreen, and that spot, to this day, still floods and fills with water during heavy rains.

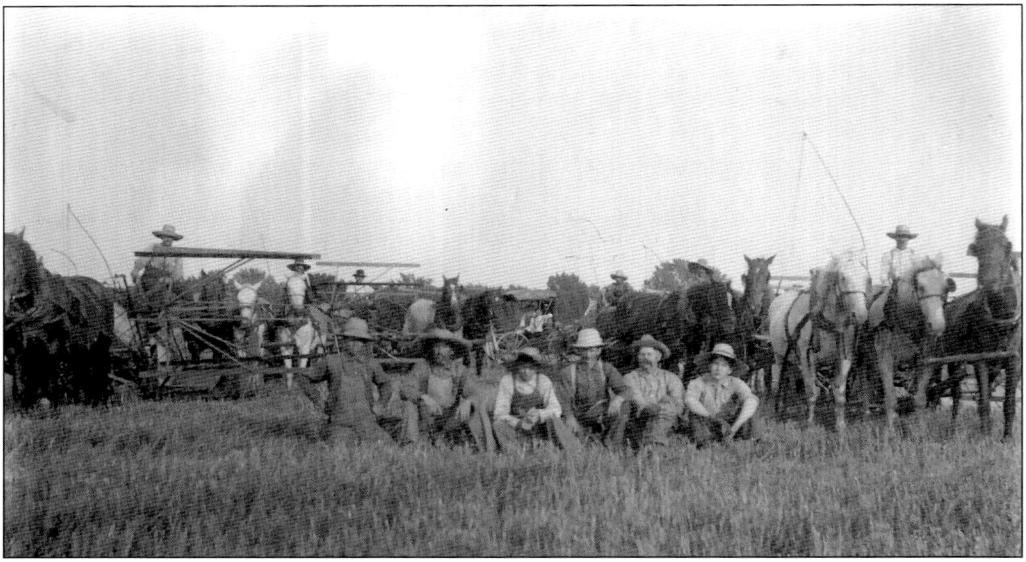

At this time, one of the hottest, dirtiest jobs on the farm was the harvesting of the oat crop. The first step in this process was cutting the oats and placing them into bundles. This was accomplished with a machine known as a binder. The drivers of the binders pictured above, from left to right, are Ira Lindsey, Henry Jimison, E. J. Lindsey, Harry Skeels, Phil Burke, and Harve Hollingsworth. These bundles of oats were then hauled to the thrashing machine. This machine, powered by a steam engine, separated the grain from the stalks and chaff. In late summer, farm families would join together to form thrashing rings. The thrashing rings would work on one farm until all the thrashing was done and then move on to the next farm. Pictured below is a thrashing ring and steam-powered thrashing machine.

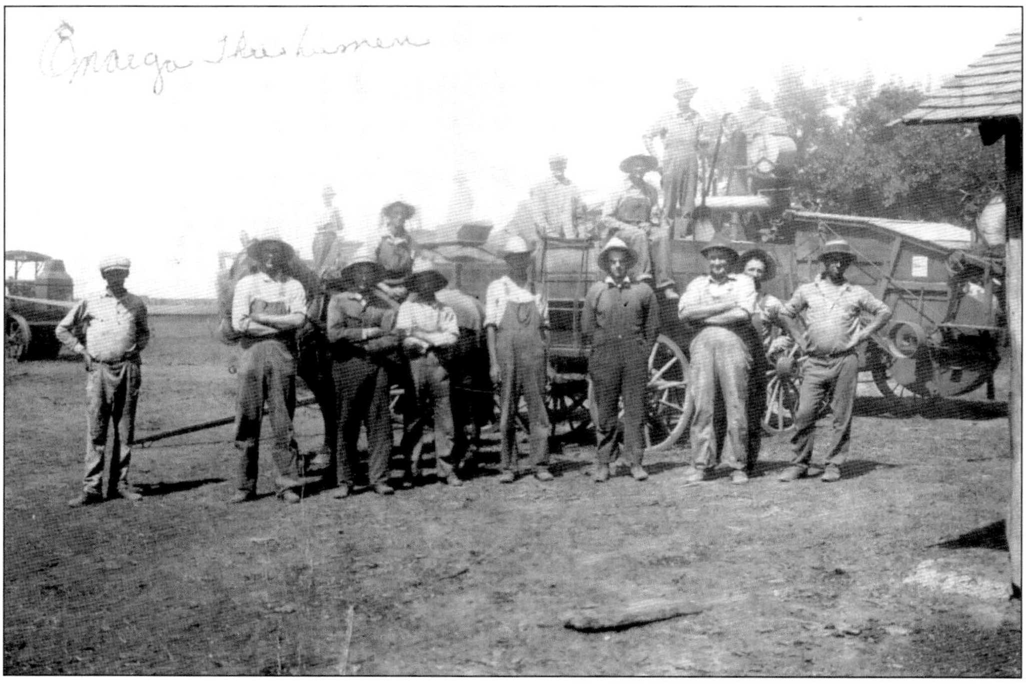

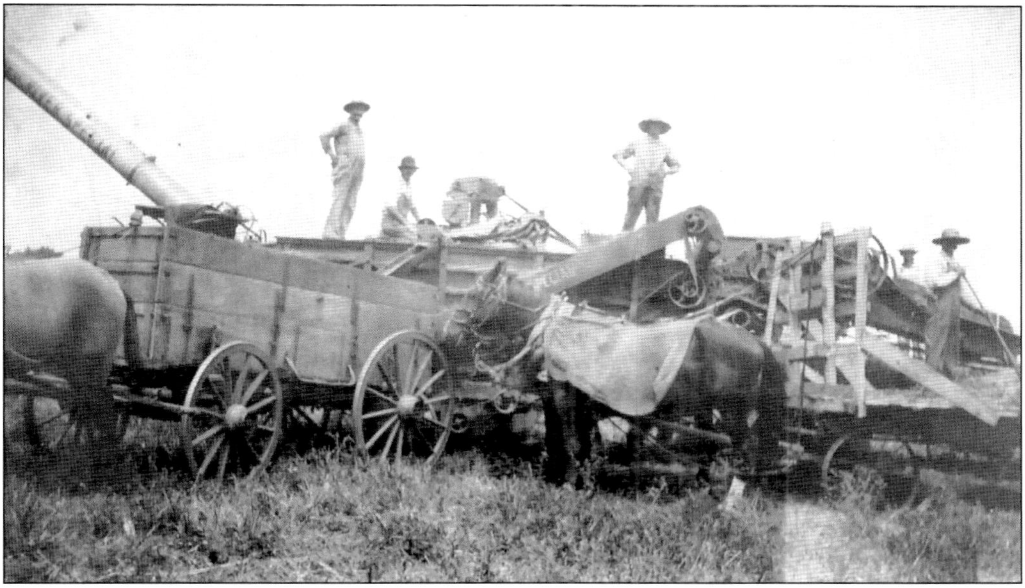

On the thrashing ring, each farmer had a job. One would shovel coal into the steam engine, others would load the bundles of grain onto racks and haul them to the thrashing machine, and others would feed the bundles into the machine. Youngsters carried water and lunches to the men. They spent the entire day at the farm on which they were thrashing, and the wife of that farmer would feed them, always trying to outdo the wives of the other members of the ring.

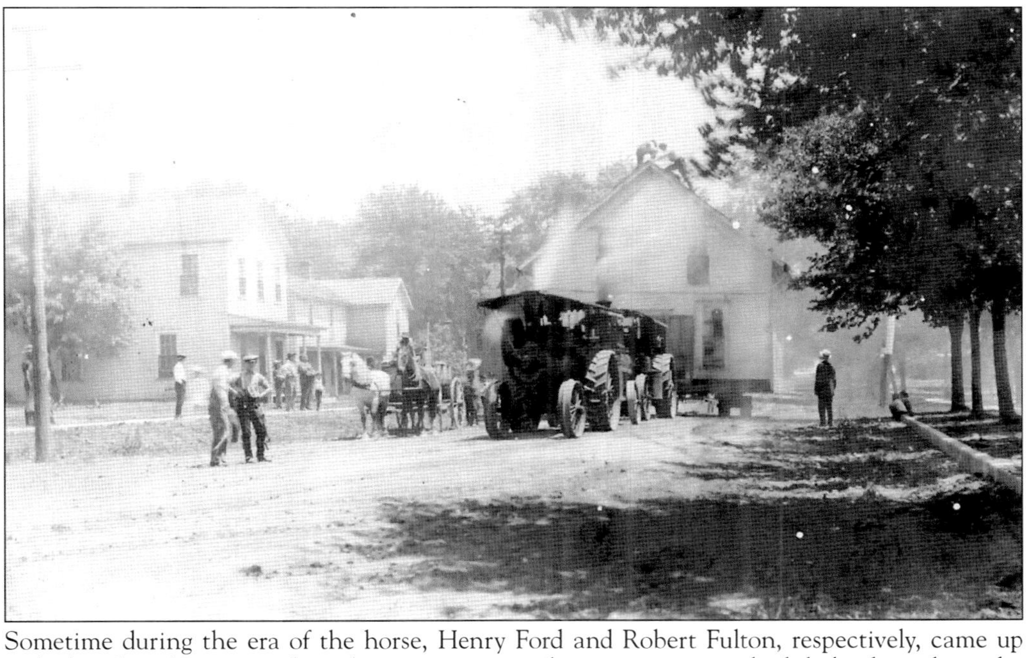

Sometime during the era of the horse, Henry Ford and Robert Fulton, respectively, came up with the idea of an internal combustion engine and a steam engine, which helped to relieve the burden of the previous sole supplier of the horsepower of that time. Here two steam engines are shown moving the parsonage of the Unity Church through Onarga.

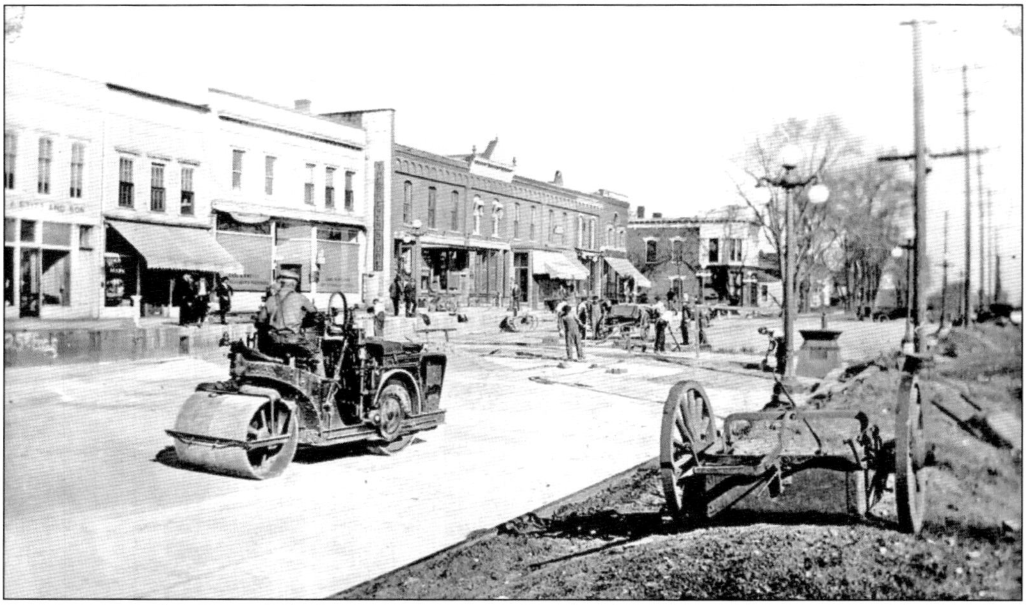

As Henry Ford's automobile became more popular, the dirt streets of Onarga, which of course turned to mud after a rain, became less and less acceptable. These pictures show the paving of Chestnut Street and West Lincoln Avenue. The picture above is titled "Paving Main Street (Circa. 1913-1915)." Note the roller compressing the sand in preparation for the laying of the brick, which is being done in the background. The picture below is of the paving of West Lincoln Avenue with the grain elevator located at the north end of Chestnut and the old hotel (on the corner of Lincoln Avenue and Route 45) in the background.

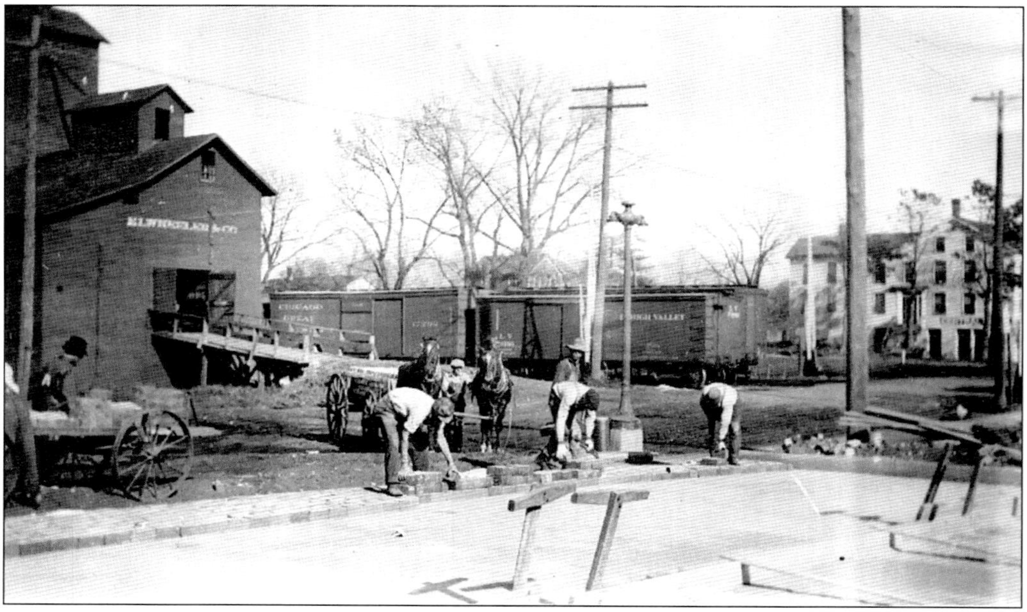

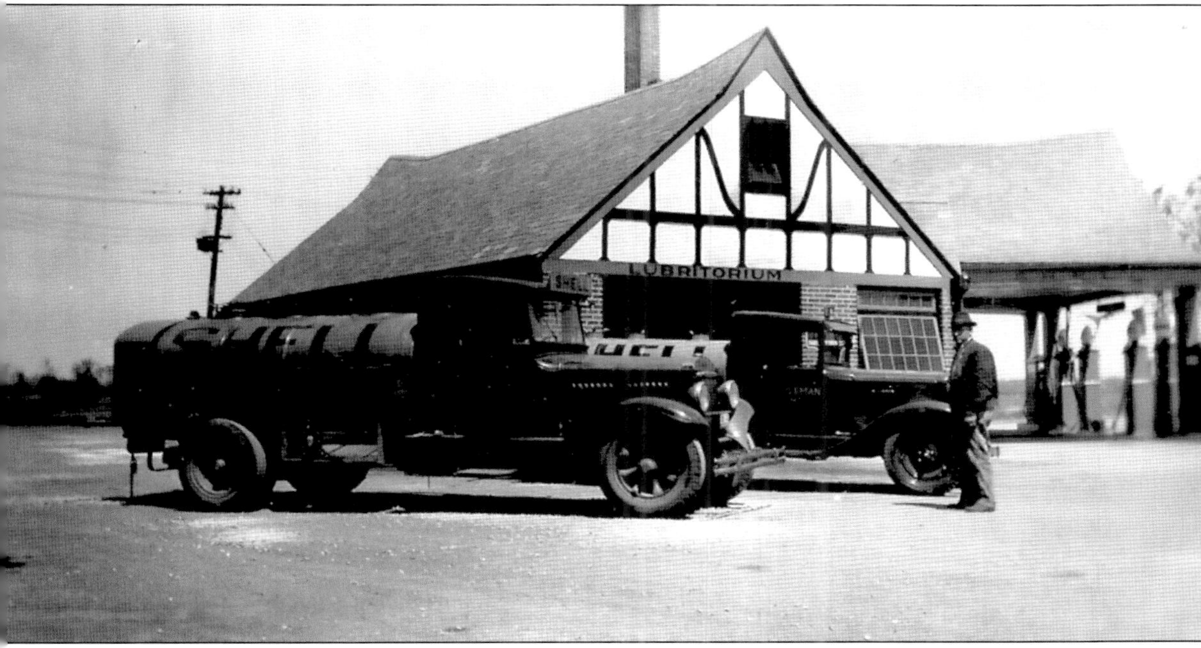

Before the advent of the super highway, Route 45 (formerly known as State Route 25) was the most direct route from Chicago to Cairo, Illinois. This route, also known as the Egyptian Trail, passed through Onarga, and Onarga businessmen responded with the creation of the stretch of road known by Onarga locals as "Gasoline Alley." Beginning at the north end of town was Carrington's Shell Station. Later Glen Eshleman operated this station. Note the "Lubritorium" over the service bay. This station was a "full service truck stop" with a café and sleeping quarters for the truckers, which were located above the service bay. Across the road was a station in front of the Onarga Nursery operated by George Townsend. Just south of this station, where Bork Nursery is now located, was a station and small café operated by Russell Hanson.

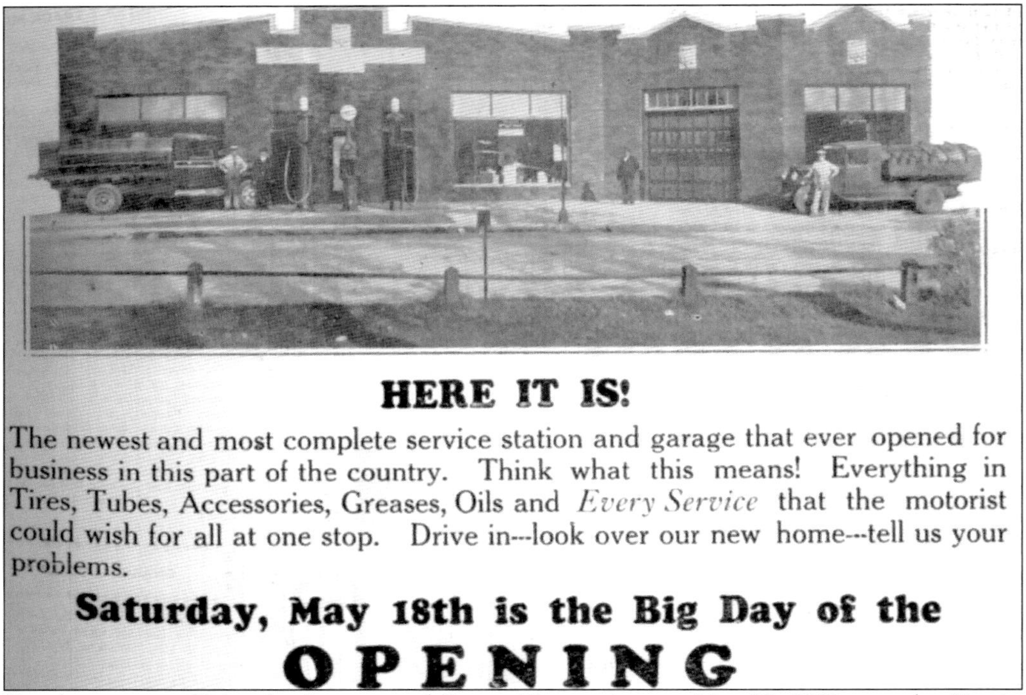

On the corner of Lincoln Avenue and Route 45, opening on May 18, 1929, was the Tarvin Brothers Shell Service Station, garage, and café, featuring curb service. The café was called the Shell Inn and in 1929 was operated by L. G. Schleichardt.

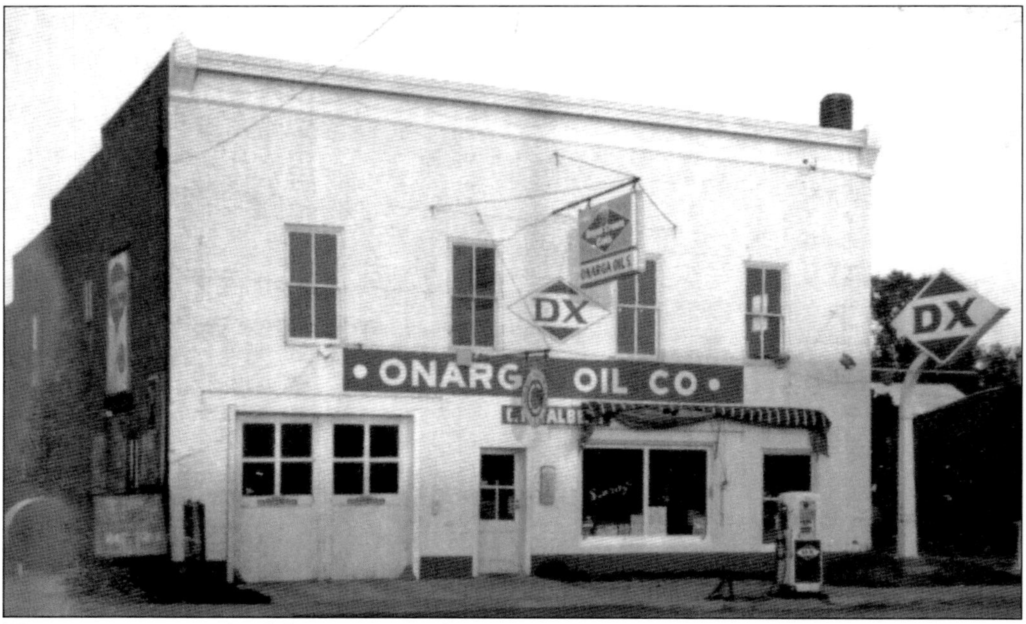

This station was south of the Tarvin Brothers, just south of the old town hall. It was originally a Farm Service Station and later was operated by Clarence Talbert, son of Lyman Talbert, whose original station was just south of the Farm Service Station.

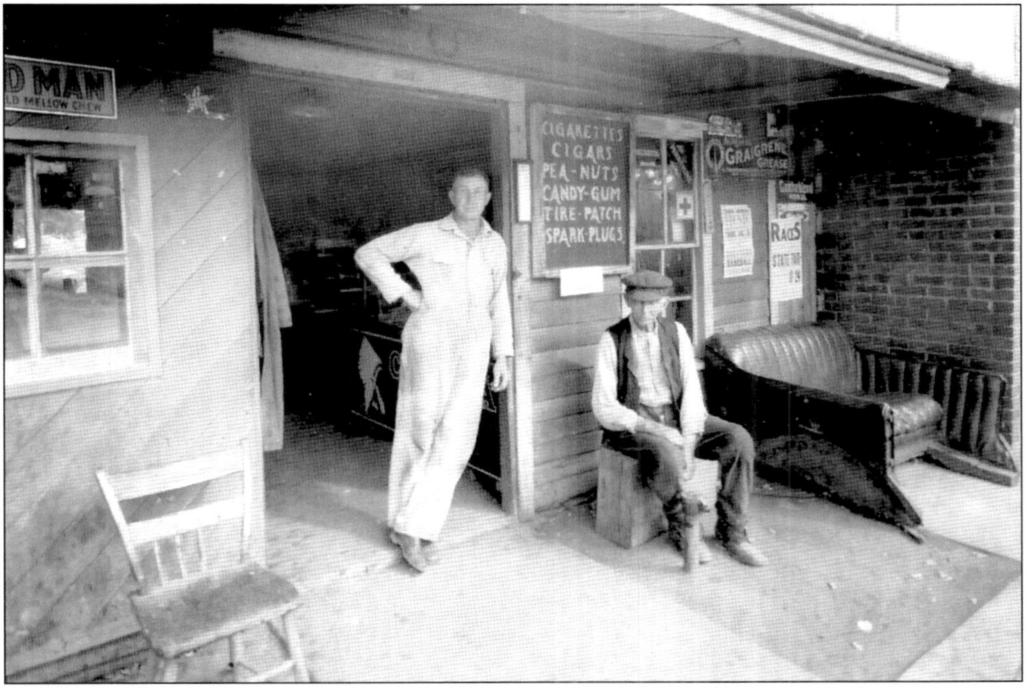

This was the original station operated by Lyman Talbert. The Talbert station operated as the Onarga Oil Company and advertised as "Located in the center of Gasoline Alley." Lyman Talbert is standing in the doorway.

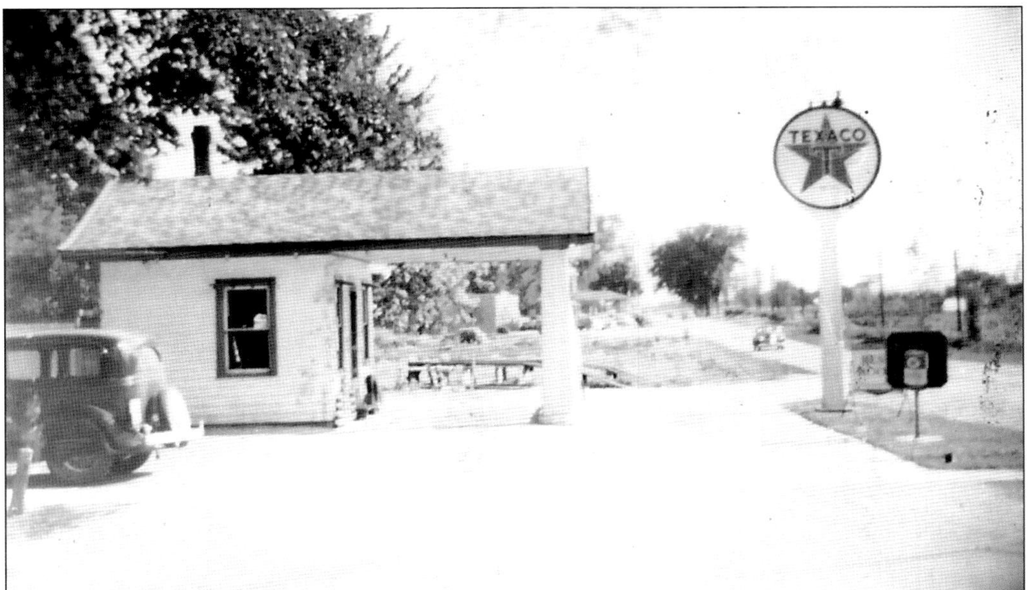

This Texaco station was located at the corner of Seminary Avenue and Route 45. At the time of this picture, it was operated by Harold Hasselbring.

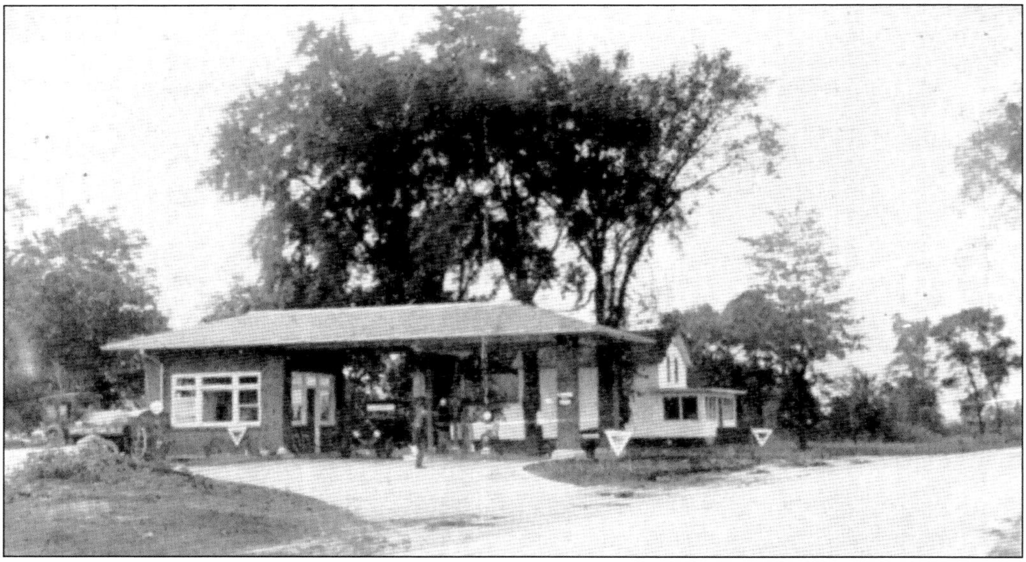

This station was at the corner of Roosevelt Street and Route 45 and, in 1929, was operated by Whiteside and Thrasher. They sold Barnsdall B-Square gasoline and kerosene.

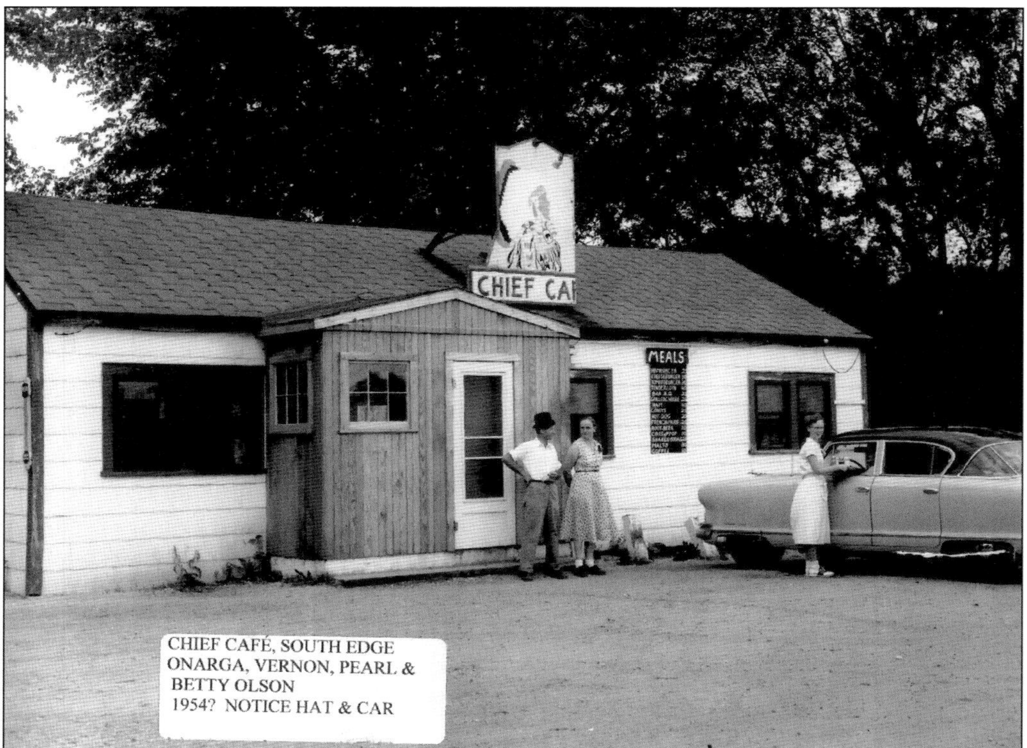

Another half block south was the H&W Station (Hatfield and Woodard). This station was operated in conjunction with a repair shop and café, known as the Chief Café (pictured above).

Eight

East Side, West Side

In May 1891, M. T. Amerman decided to start a new business in addition to his grocery business. He began the M. T. Amerman Undertaker and Embalmer Service. His services included embalming and preparing the body at the deceased's home. All the visitations and funerals were also conducted at the family home. M. T.'s two sons, Harry and Fred, joined their father in the business in 1904 and 1906, respectively. In 1925, M. T. Amerman died at the age of 66. In memory of their father, Fred and Harry built the Amerman Mortuary.

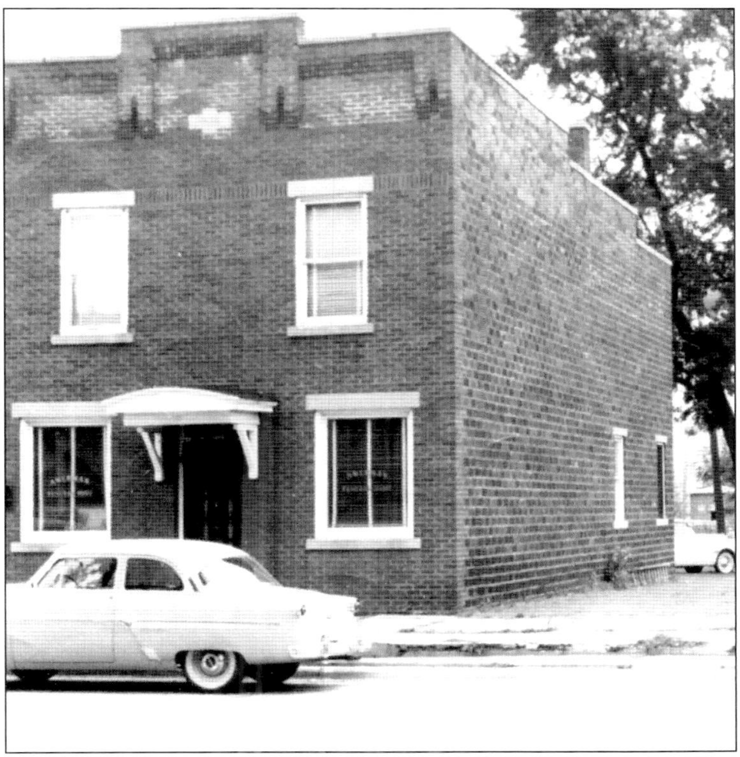

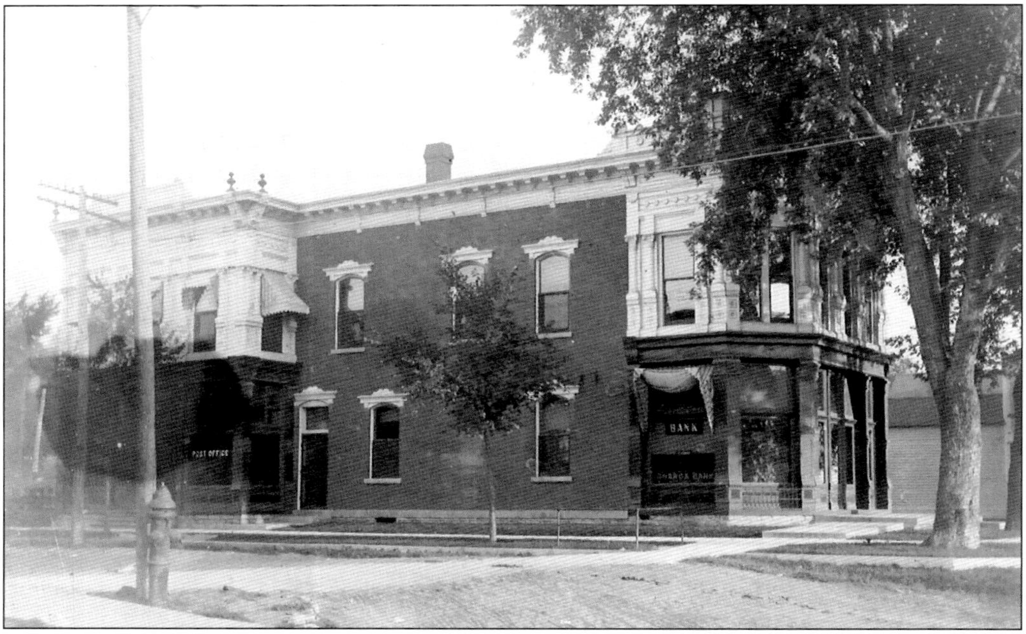

The David Durham family lived near Terre Haute, Indiana. After the death of their father, they moved to Onarga because of the Grand Prairie Seminary and the fellowship of the Friends Church (Quakers) that was maintained there at the time. Brothers Ben, Ezra, and William Durham started the Durham Bank after their graduation from Grand Prairie Seminary.

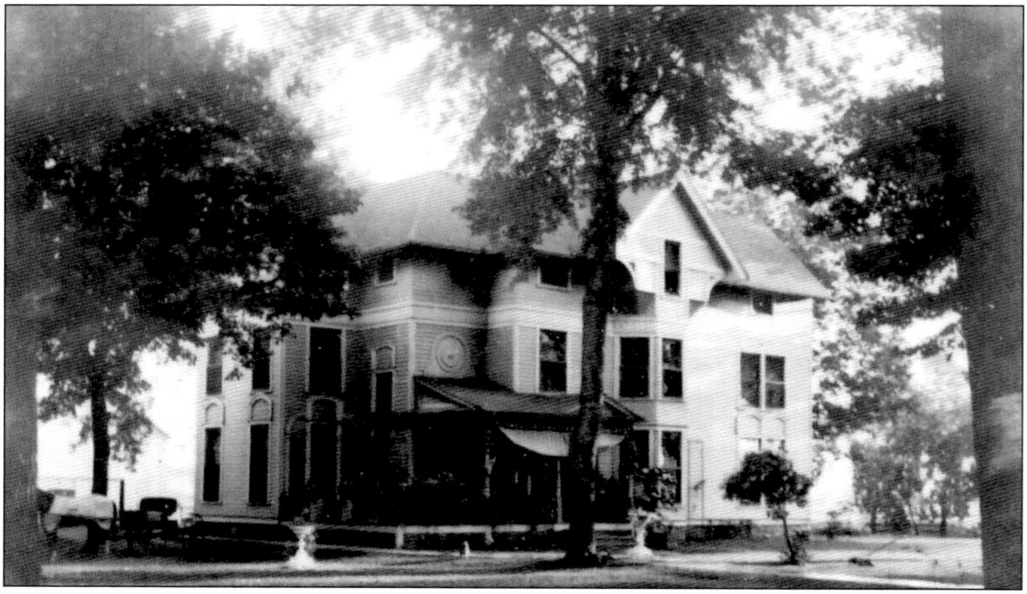

William and Mary Josephine Durham left this home in Onarga in 1915 to move to Los Angeles, California. In October 1925, they sold their Onarga home and 20 acres surrounding it to the Village of Onarga for $1. The deed record stipulated that the house and 20 acres were to be used to provide a park for the town and that if at any time thereafter the acreage was not used as a park then the real estate would revert to the Durham family heirs.

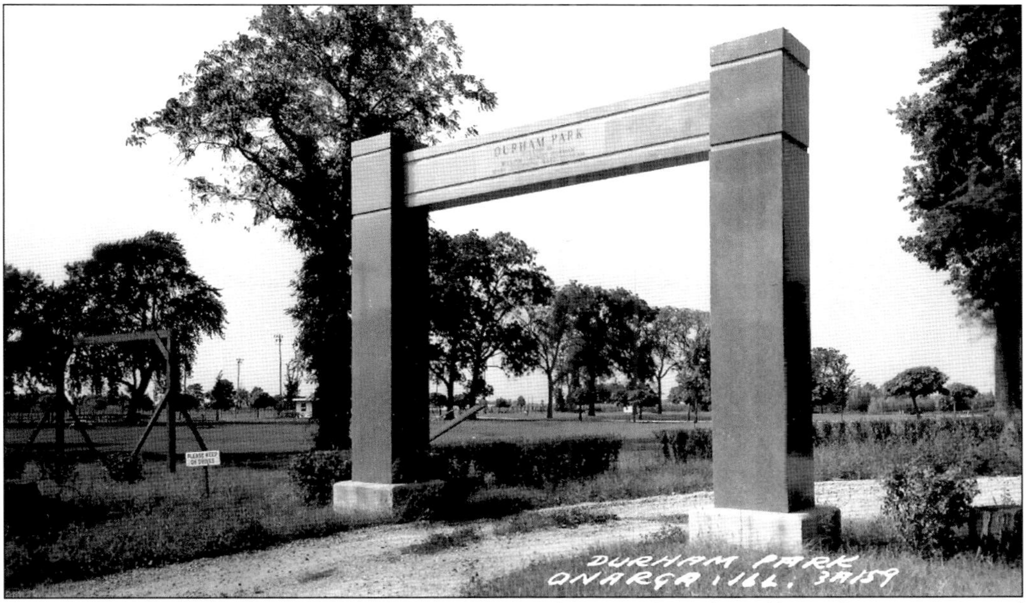

The future success of Durham Park was assured in July 1950 when the Village of Onarga received two gifts from William and Mary Durham. The first was a gift of $8,000 to erect this granite arch at the entrance to the park and to enclose the park with a woven wire fence. The second gift was a 240-acre farm near Rankin. The income from the farm was to be used for the development of the park and recreational facilities for the community.

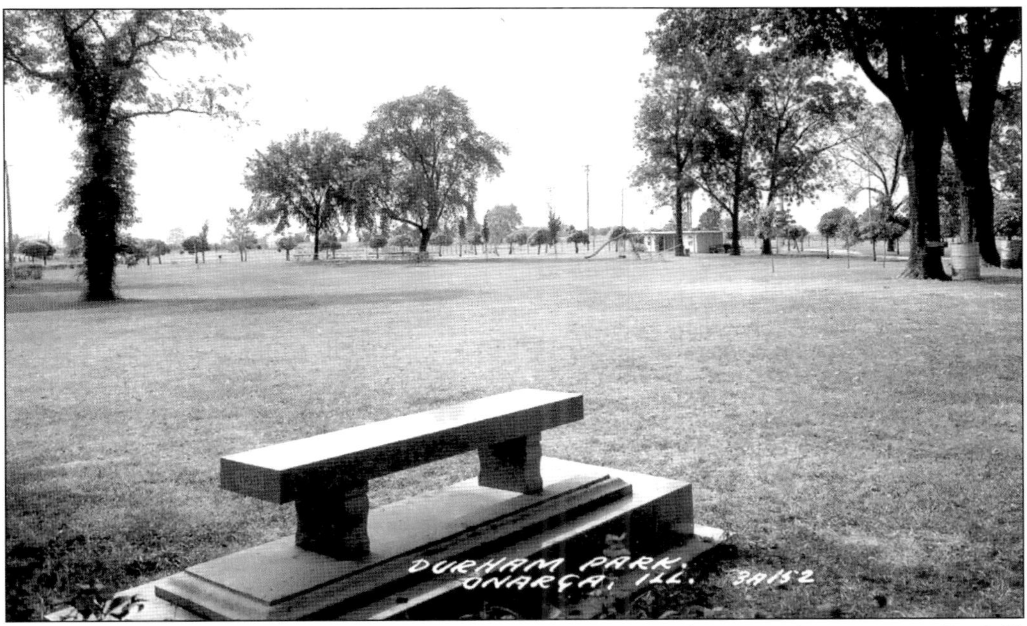

This marble bench was dedicated in 1950 to the memory of Onarga businessman Fred K. Amerman and his son, Sgt. Bruce Amerman, who both died that year. Just north of the bench and out of the photograph is a large concrete water fountain with a plaque that reads, "Presented by John Cox & Sons, 1933."

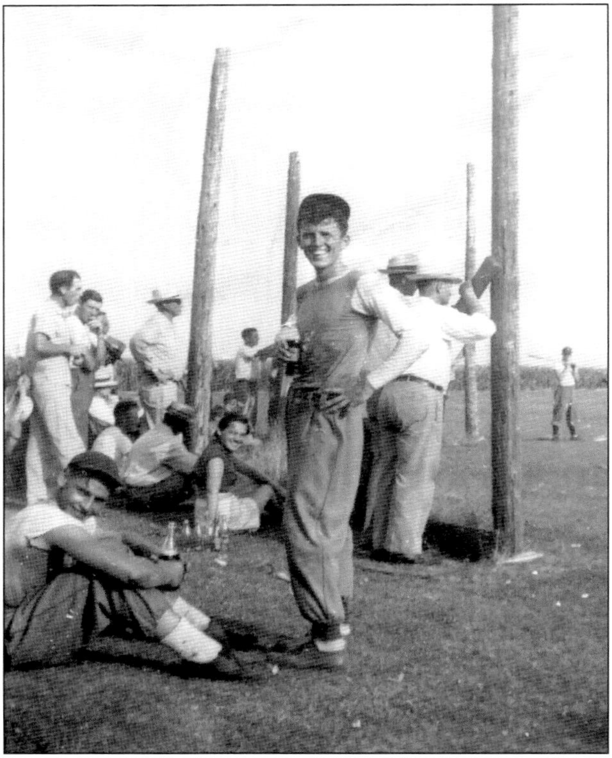

Shortly after World War II, some of the returning veterans formed a baseball team. Wayne Lee, pictured here (on right) with Dick and Margaret Dannehl, recalled that the park was not mowed or kept up well at this point. A few hours before a game, Dick and Wayne would borrow a manual reel mower from Clarence Talbert and push mow the outfield.

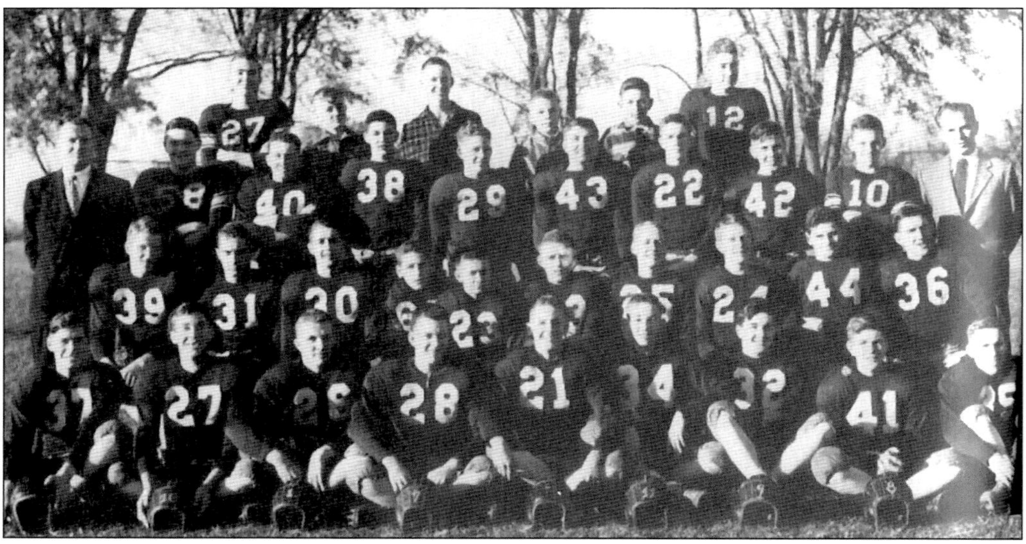

The 1949 Onarga High School football team was the first to have the privilege of playing at the new Johnson Field at Durham Park. Harold Lathrop, third from the left in the first row, was the first to score a touchdown there. The field was built with volunteer labor. Dr. Johnson donated the lights for the field, earning the honor of having the field named for him.

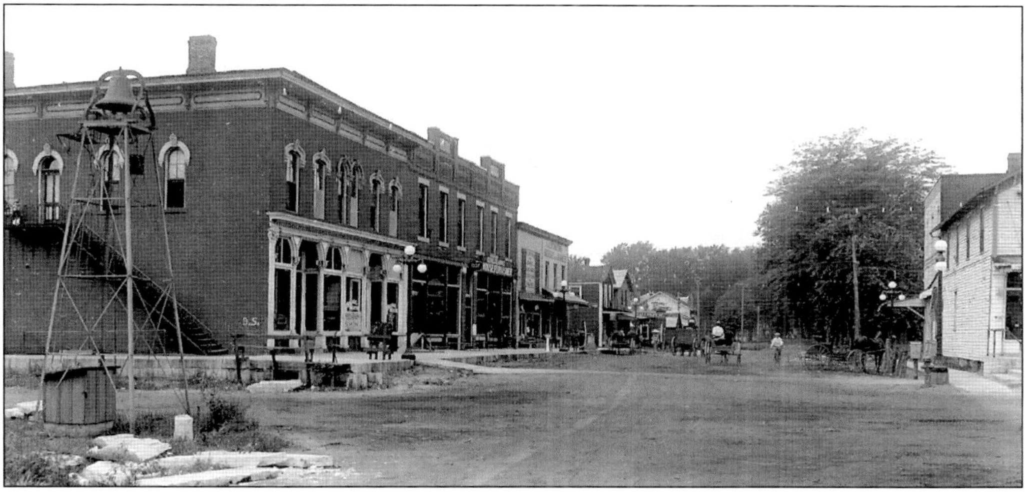

Originally Brown and Company Hardware and Furniture, this building was modified and became the Modernistic and then the Mode Theater. The idea of a theater was hatched in 1933 when the Military School Auditorium was leveled by a fire starting in the projection room. Irvin Gromell and associate John Egley began the Modernistic Theater. Gromell also purchased the building next door and converted it into a tearoom. On July 7, 1935, the Modernistic opened showing "Folies Bergere" starring Maurice Chevalier. In August 1937, Gromell leased the building to the Kerasotes Brothers of Urbana. They changed the name to the Mode. Note the fire bell that stood at the corner of West Seminary Avenue and South Chestnut Street. Pranksters even rang the bell when there was no fire.

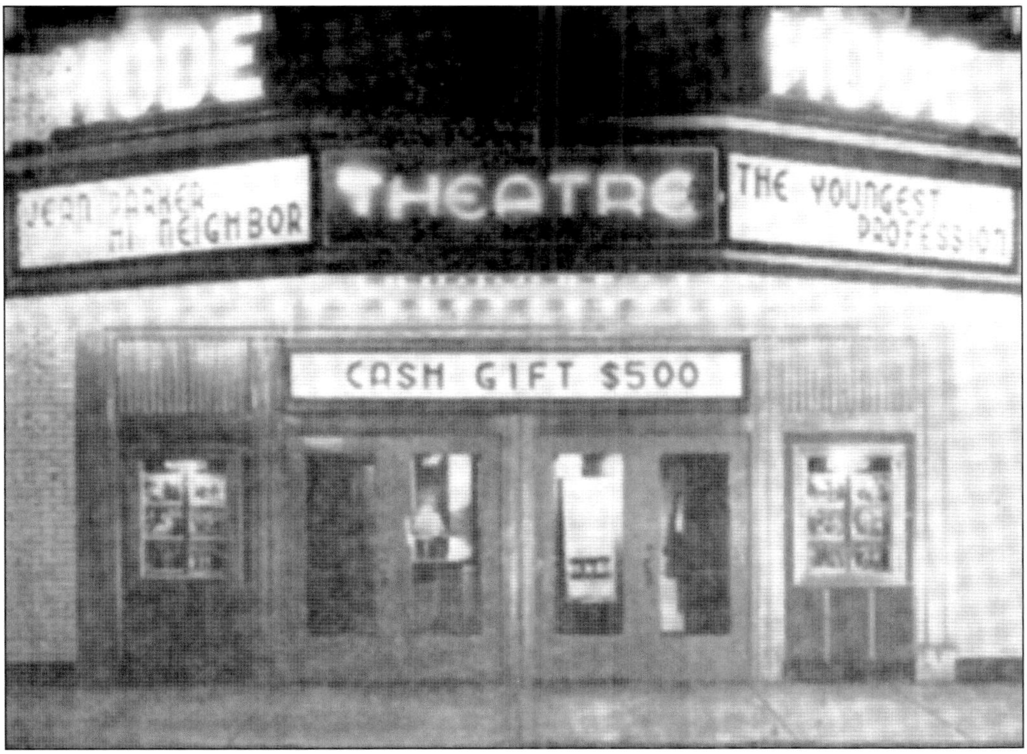

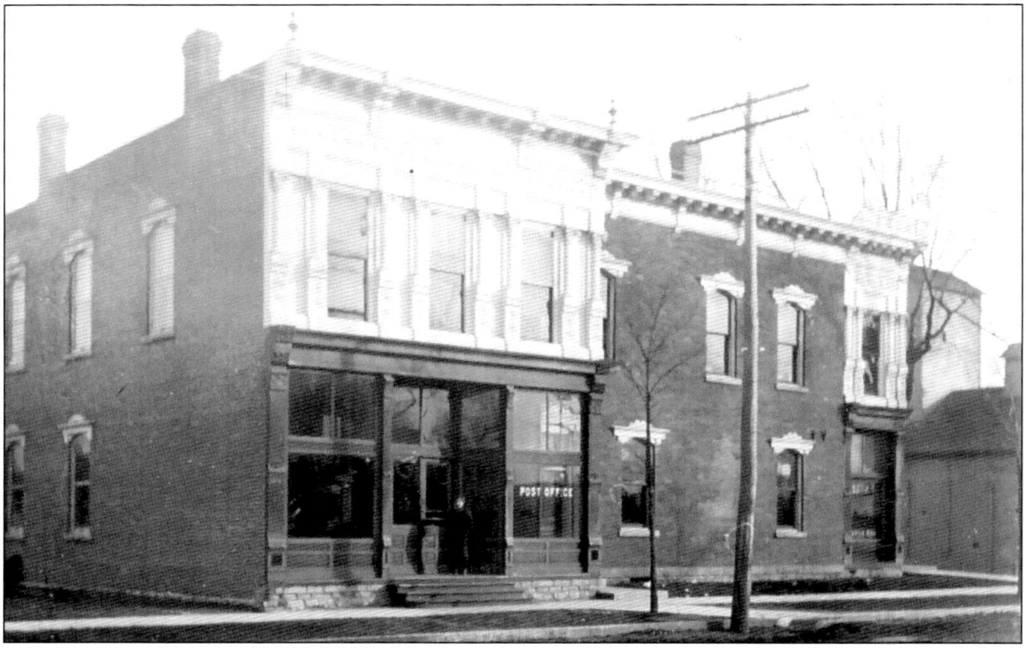

At one time, mail was dispatched by train where mailbags were hung for pick up. Postal records show that the Onarga Post Office was established on March 24, 1854, with Townsend W. Gardner appointed postmaster. The post office was located in the Durham Building at the corner of North Chestnut Street and West Lincoln Avenue. Other businesses were the Durham Bank; M. K. Smith, attorney, and later Mr. Thomasen; Illinois Bell Telephone Office; Dr. J. L. Shawl's office; Esther's Beauty Salon; and numerous restaurants.

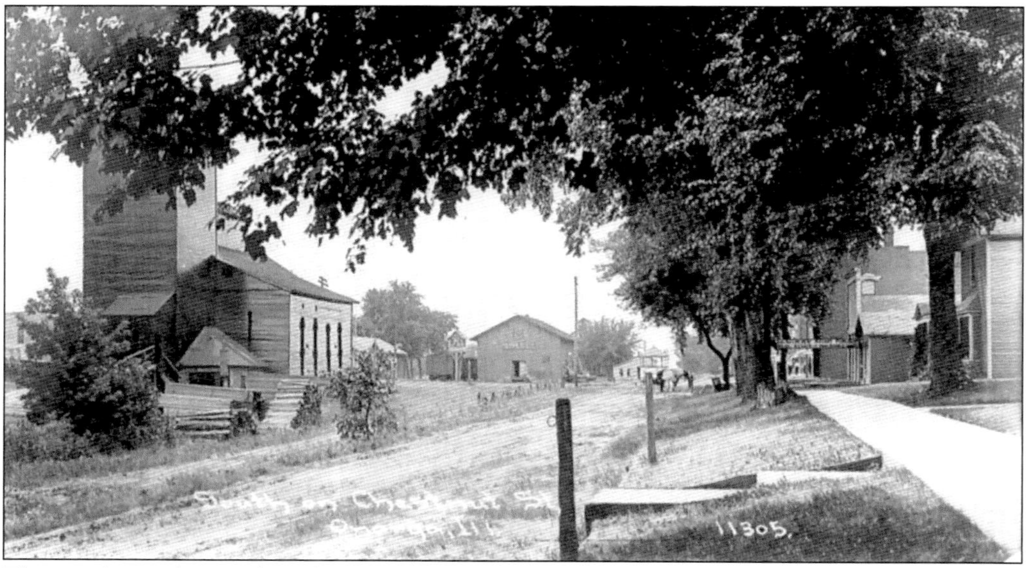

The warehouse for Booth and Stitt Lumber can be seen on the east side of Chestnut Street along with the E. L. Wheeler elevator. Wheeler ran a second elevator that was located south of Seminary and Chestnut. There was also a long line of coal bins as coal was the main source of heat at that time. On the roof of the second elevator was a large, bronze weather vane of a horse.

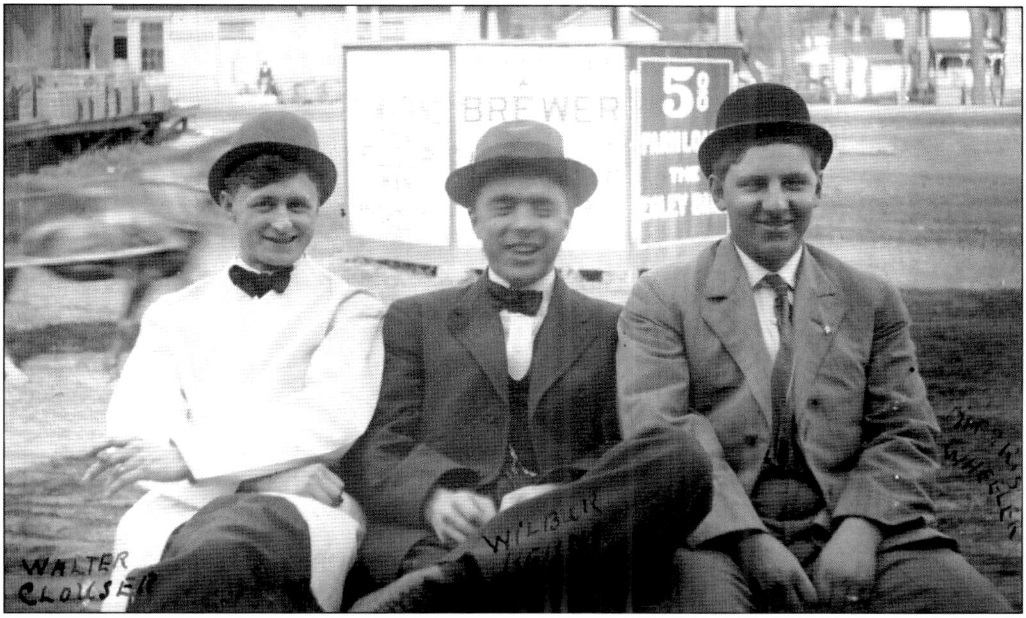

This photograph was taken on Onarga's main street in front of the advertising gazebo and depicts Walter Clouser the barber, Wilbur Kerns the banker, and Morris "Boy" Wheeler from the elevator.

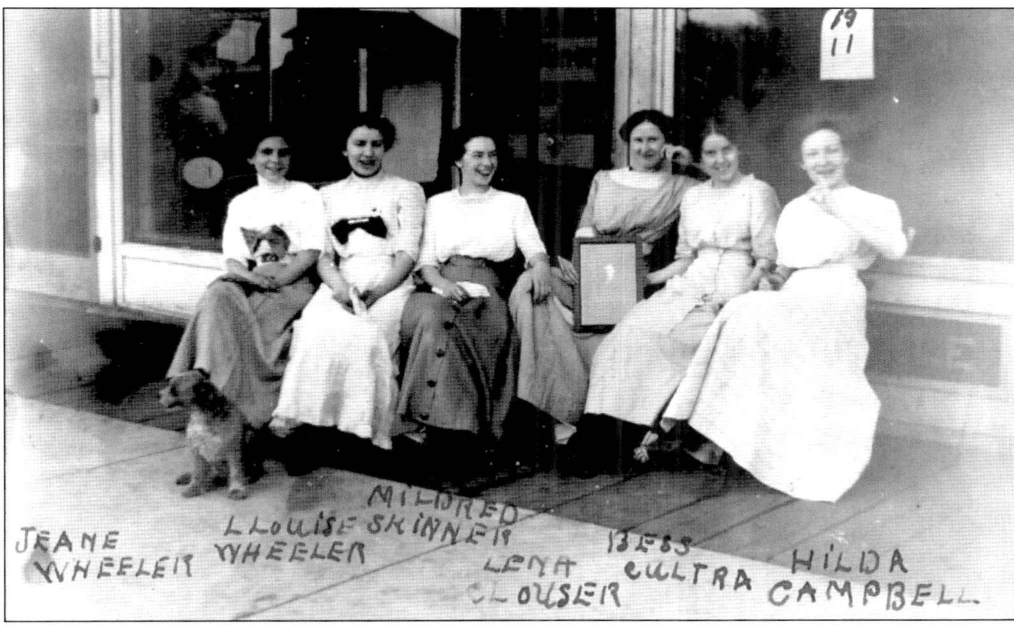

This 1911 photograph depicts Hilda Campbell and Bess Cultra, proprietresses of the C&C Millinery Store. From left to right are Jeane Wheeler, L. Louise Wheeler, Mildred Skinner, Lena Clouser, Bess Cultra, and Hilda Campbell. It was fashionable to display the latest styles in hats in a glass case outside the storefront.

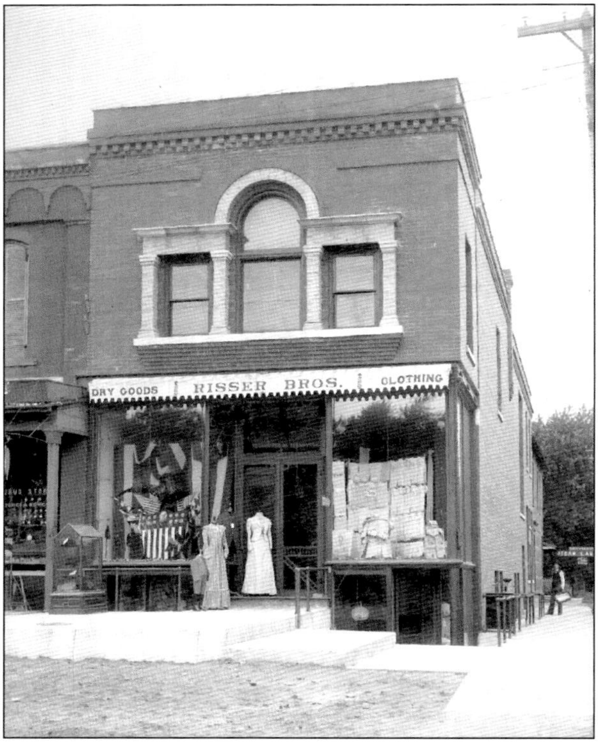

The Risser Mercantile Store was located on the corner of West Lincoln Avenue and North Chestnut Street. The Rissers were at one time in partnership with William Pierson. These photographs were taken of the mercantile store in the early 1900s. Note the glass millinery case. Special invitations were sent to the ladies of Onarga to view their spring and fall chapeau specials.

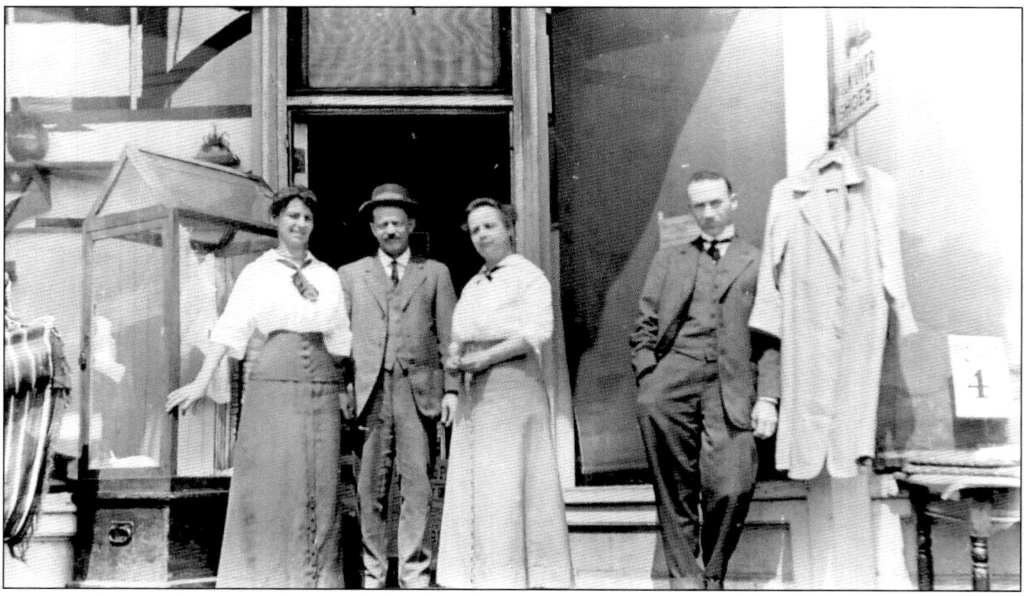

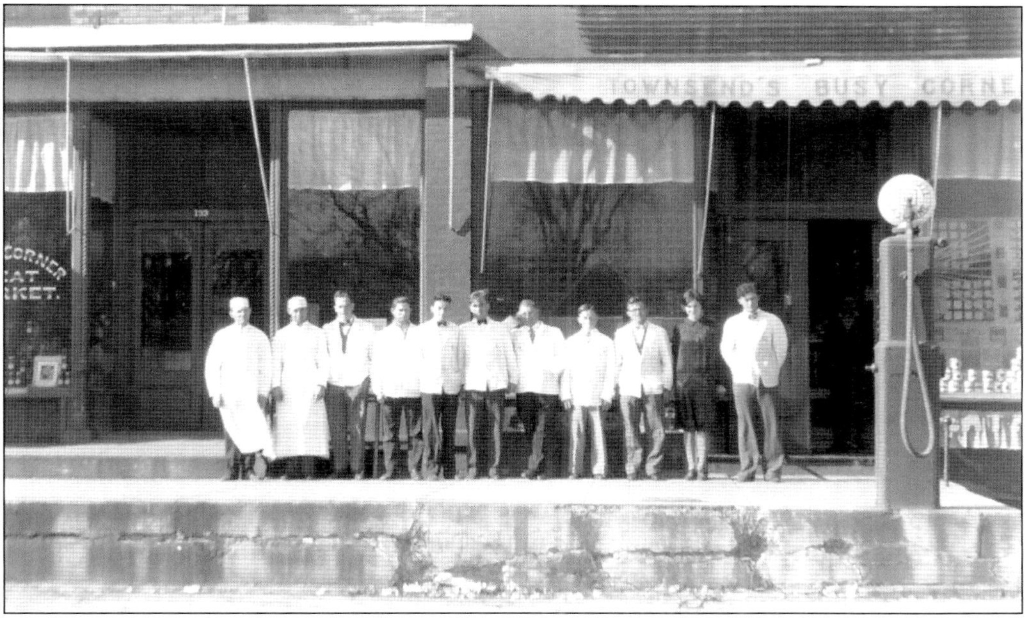

South of Lincoln Avenue on Chestnut Street was the Ted Townsend Grocery Store and the Busy Corner Meat Market. Note the Barnsdall Gas Pump, which sat right in front of the Townsend Grocery Store. The above photograph depicts the employees of the Townsend's Busy Corner Grocery Store and Meat Market. To the south of the Busy Corner were Sparnell's 5 and 10 Cent Store; Charles Krause's Drug Store; and in the same building, Ira Furby's watch repair and jewelry store. There was also the Stitt's Hardware; Dr. Hemala's office; the Leader and Review; Jack Craig Cleaning and Pressing; Lawhead's Photo Shop; and John Setinsky, tailor. Other businesses were Brewer's Clothing Store, Billy Fickle's Electrical and Fix-It Shop, Clark Cook's Restaurant and Hotel, and Dad Carney's Barber Shop.

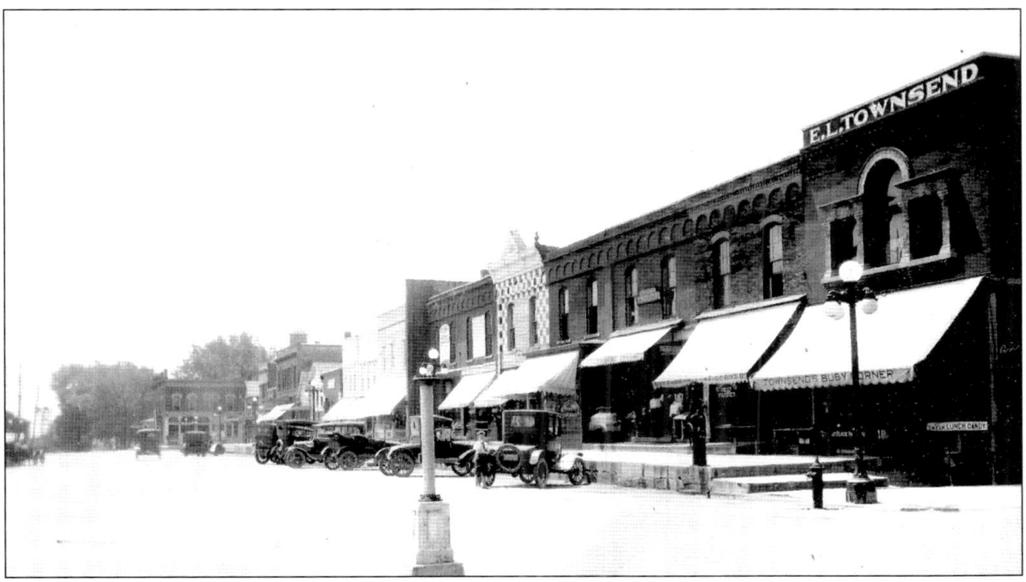

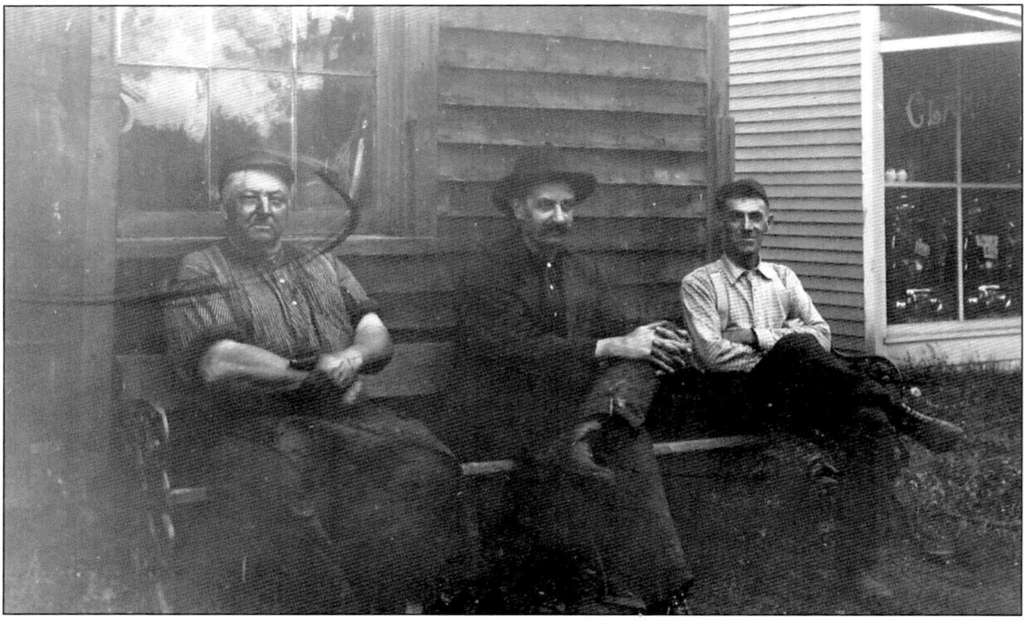

This photograph shows Cal Burkhalter, who ran a blacksmith shop, and George and Gaylord Clarke, who ran a hardware and secondhand store. Their businesses were located on the north side of East Lincoln Avenue.

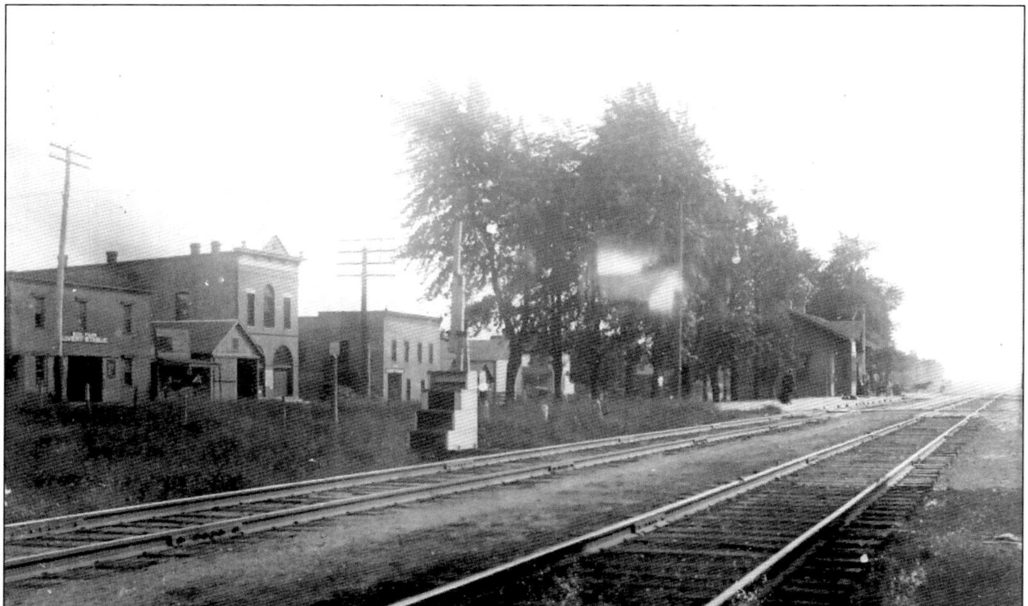

This photograph also shows the east side of Onarga: Baylor's Livery later purchased by Ed Farr; the Onarga Town Hall—with the Masonic lodge upstairs; the local calaboose behind the town hall; Hugh Ishmiel's Blacksmith shop; and Sam Moon's Livery and Undertaking. The Illinois Central Railroad depot and freight house was on the east side of the tracks as well.

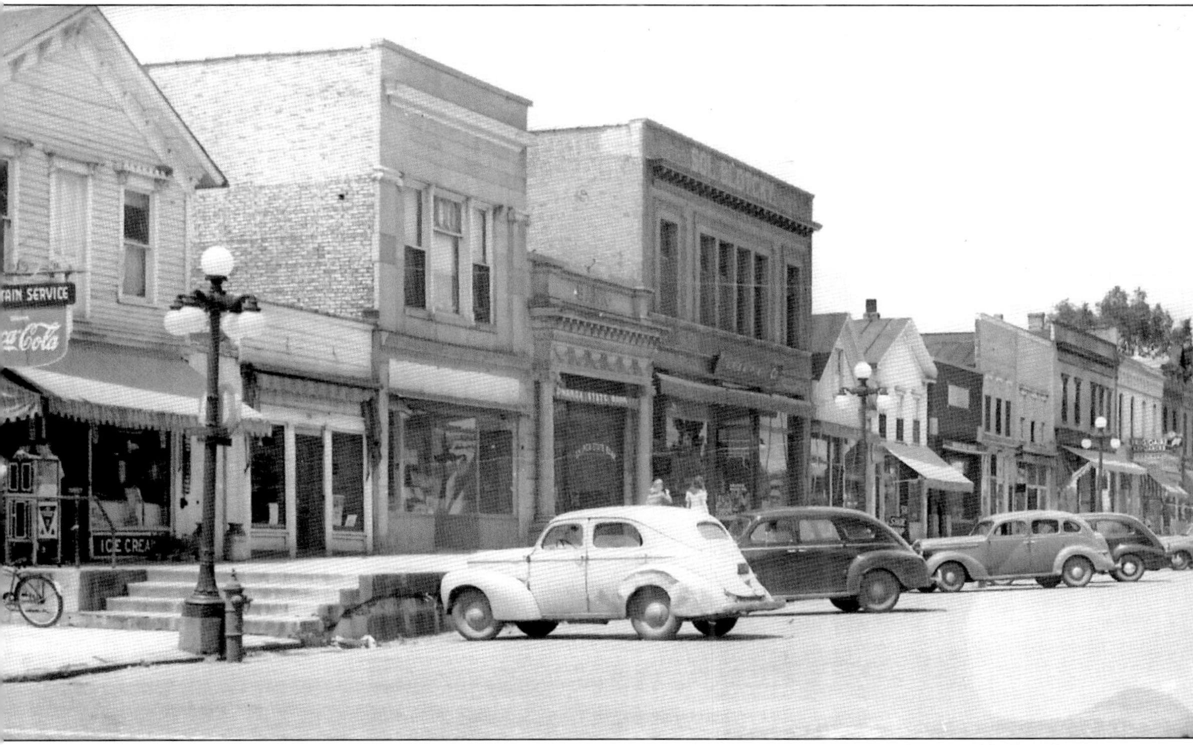

The Robb Drug Store was sold to George Rabe in June 1929. The business was then called Rabe's Drug Sundries and sat on the south end of Chestnut Street. Rabe had an outdoor popcorn machine, and local residents recalled that the smell drifted right up Chestnut Street. This photograph shows the cast-iron streetlamps and street signs attached. Other businesses in the 1930s were the Onarga State Bank; Onarga Mercantile; Albert Kanosky Grocery; A&P Tea Company; Townsend and Olson's; C. L. Krause Drugs; Leader and Review newspaper; J. W. Click, barber; Clifton and Whiteside; Glenn Cox Plumbing and Heating; W. E. Yocam, Feed, Coal, Produce, and Implements; Booth Lumber Yard; S. C. Moon, funeral directors; E. L. Wheeler and Company, grain, coal, and seeds; John Pugh Garage; and Hahne Auto Service. S. S. (Sandy) Foley ran a blacksmith business, the Onarga Bakery produced Purity Bread, and Ortman's Cafe advertised that he was "the oldest restaurant man in town."

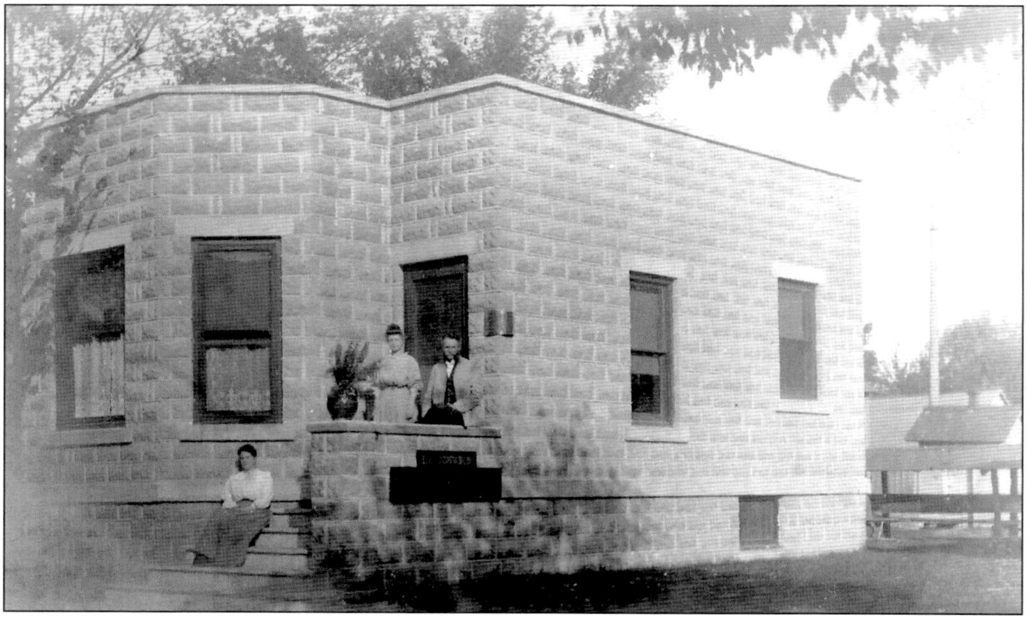

Dr. I. B. Johnson's Dental Office sat on the north side of West Lincoln Avenue. There was a lit croquet court, a popular sport of the time, behind Dr. Johnson's office, which can be seen in this photograph. One of the watering troughs for horses stood at the corner of West Lincoln Avenue and Chestnut Street. The other one was about halfway down the street on the east side.

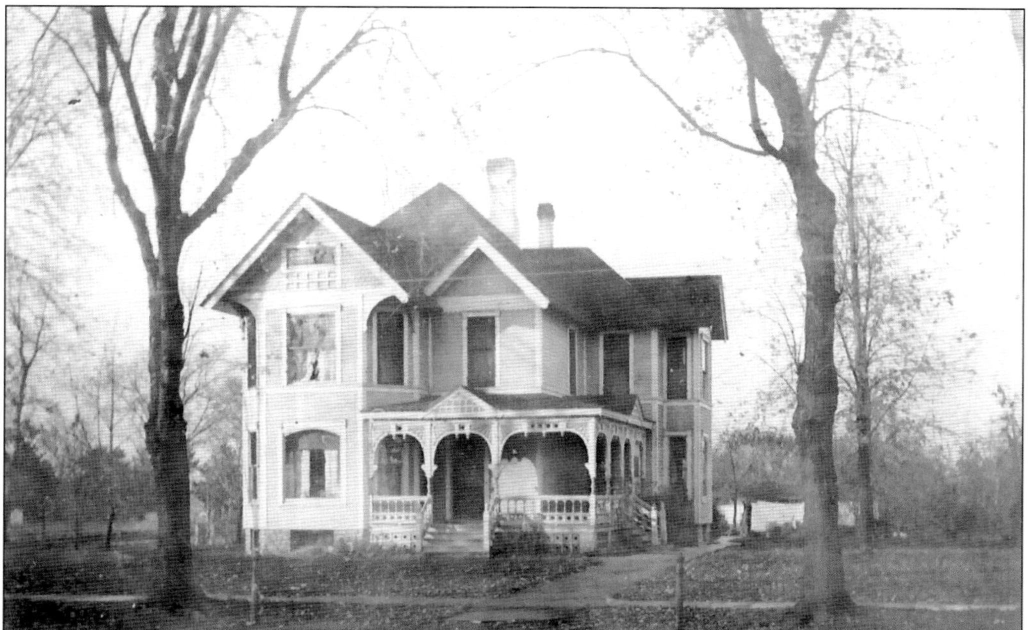

Dr. Ira Palmer had his physician's office set up in his home, which was located on West Lincoln Avenue and North Evergreen Street. Other Onarga doctors and dentists were Dr. Hemala, Dr. Birch, Dr. Yazarian, Dr. Shawl, Dr. Burgett, Dr. Search, Dr. Harper, and Dr. Killop.

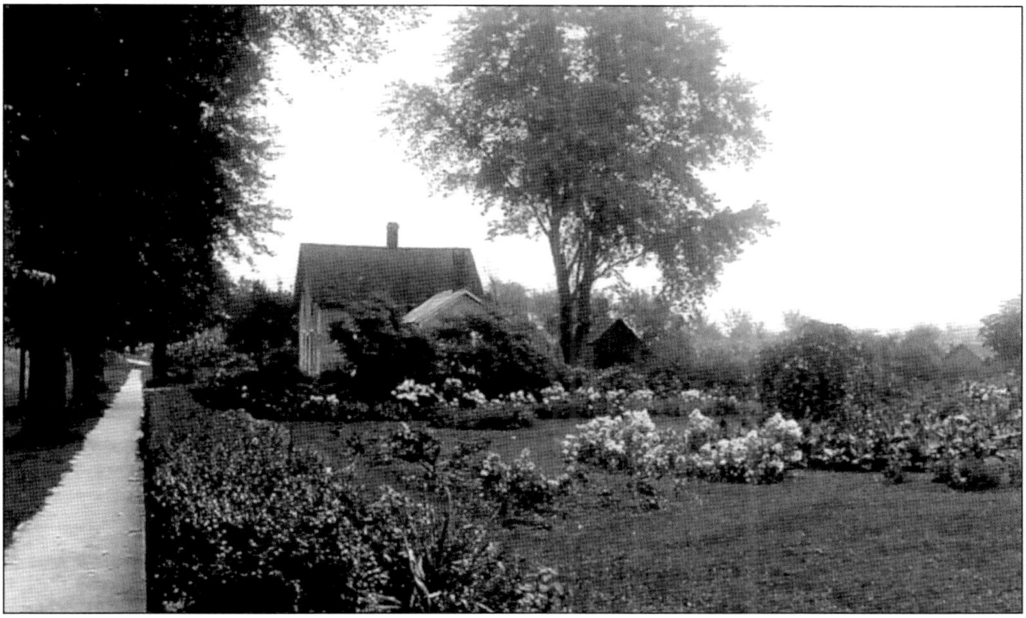

Founded in 1865 on what was once the hunting grounds of the Iroquois Indians, the Onarga Nursery is rich in tradition and family heritage. Robert Blaine Cultra purchased a small fruit farm in the northeastern part of Onarga when he returned from the Civil War. He spent the next 20 years walking through the surrounding rural areas selling strawberry and raspberry plants and fruit trees. He would spend the nights in his customers' homes as he journeyed about. This was the beginning of today's Onarga Nursery Company. The above picture shows the Onarga Nursery's original business office. The picture below shows the brick building built in 1934. The Onarga Nursery participated in many events that were part of America's history. Onarga trees helped to form the World's Fair Garden at the 1933 Century of Progress International Exposition in Chicago.

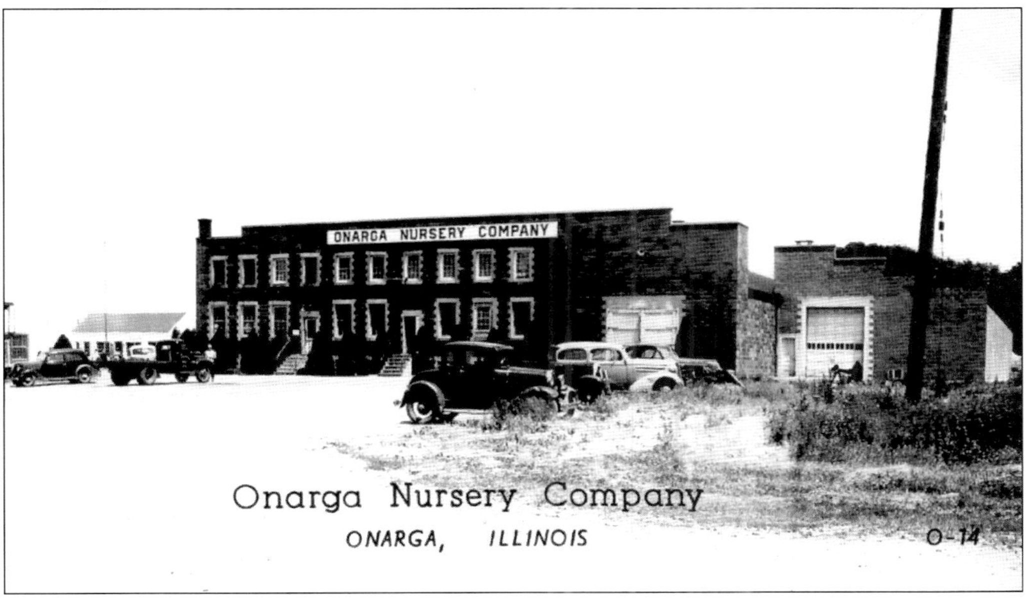

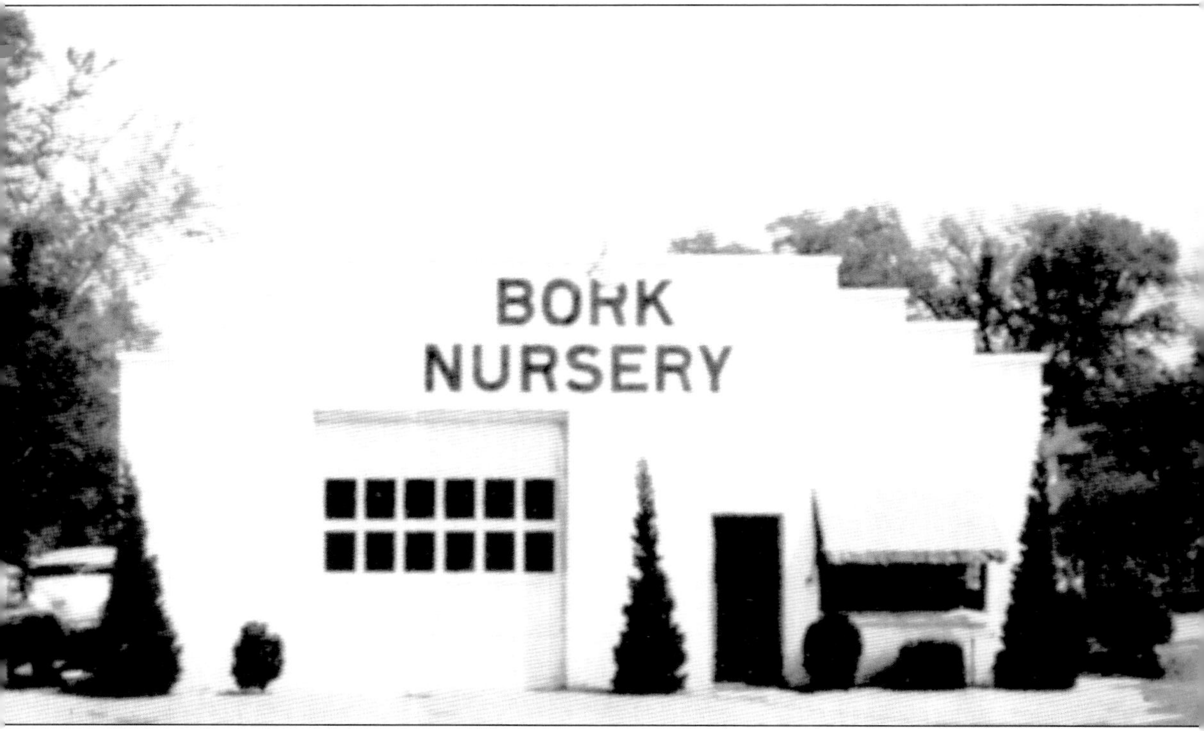

In 1946, Leslie Bork Sr. borrowed a truck from his father to buy and sell nursery stock. This was the beginning of Bork Nurseries, Inc. He later rented two acres of land and used his garage as a warehouse. A tractor and seven acres of land were purchased in 1948, and the first storage building was constructed in 1949. It was 36 feet by 60 feet. The company's motto was "Tradition, service, quality and dedicated employees is what defines our history and our success." At one time, Onarga was known as the nursery capital of the world. Another nursery in Onarga was the Cultra Nursery, owned by Ronald R. and his son, Randy. Established in 1952, this nursery was located on East Roosevelt Street. They specialized in landscaping and wholesale quality nursery stock. Perry Price Landscape Service was founded in 1946. During the early years, Perry's brothers, Walter and Fred, worked for him part-time. Jesse "Turtle" Ireland started a nursery business in 1950 primarily as a wholesaler of nursery stock. He had been a salesman for the Onarga Nursery.

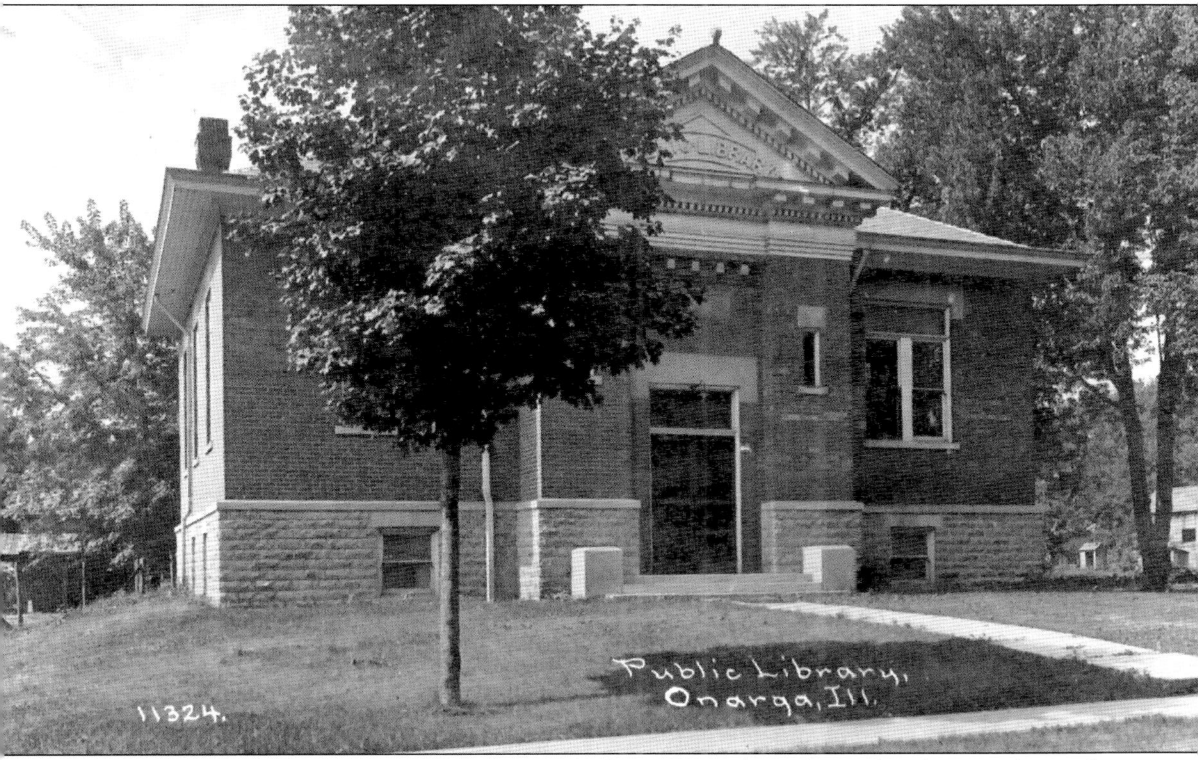

The seeds for the Onarga Community District Library were planted in 1858 when residents of the village of Onarga felt that the citizens needed a source of reading materials and organized a library association. The library had 150 volumes of donated material. Membership shares were fixed at $5, and membership in the association was gained by paying that amount in cash or books. In 1862, a lot was purchased and a building costing $164.44 erected. In 1873, the association voted to donate all its property to the village, providing the village would levy a tax to maintain the property and run the library. The village accepted the board's offer. In 1906, the library board recommended that the village accept the offer of philanthropist Andrew Carnegie. If the village would maintain the library at not less than $500 per year and donate a site for the building, Carnegie would give the village $5,000 to erect a building to house the Onarga Free Public Library. The beautiful redbrick building was erected in 1907.

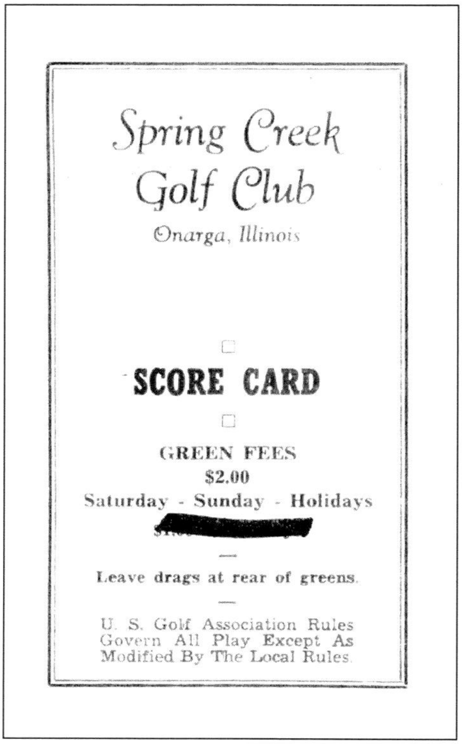

Spring Creek Golf Club

Onarga, Illinois

SCORE CARD

GREEN FEES
$2.00
Saturday - Sunday - Holidays

Leave drags at rear of greens.

U. S. Golf Association Rules Govern All Play Except As Modified By The Local Rules.

A well-dressed golfer wore long stockings and plaid knickers—the louder the better. Bobby Jones and Walter Hagen made the game so exciting that a group of enterprising businessmen developed a nine-hole golf course. Rules and by-laws were written, and in 1925, the Spring Creek Golf Course came to fruition. In 1926, a clubhouse was constructed with donated labor, both common and skilled, by Gleason Thorne and Son Construction.

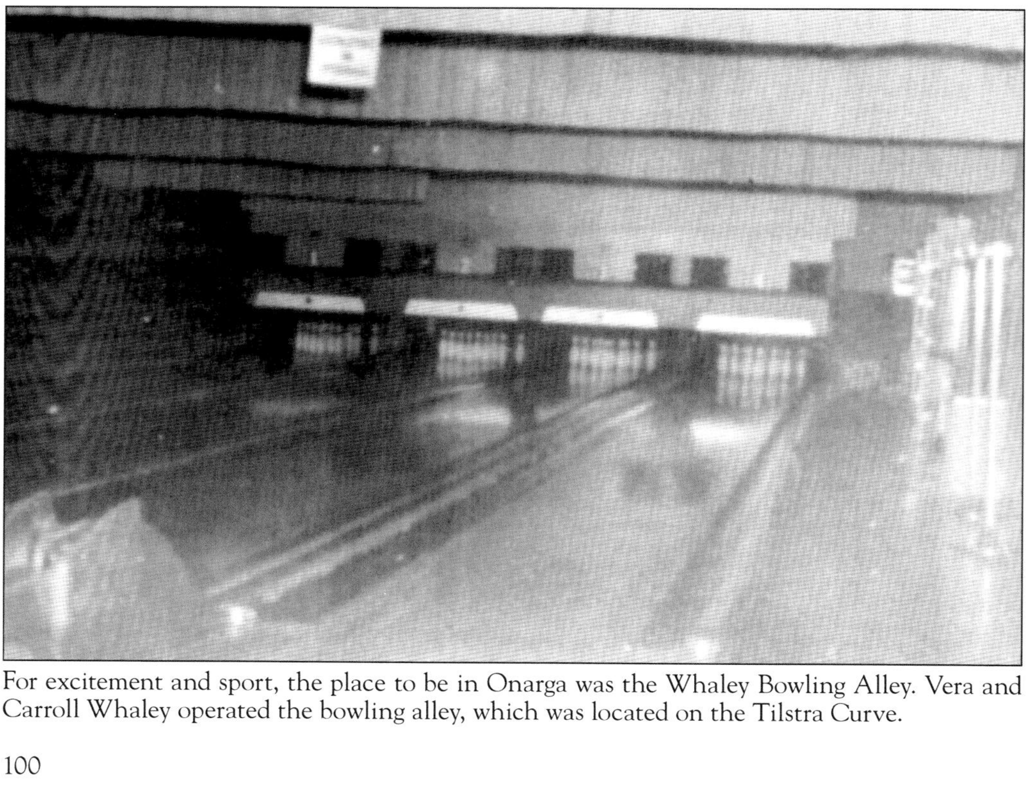

For excitement and sport, the place to be in Onarga was the Whaley Bowling Alley. Vera and Carroll Whaley operated the bowling alley, which was located on the Tilstra Curve.

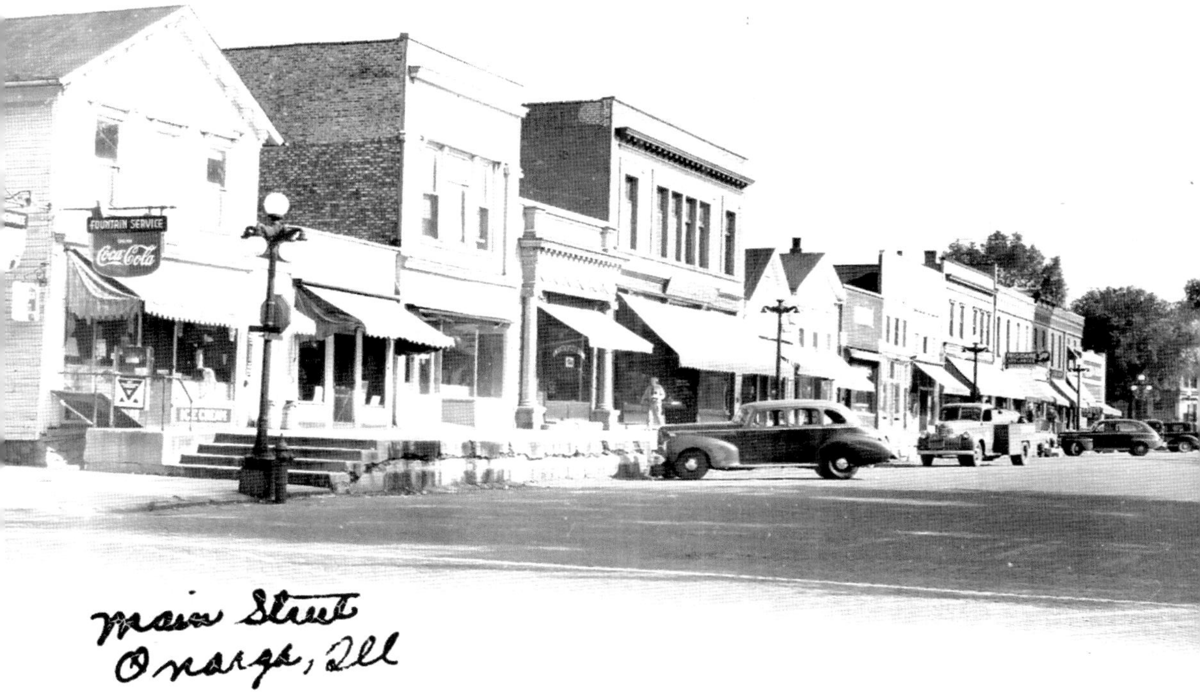

The Onarga State Bank was authorized to commence business on January 30, 1918. James Kewley, Wilbur Kerns, and Henry Knoche were granted permission to organize the banking association. One of the focal points of the Onarga State Bank was its beautiful domed, stained-glass skylight. The Onarga State Bank is the fourth building from the left in this photograph. Also seen in this photograph is the Onarga Hatchery run by Russell and Madelyn Enz. The Onarga Mercantile Company was opened on April 27, 1912, by Sol Blotcky, who came to America at the age of 16. In the 1950s, Ryan's 5¢ to $1 Store opened in the Mercantile Building. Another business that started up in the 1950s was the Louis Melind Company. The stamp-manufacturing plant was completed in May 1951 and employed many people from the area. Also, Robert (Bob) Brown ran a fertilizer business in which he applied anhydrous and phosphate to farm ground.

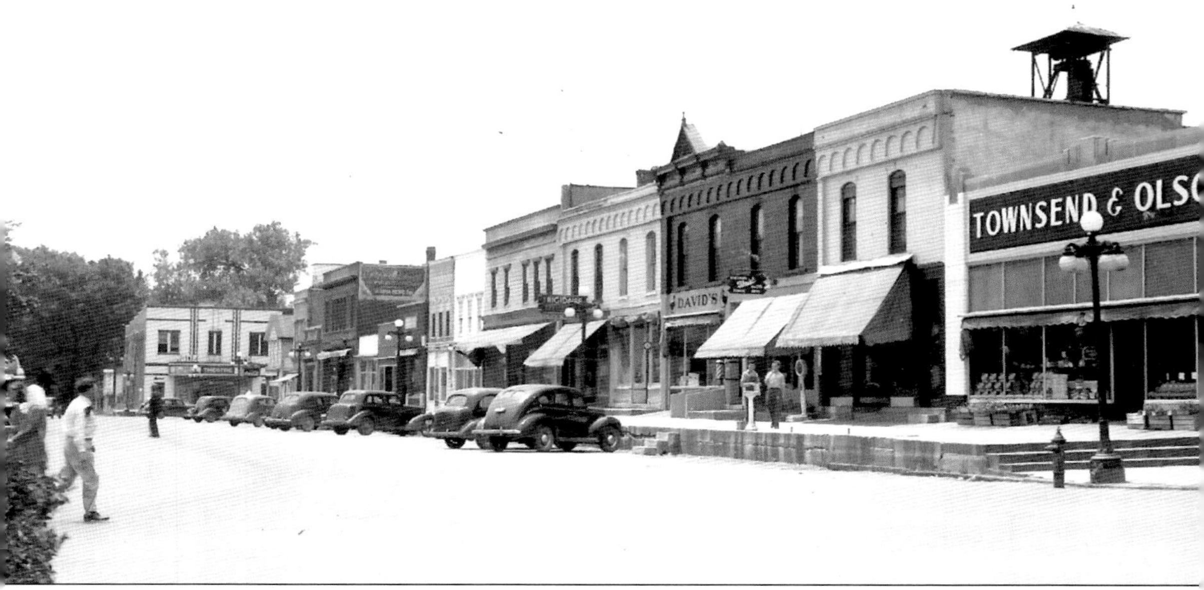

Onarga's first newspaper was the *Mercury* in 1859. Next, in 1865, was the *Onarga Advertiser*, which later merged with the *Grand Prairie Review*. The *Onarga Review* began in 1865 and the *Courier* in 1870. The *Onarga Leader-Review* was first published in 1872. In April 1939, the *Leader-Review* was purchased by Marvin Craig of Fairbury who popularized the journal with his unique brand of humor. Other long-lasting Onarga businesses were the Farmer's Pioneer Mutual Insurance Company (which moved to Onarga in 1937 but had been organized in 1874) and the Onarga Mutual Building and Loan, which was founded in April 1887. Another business was the Ficklin Machine Company. Roy Ficklin began repairing farm equipment in the late 1930s. Joined by his son, Roy Lee, in 1946, they continued in the equipment repair business, custom corn shelling, and eventually farm wagon design and manufacturing.

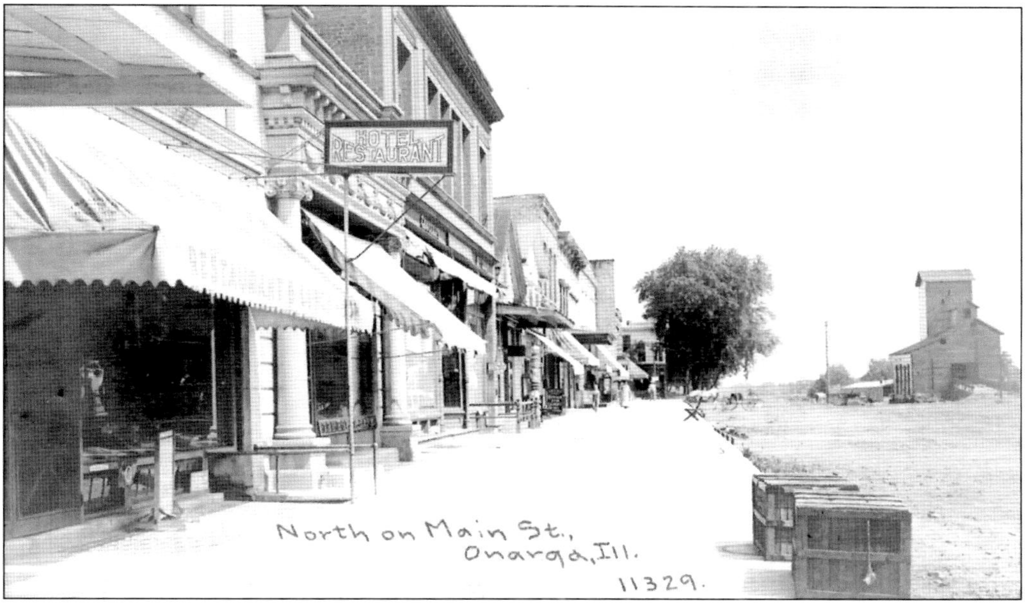

This 1915 photograph depicts Onarga facing north on Chestnut Street. The wooden crates in the forefront of the photograph are for ice for the hotel and restaurant. In this photograph, directly in front of the hotel and restaurant, are the glass circles that were embedded in the concrete sidewalk to allow sunlight to filter to the basement businesses. In the middle of Chestnut Street was a brick firewall.

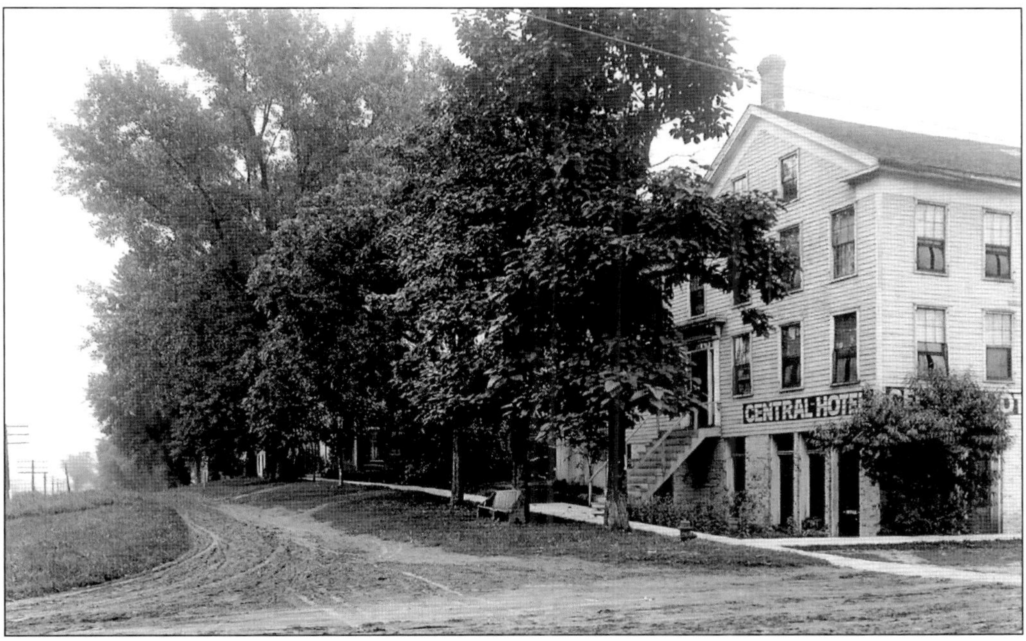

The Central Hotel sat at the corner of Oak Street (Route 45) and East Lincoln Avenue. The Central Hotel was originally the Hotel Roney. Many wonderful dinner parties were held at this hotel. This photograph was taken on August 11, 1915. Eventually, the Central Hotel was razed and a doctor's office was built by Dr. Hemala in its place.

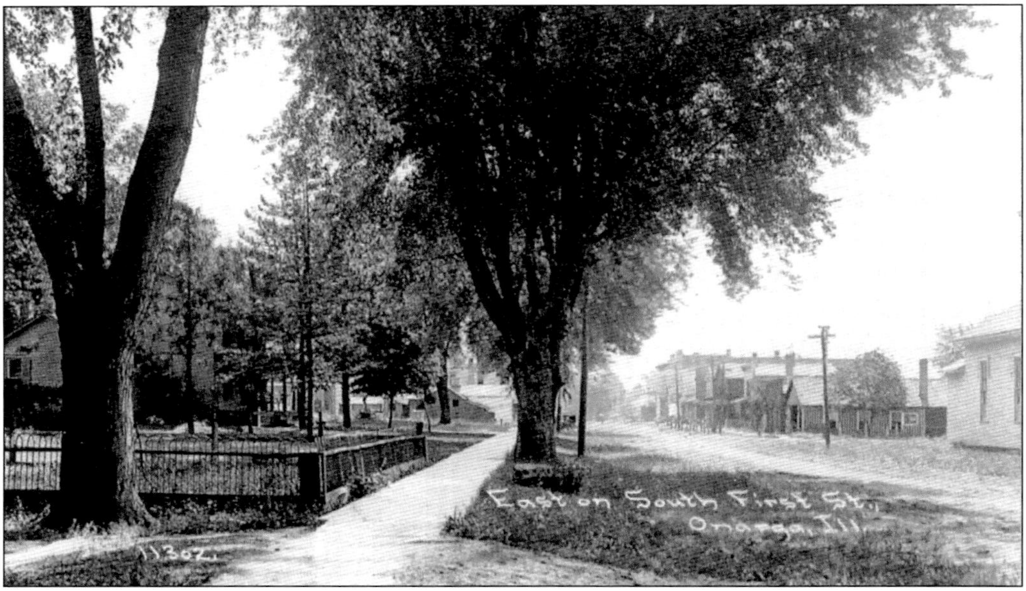

On the far right of this photograph is the Pilgrim Holiness Church, which sat at the corner of South Walnut Street and West Seminary Avenue. The next building on the right belonged to S. S. (Sandy) Foley, the blacksmith. The houses on the left were torn down, and the lots became part of the Onarga Public School yard. The photograph is labeled "East on South First." Onarga's streets were later changed to the names of trees and presidents.

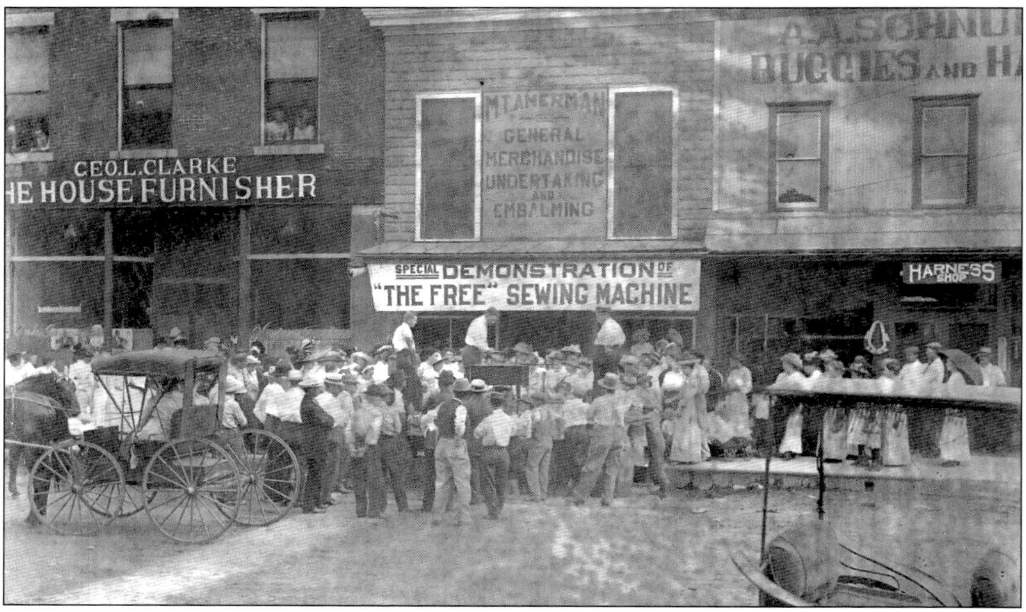

M. T. Amerman invited the public to a grand demonstration of a Free sewing machine on Saturday, July 26, 1913. A free sewing machine was given away that day. The individual had to be present to win. The Free sewing machine, in addition to being fully warranted, was insured for five years against breakage, wear, fire, tornado, lightning, and water. It seems Amerman's demonstration was a grand success.

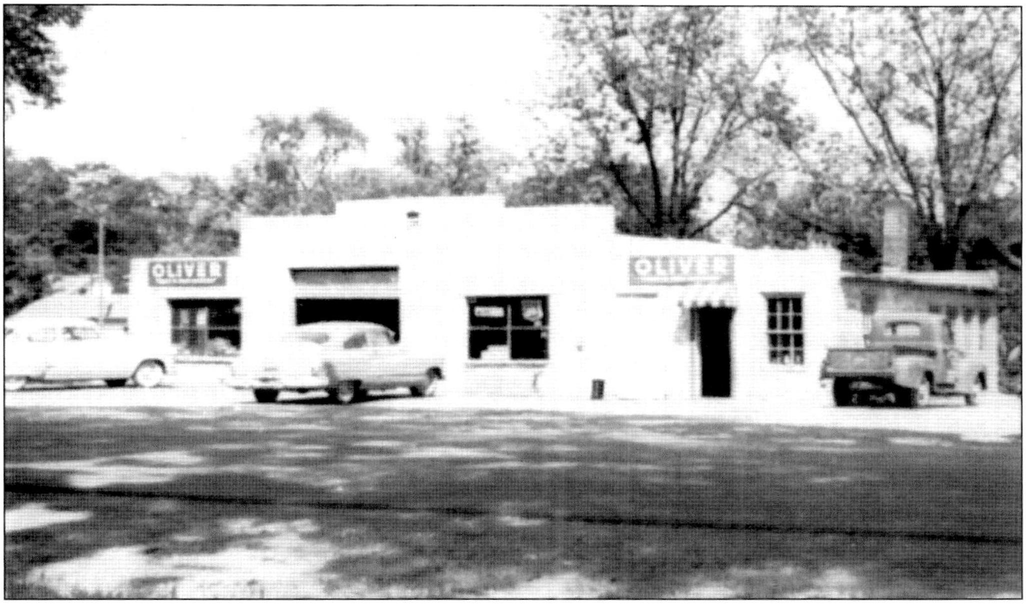

Kinley Hynd ran the Hynd Equipment Company in the late 1940s and 1950s. He specialized in the sale and repair of Oliver farm equipment. Don Morgan and Benny Eheart were employees, and Kinley's wife, Ila, was the bookkeeper for the business. Kinley eventually sold the business to Harry Hockersmith.

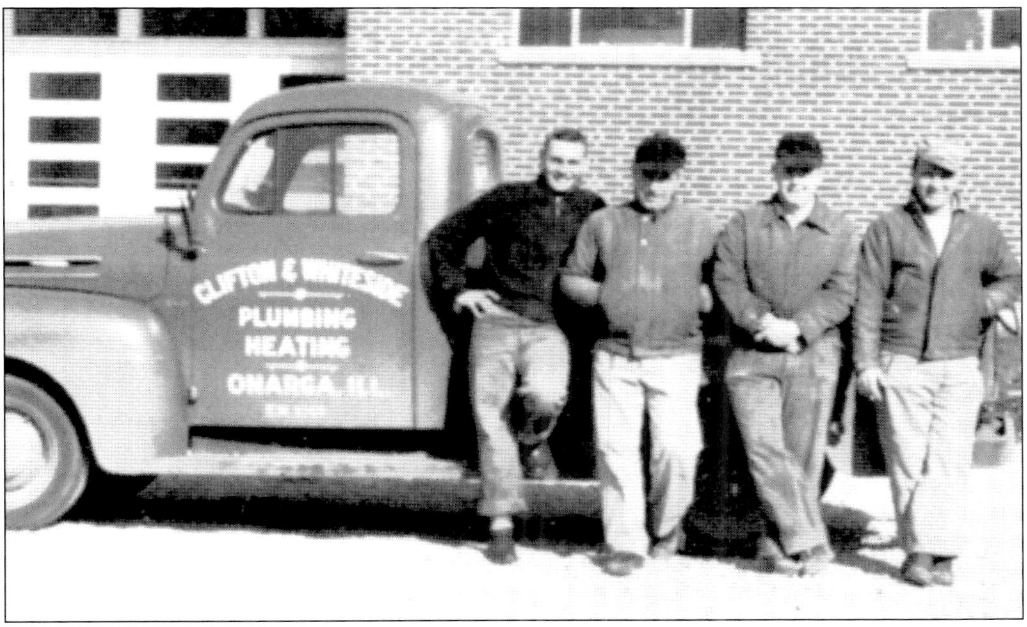

In the 1920s, Stitt and Zirhut were partners in a plumbing business. George Clifton worked for them. Later Howard Whiteside joined them. In 1925, Clifton and Whiteside went into business for themselves, and this partnership lasted until 1954 when Clifton retired due to health. Whiteside's secretary was Erna Mae Danforth, and employees over the years were Dick Dannehl, David Danforth, Don Schnurr, Earl Frye, Lawrence Link, and Lester "Peanuts" Dannehl.

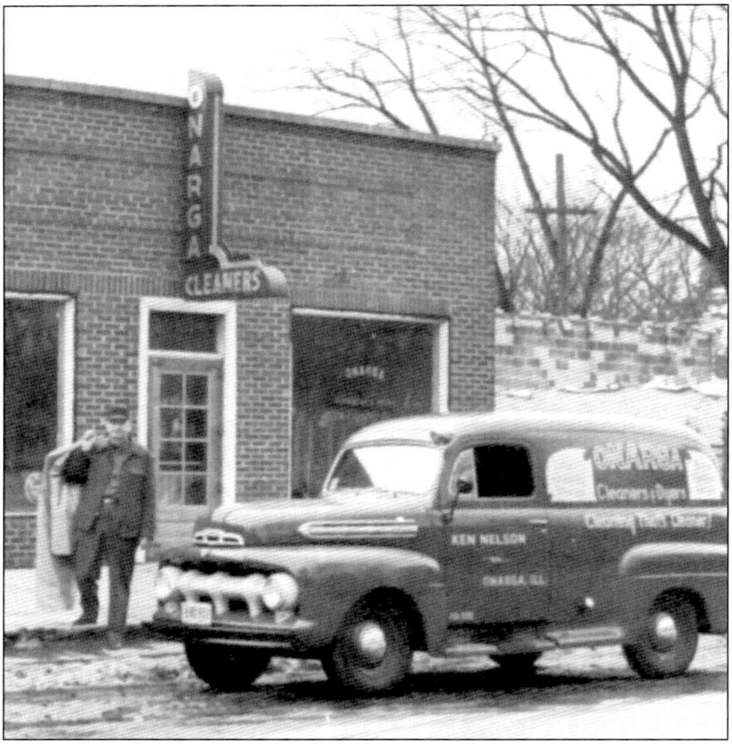

Onarga Cleaners and Dyers was first established by Clifford Landwer in 1945. In the 1950s, Ken Nelson took it over. They offered free pickup and delivery in Onarga on Wednesday and Saturday mornings.

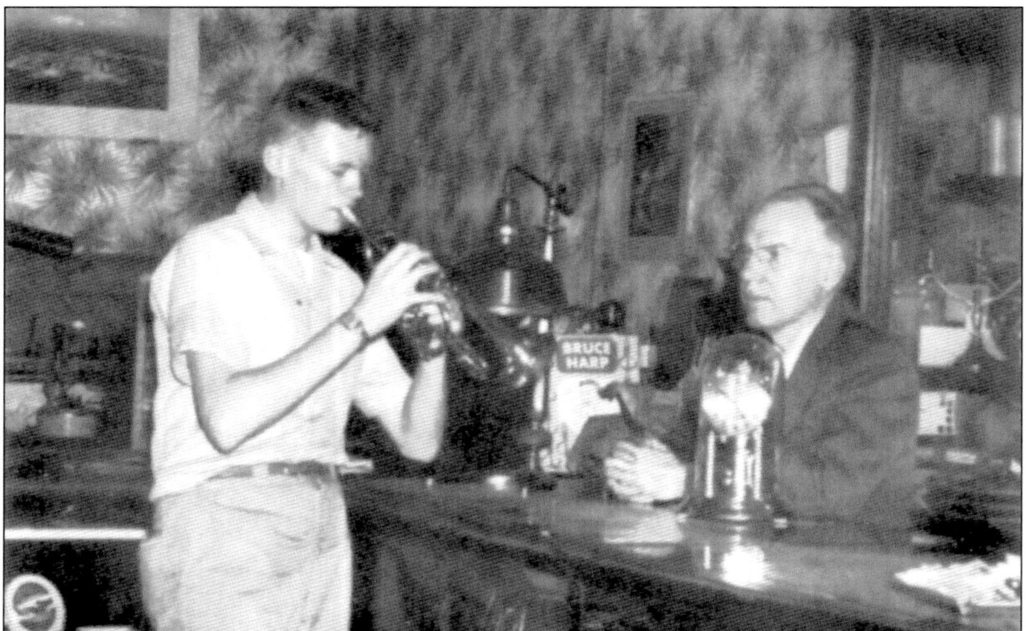

Homer's Jewelry and Music Store offered a full line of jewelry and silver plus band instruments and all types of accessories. Customers could even rent a band instrument, which gave them a chance to test their child's musical talent before making a purchase.

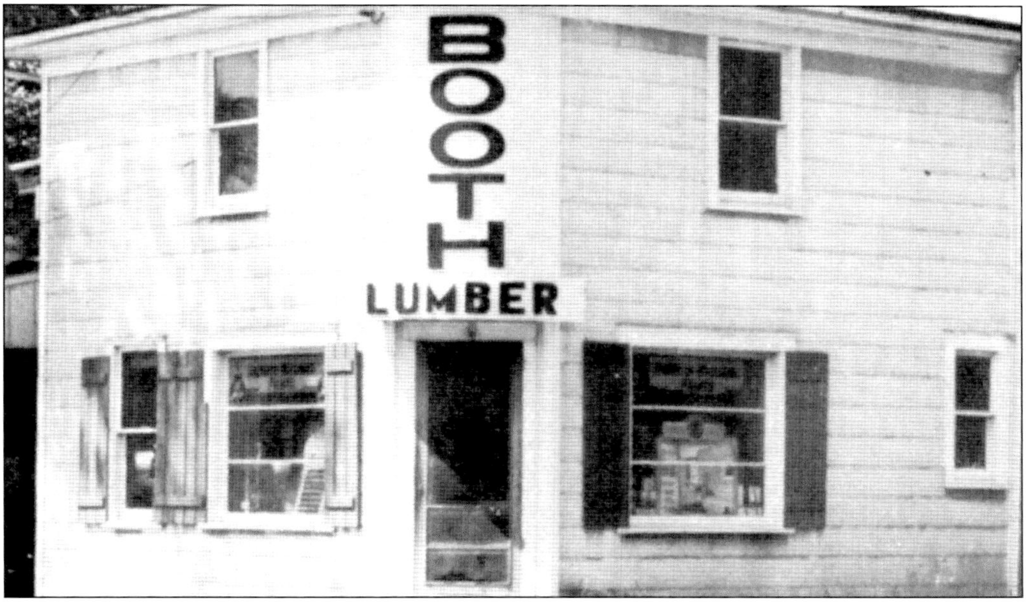

Booth Lumber Yard originated in the Booth-Stitt Hardware Store on North Chestnut Street and was owned by Charles Booth. When Charles died, George, who was a teacher, came home to take over the business. He liquidated the hardware store and bought the lumberyard on South Chestnut Street from George Egley. This business provided the best of service and stock to this community. In 1938, George was joined by his son, Charles Booth.

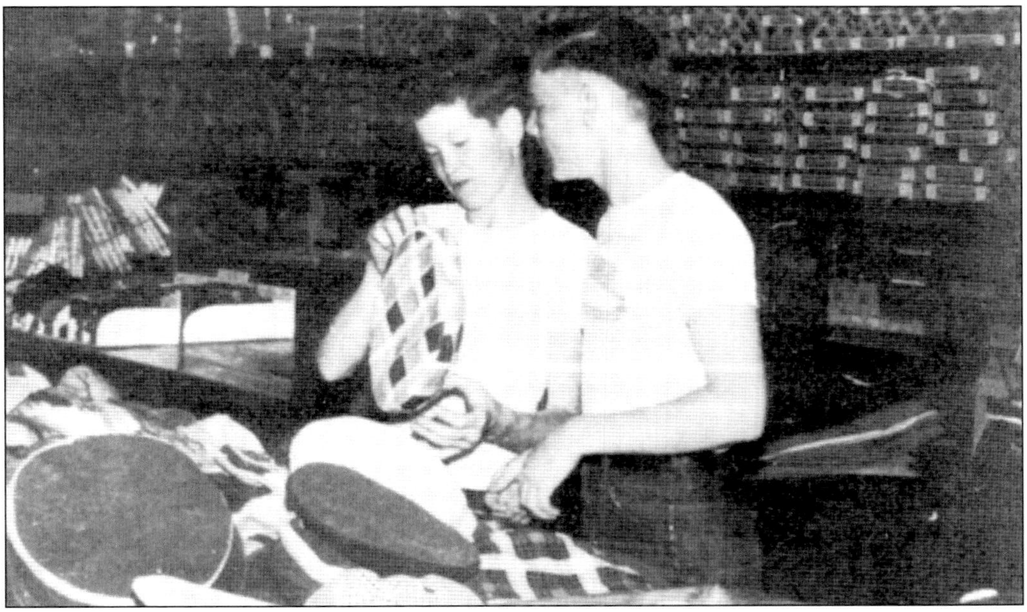

Schnurr's Quality Store offered men's and boy's clothing along with canvas products and Evinrude motors. "We have the clothes for nearly every activity; sport shirts in a variety of styles and colors, slacks for dress and slacks for rough wear. If it is clothes for vacation or sport comfort . . . yes, and even for business, come in today and make your selections from a large stock of merchandise."

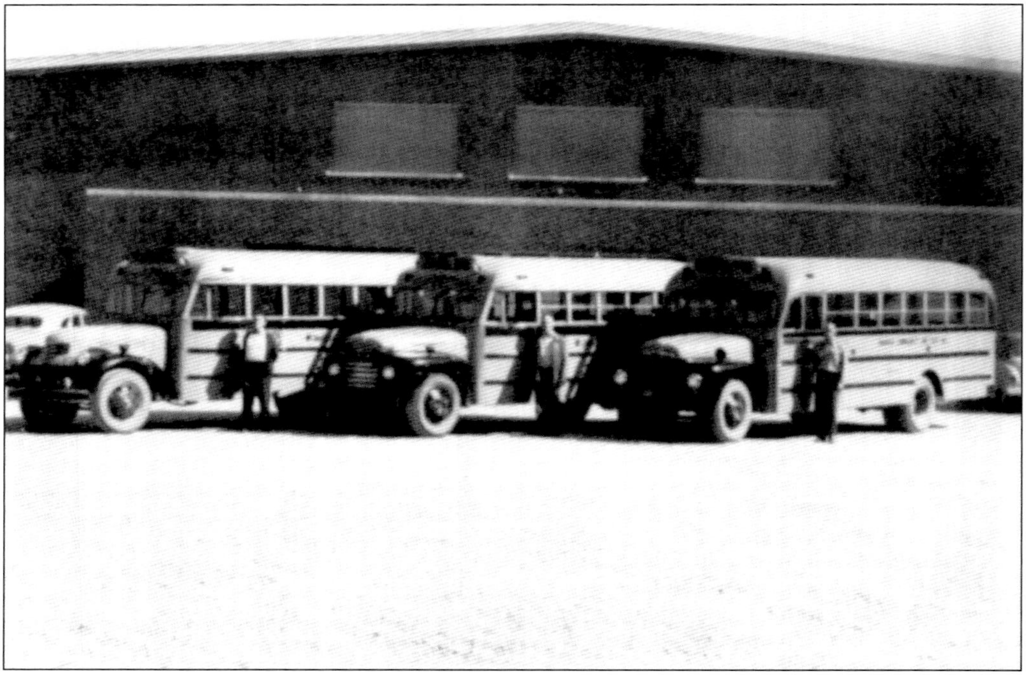

Poskin's Bus Service, owned and operated by Vincent (Vinnie) Poskin, was a very important part of Onarga. The Poskin's Bus Service started busing the Onarga students in 1942.

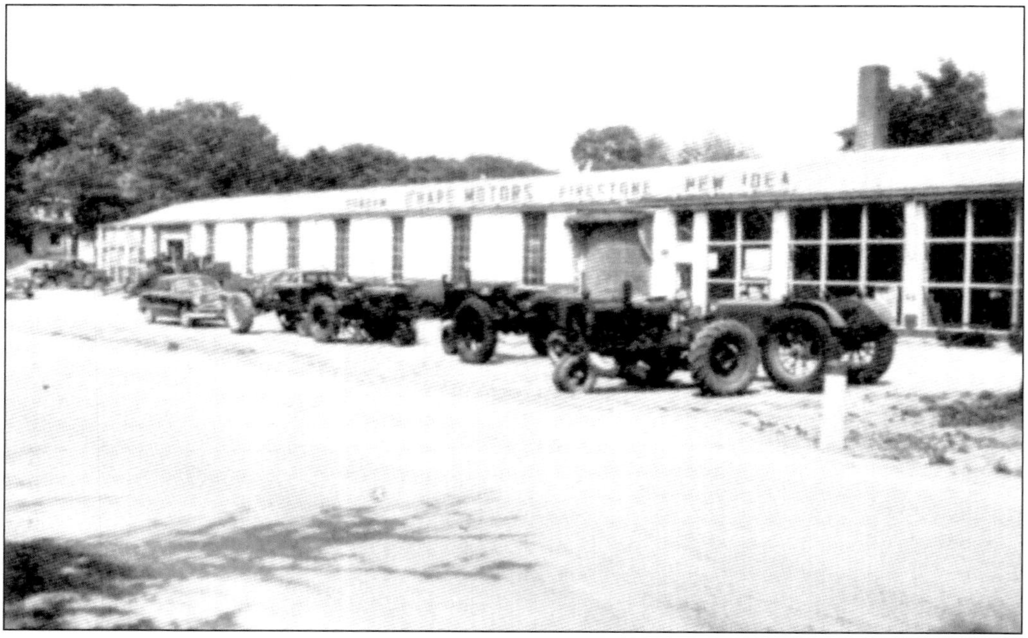

The O'Hares ran a Ford Car Agency where they sold and serviced Ford cars. They were also an Allis Chalmers implement dealer. Later they manufactured and sold Crownline Boats. The O'Hares employed many, many people from the Onarga area, and their business was located on the east side of Oak Street.

Nine

PRIDE, HONOR, AND FREEDOM

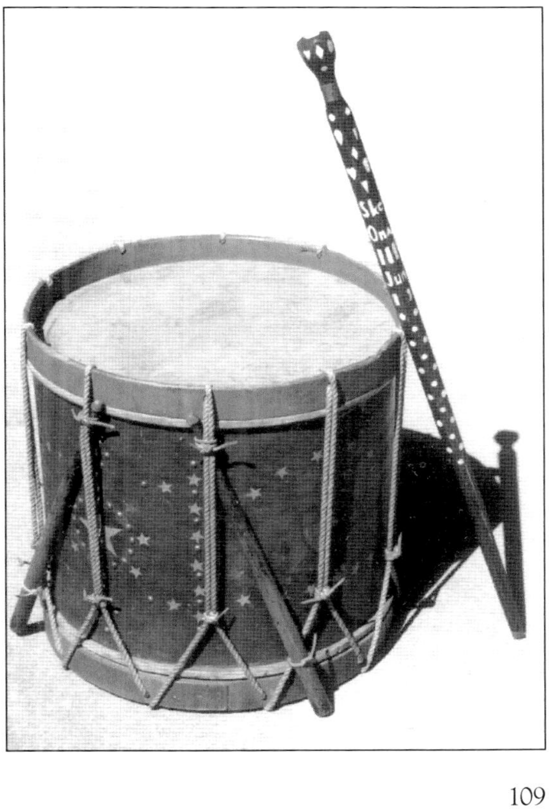

This drum is very special as it was likely carried by Company D of Onarga soldiers in the 113th Illinois Infantry. A drummer was a very important part of the U.S. Army, as he established communication and kept order among the units in the fields. Many campaigns would have ended in failure if not for the drummer. When in the field, drummers followed units onto the battlefield, beating out cadences and signals to fire, cease fire, and charge since it was nearly impossible to hear an officer's voice over the din of battle.

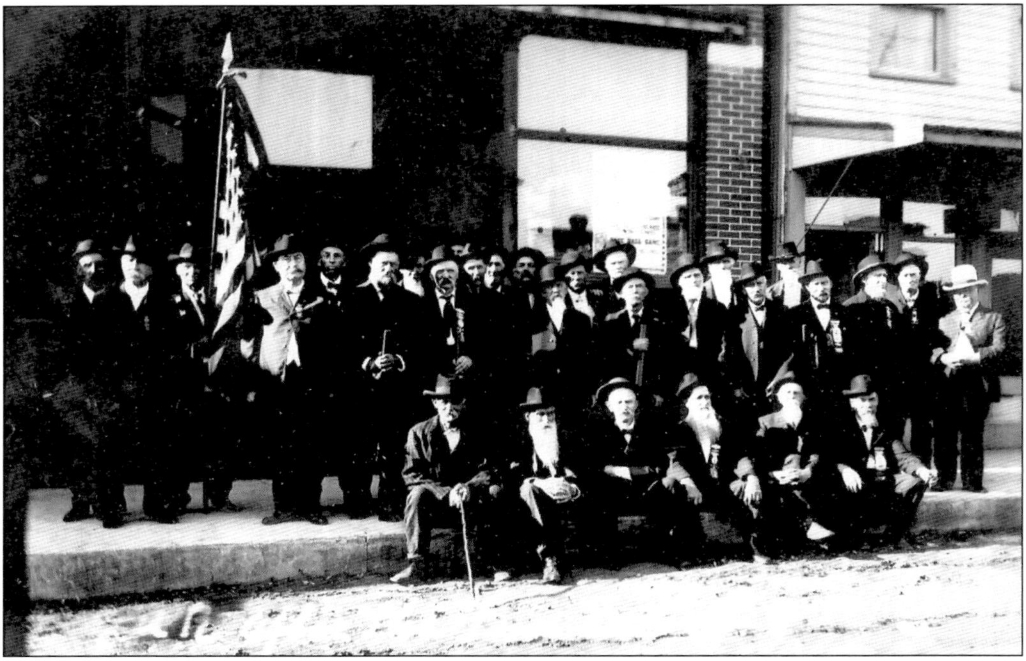

After the Civil War had ended and the soldiers who survived the war had gone home, they began to miss the friendships and camaraderie that they had shared during the war. The Grand Army of the Republic (GAR) was founded on April 6, 1866. To become a member of the GAR, a man must have served between April 9, 1861, and April 12, 1865, and must have been honorably discharged. The above photograph depicts Onarga's GAR taken after a funeral for one of the "old-timers." The photograph below was taken on May 30, 1907, and is titled "Old Soldiers," showing Snapp, Farr, Merideth, Campbell, Dr. Palmer, Schnurr, Farrington, G. R. Palmer, O. Townsend, Owens, Waide, Mears, Fickle, Kay, Eversole, Frazee, Laughlin, Holmes, David, Skeels, Frisbee, and Gilbert.

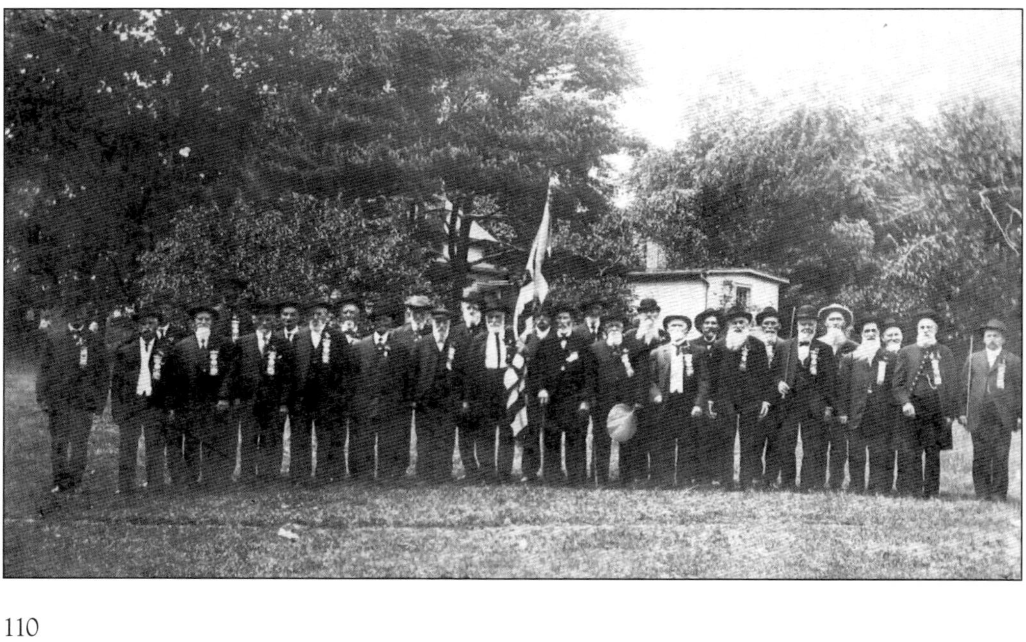

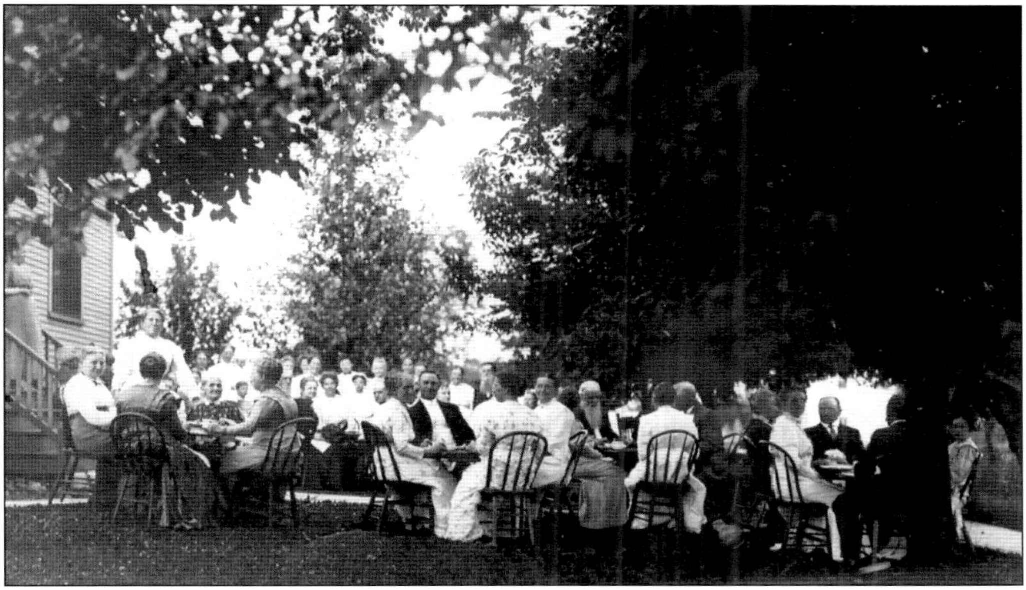

This photograph depicts the 1912 Onarga GAR reception held at Fannie Talbert's home on East Seminary Avenue. The GAR's three cardinal principles were fraternity, charity, and loyalty. From Abraham Lincoln down, state and federal leaders had promised to care for "those who have borne the burden, the widows and orphans." Men who had lived together, fought together, foraged together, and survived had developed a unique bond.

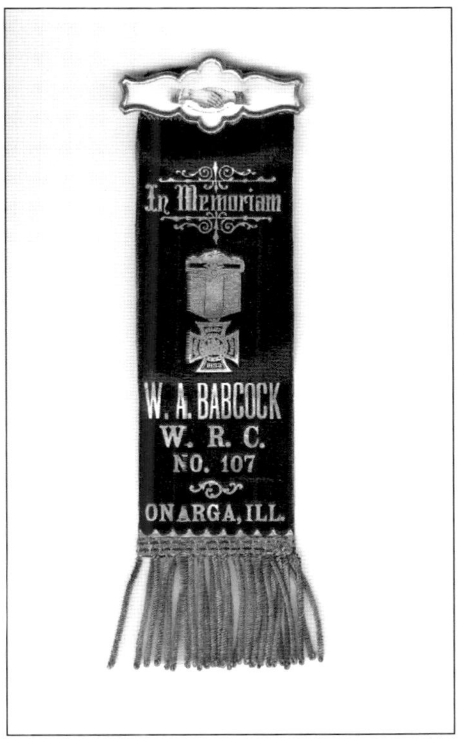

GAR organizations were called posts. Onarga's post was named for William A. Babcock, who was a Civil War doctor and surgeon. He was on the staff of the 76th Illinois Volunteer Infantry in the great war of the rebellion. Dr. Babcock returned to his home in Onarga after the war and died on April 7, 1875, of paralysis.

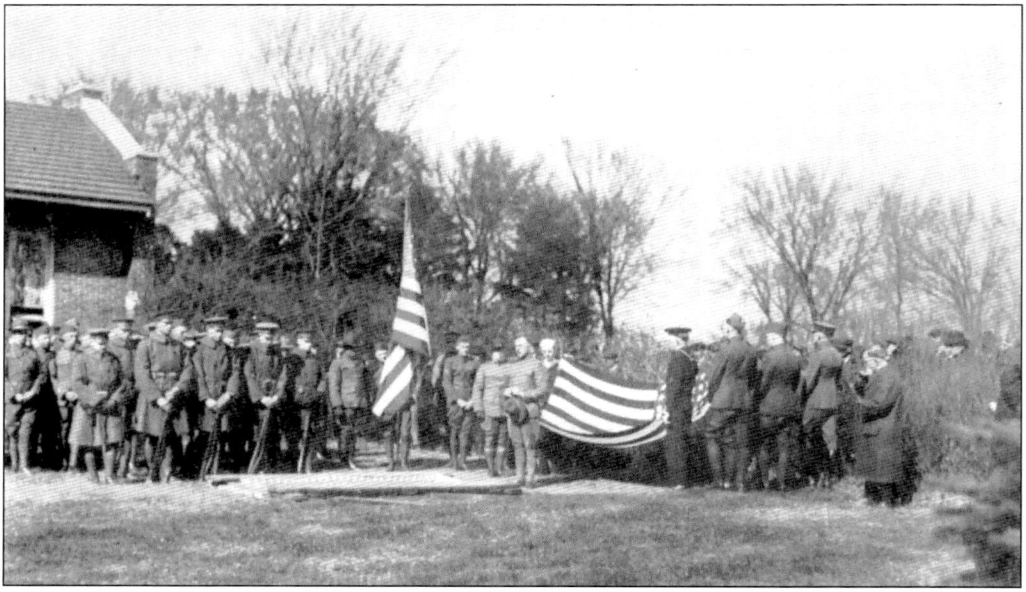

As they had in the Civil War, many of Onarga's young men responded to the call when the United States entered World War I in April 1917, and several died in the conflict. The above photograph shows Onarga Military School cadets participating with the Onarga American Legion at the funeral of Pvt. Ray Perry, an Onarga man who was killed near Stenay, France, in November 1918. Notice the cemetery chapel, built in 1913, in the background. The cemetery association deeded this portion of land north of the chapel to the Onarga American Legion. The funeral for Private Perry was held in the military school auditorium on April 10, 1921. The photograph below shows the funeral procession making its way from the auditorium to the cemetery.

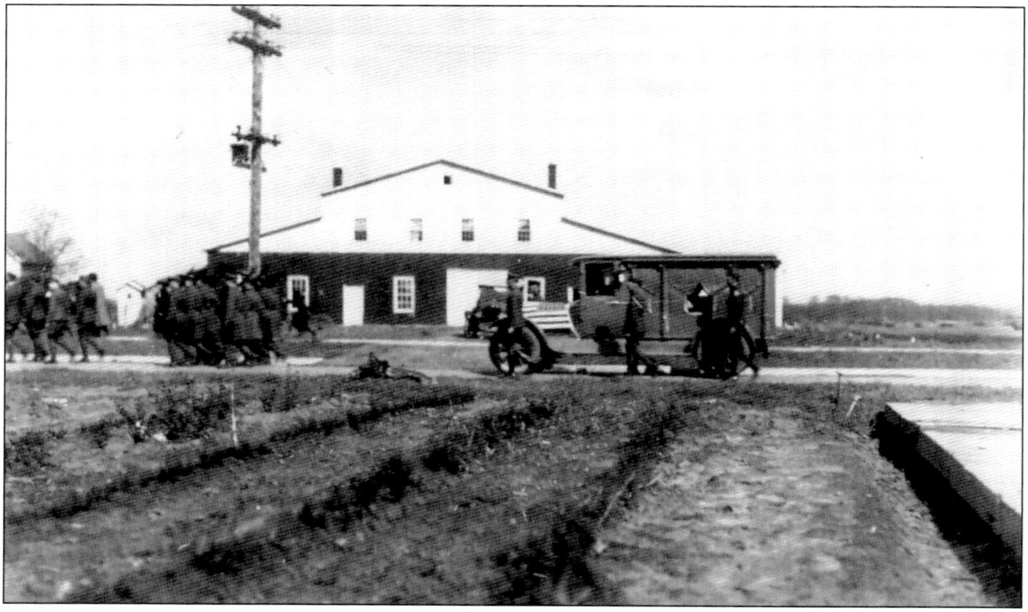

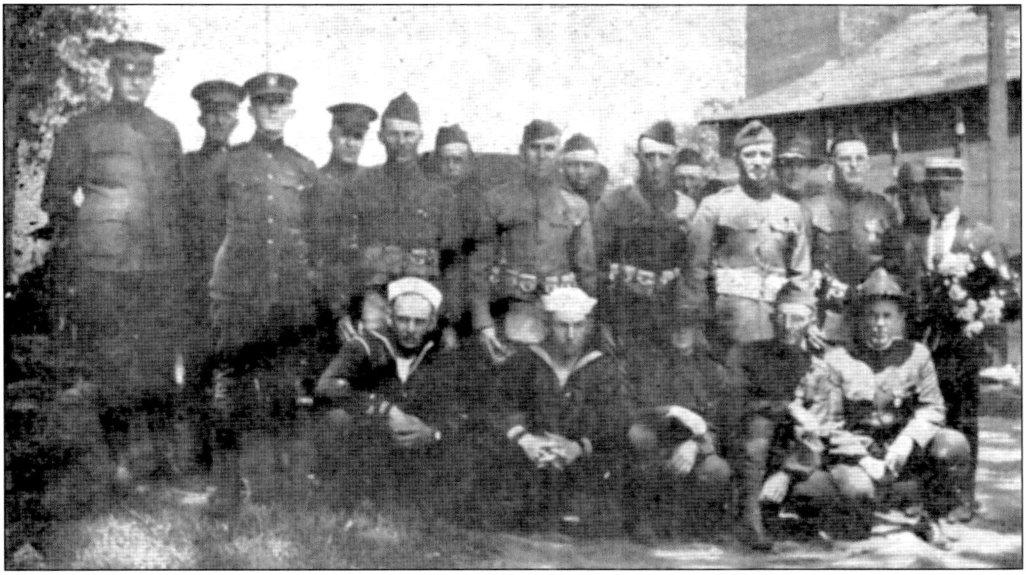

In 1919, the American Legion was chartered by the U.S. congress as a patriotic, mutual-help, veterans' organization. In February 1920, 23 Onarga, Gilman, and Thawville veterans of World War I applied for a charter to form a post in Onarga. Onarga American Legion Post 551 was granted a charter on September 28, 1920. The above photograph, which was featured in a 1944 Legion Christmas greetings publication, is of unidentified legion members in 1923. The photograph below features the 1944 Legion members, from left to right, (first row) Edward Miller, Archie Fisher, Herman Peters, Charles Warnock, Bert Olson, Robert Knoche, Claude Ludwick, Leonard Havland, George Onken, and Edward Davis; (second row) J. Emer Hicks, Byron Blotcky, Chauncey Booth, Corwin Rickards, Victor White, Andy Crozier, Harry Fryer, Ermon Keever, and Morris Wheeler; (third row) Todd Frazier, John Stienecker, Royal Krause, Fred Wand, Claus Sterrenberg, Clyde Talbert, and Rudy Wulff.

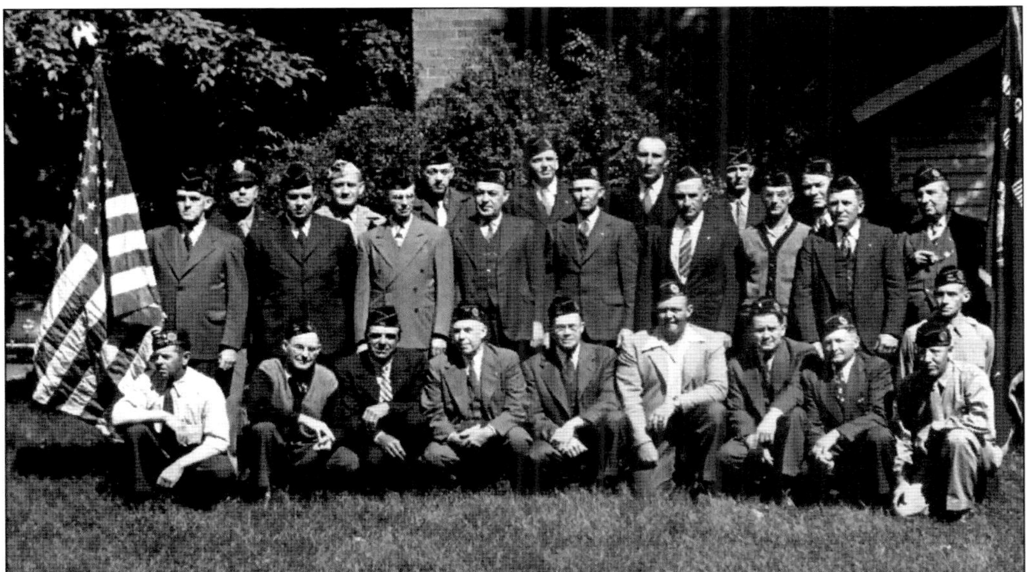

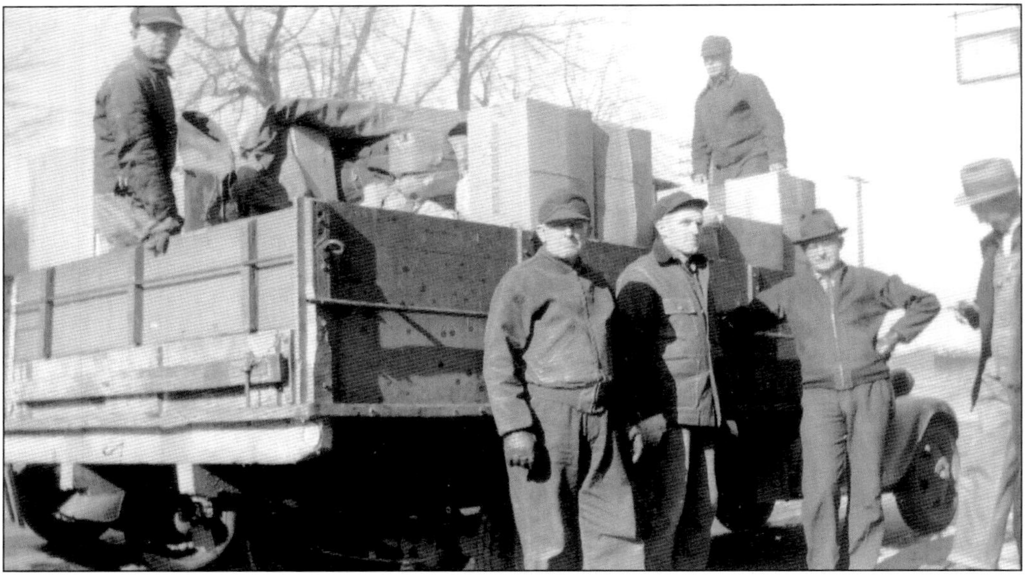

Due to the Pauper Relief Law, which took effect in September 1931, an emergency existed in Onarga. The American Legion felt that steps should be taken at once to meet the situation. Interested parties met on Tuesday, September 15 at the Onarga Military School Auditorium to discuss ways and means of caring for those who were in need. This photograph shows the American Legion delivering goods as a result of this law.

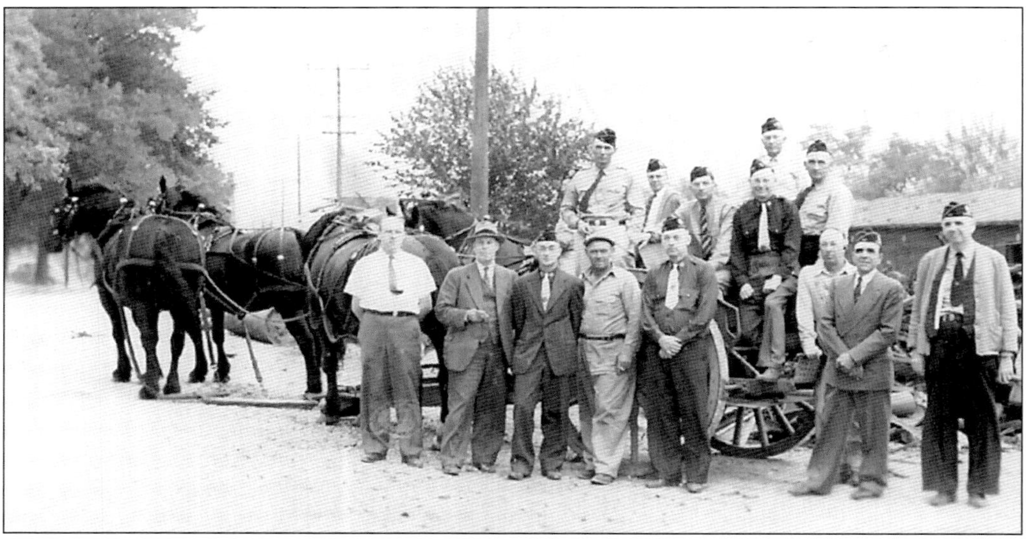

Onarga's scrap salvage efforts were very gratifying. A total of 340 tons of scrap iron were gathered for the war effort and another 600 pounds of brass, copper, and other metals. One thousand pounds of discarded but usable clothing was collected. Fur coats and some odd fur pieces were sent to the Merchant Seamen's Vest project and made into fur-lined vests. This photograph depicts the American Legion scrapping Onarga's big gun.

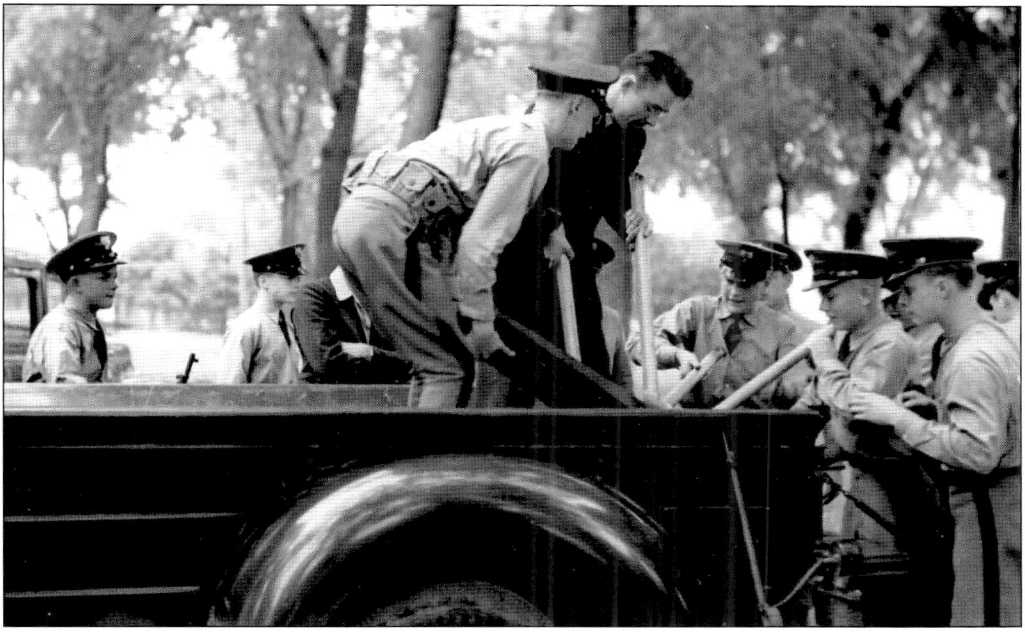

The Onarga Military School also provided support to the World War II effort. The above photograph shows the cadets loading their donation to the scrap drive—the two Gatling guns that had been sitting in front of the administration building—on a truck owned by the Amerman Brothers. The photograph below shows the guns being driven west on Seminary Avenue to the scrap drive location in the downtown area. Notice the sign stating, "OMS' Gift Gatling Guns to Gather Huns." Although the term *Huns*, meaning barbarians, was not a very complimentary nickname for German soldiers, it was widely used in the Allied countries during both world wars.

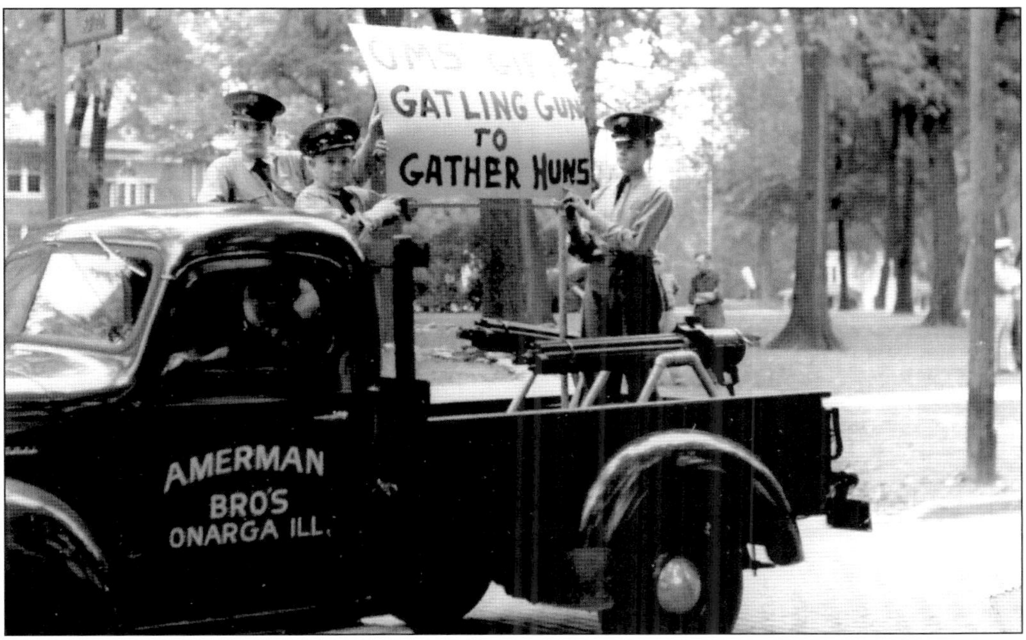

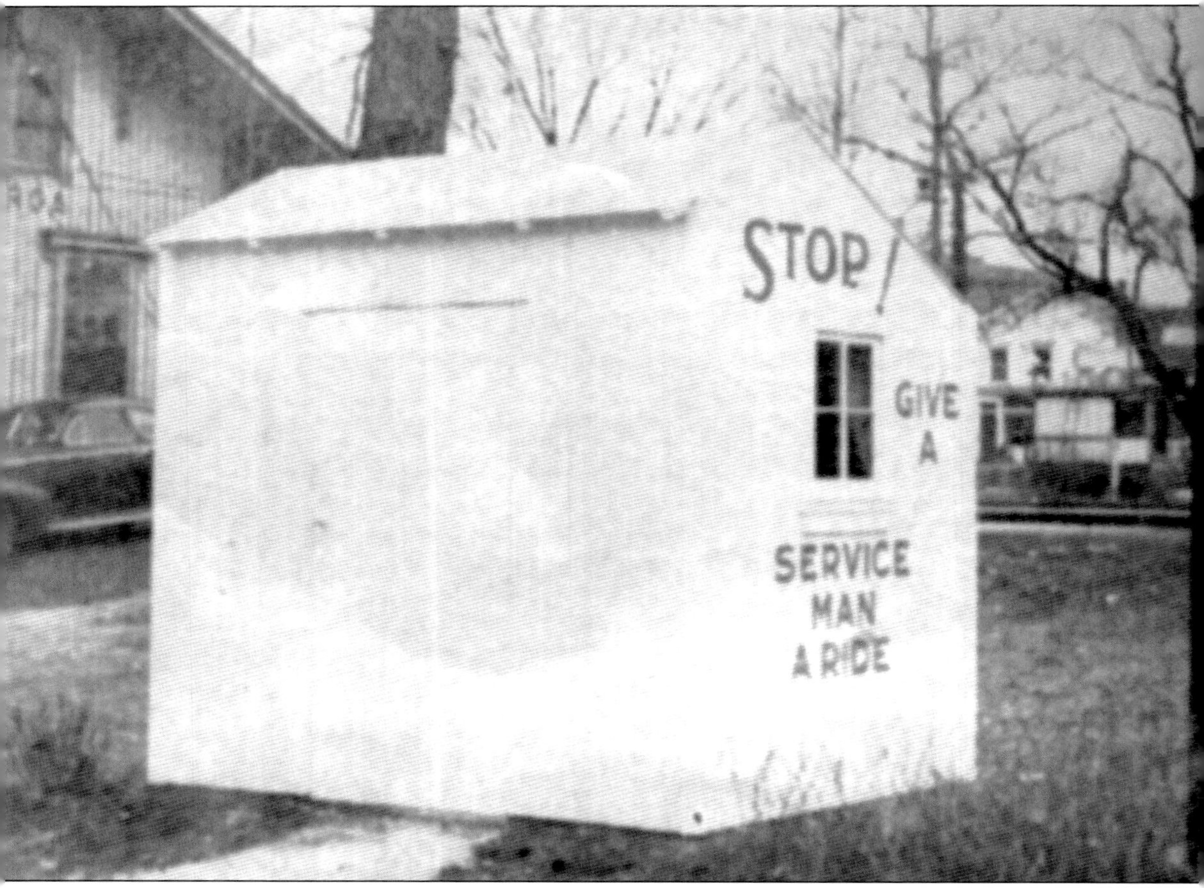

The Legion Shack stood under the "Onarga" sign and kept the hitchhiking servicemen from freezing along the road. The shack was used day and night the year round. Painted on the side of the shack was "Stop! Give a service man a ride." Onarga has always been extremely proud of its servicemen and servicewomen. Several families had two, three, four, or five children in the service. From scrap drives to war bond drives to Christmas parties for the children of the servicemen and women, Onarga kept the home fires burning. The disappointments and obstacles of war bound Onarga in friendship and fellowship, which have lasted a lifetime.

Ten

Yankee Doodle Came to Town

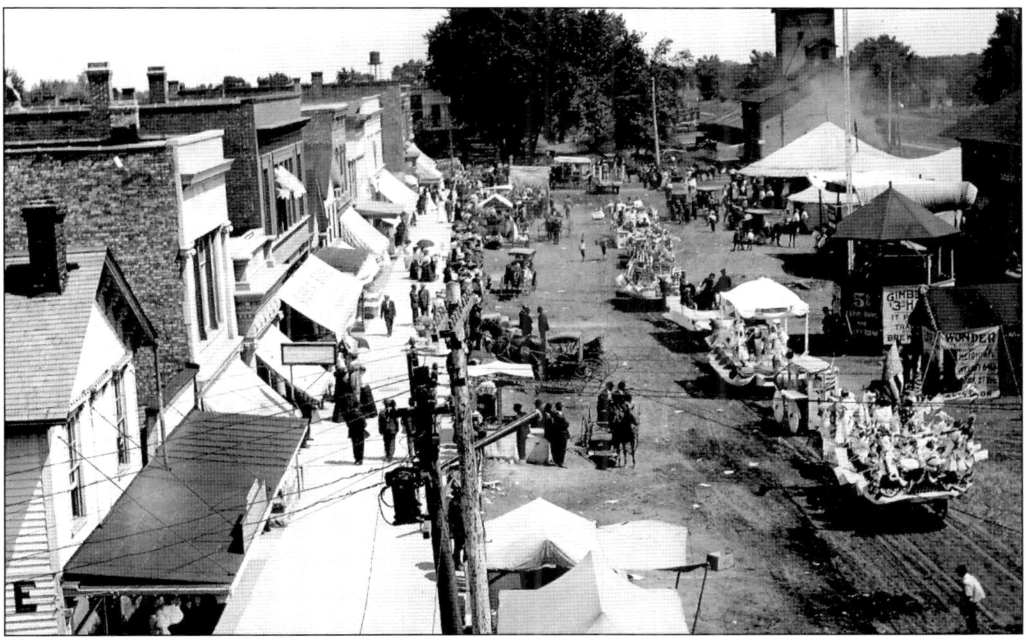

Onarga has always celebrated the Fourth of July with great gusto. The above picture depicts Onarga's Independence Day parade held on July 3, 1909. The parade lineup was as follows: the Women's Relief Corp, Campbell's, Booth's, Carter's Leader and Review, Krause, and Lovett's. The Fourth of July parade has been held almost every year in Onarga. The parades included marching bands, fife and drum, veterans marching or riding, and specially decorated cars and floats.

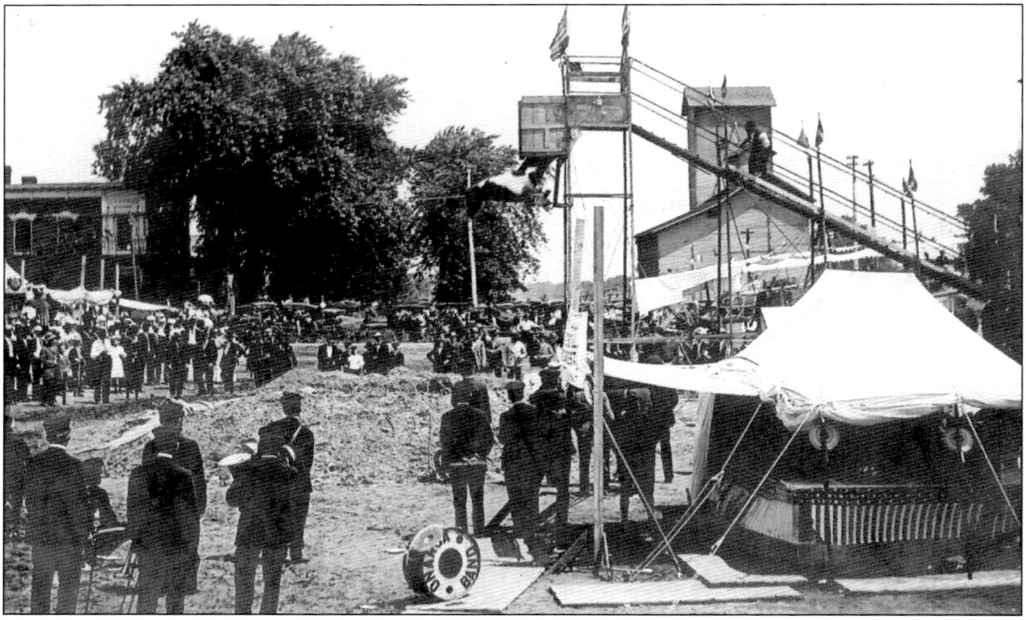

A diving horse was an attraction that was very popular beginning in the mid-1880s. A horse would dive into a pool of water, sometimes from as high as 60 feet up. A large ramp and tower were constructed of wood and steel. These photographs show a diving piebald horse exiting the ramp and also in motion. Note the Onarga Band in the foreground of the photograph. This was a most popular attraction for the Fourth of July celebration in Onarga, as attested to by the hundreds of onlookers and buggies in the photograph.

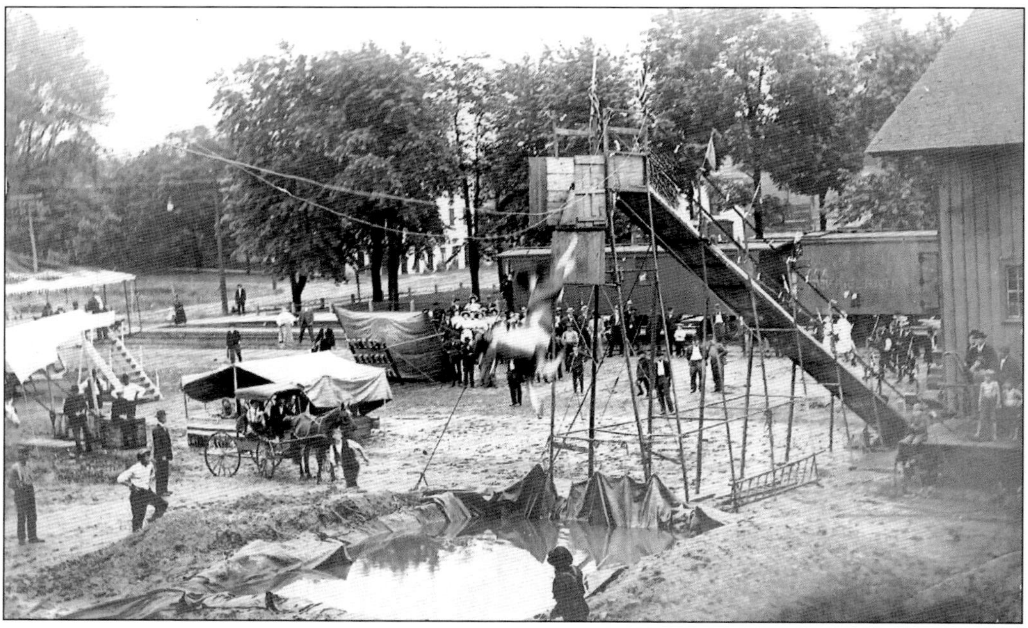

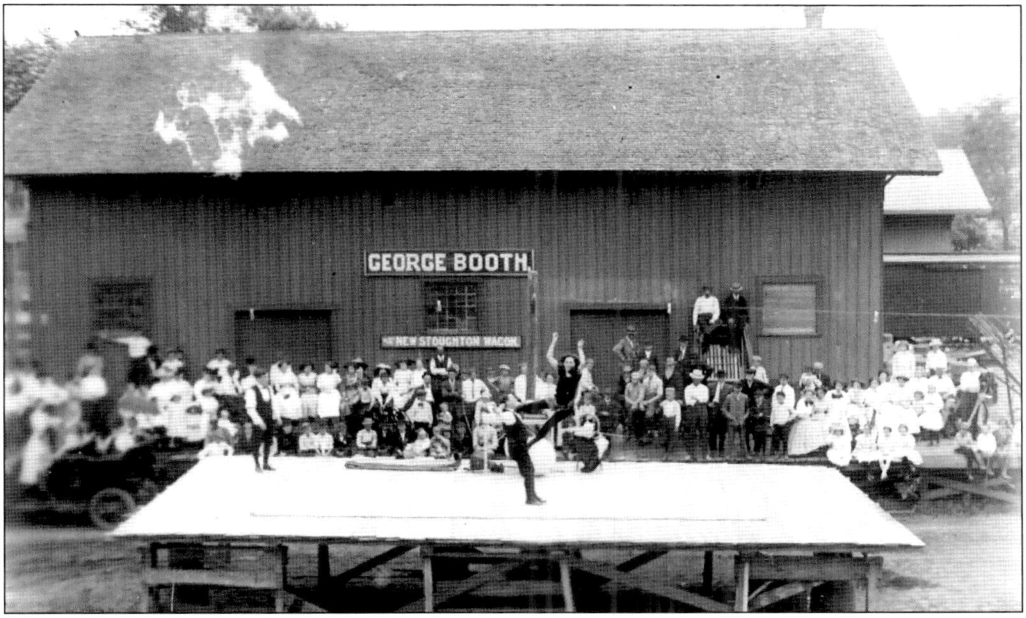

These tumbling acrobats were part of the Fourth of July celebration in Onarga. A wooden platform was constructed in front of George Booth's lumber business located on the south end of Chestnut Street. Onarga has always had a love affair with Independence Day and celebrated with vigor and overwhelming pride. The acrobats were a favorite Fourth of July act enjoyed by all. Other activities in Onarga on the Fourth of July were games such as tug-of-war, potato sack races, and watermelon-eating contests. Of course, softball as well as kitten ball was also popular and very competitive. Kittenball teams were Ridge Runners, Onarga Nursery, Del Rey, Corn Huskers, Lincoln Avenue, Gasoline Alley, North Main, South Main, Christian Church, Farmers, Ridgeville, and Poverty Row.

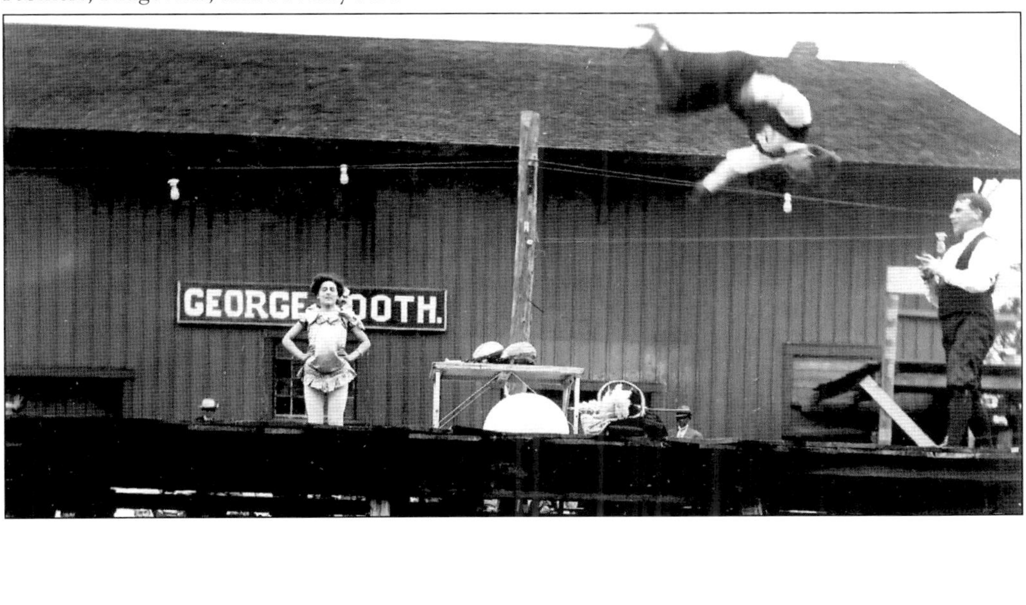

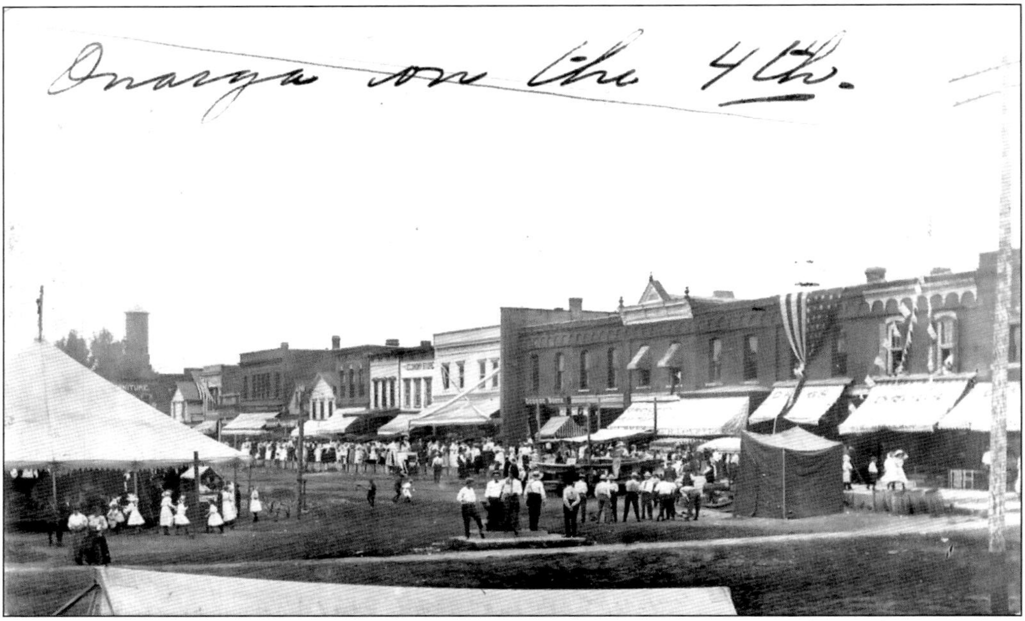

A patriotic symbol, the American flag can be seen many times in the above photograph of "Onarga on the 4th." Onarga flew the symbolic colors—red for courage, white for liberty, and blue for loyalty—in this photograph, which was taken on July 4, 1910, and shows much activity on Onarga's main street. The photograph below depicts boys identically dressed and sporting umbrellas advertising Carl B. Brewer's Department Store. Brewer's motto was "It Pays to Trade With Brewer." This photograph was taken just prior to the Fourth of July parade. A banner hanging on the front of the Economy Store advertises "Victor Talking Machines."

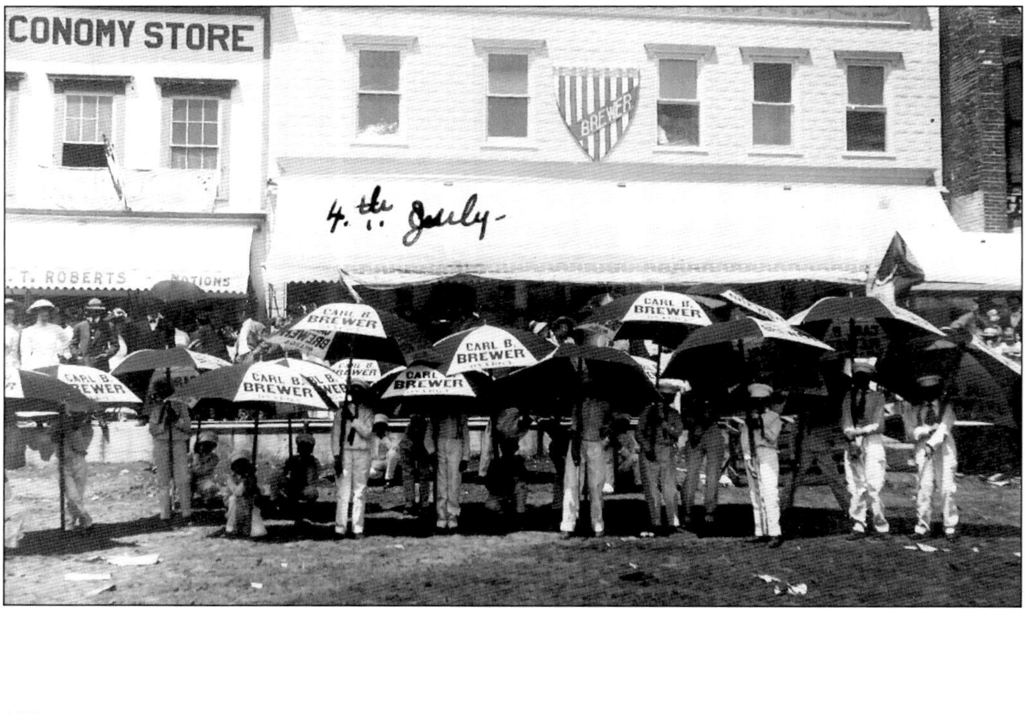

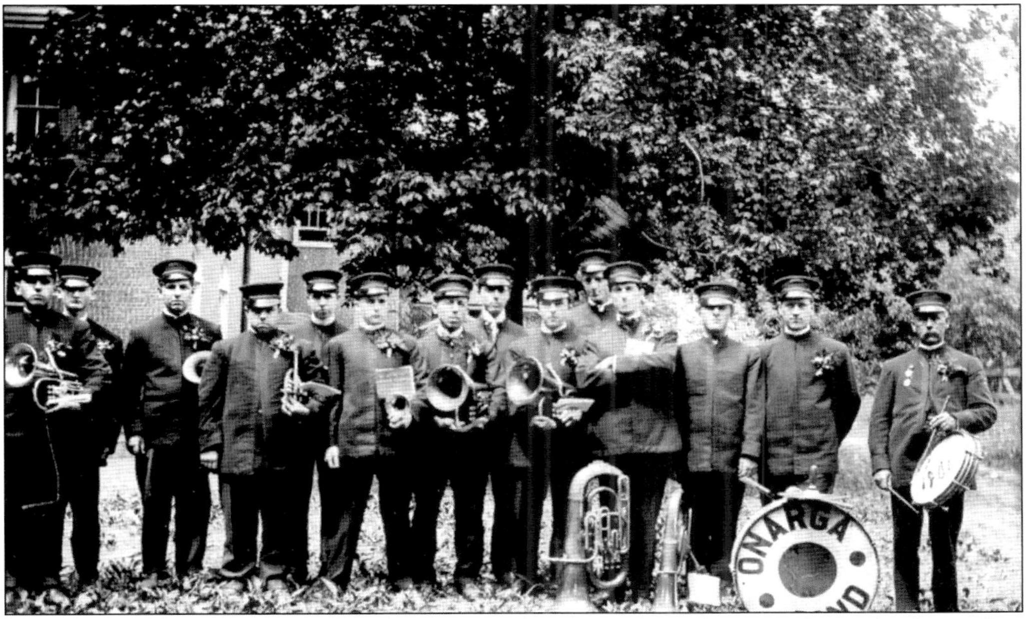

This photograph taken in 1909 depicts the Onarga Band. From left to right are leader Wilbur Kerns, McQueen, Ponton, Wheeler, Burkhalter, Whiteside, Lundy, Fickle, Kerns, Stitt, Gould, Collins, Stearman, Townsend, and Lief. The Onarga Band played for many of Onarga's Fourth of July celebrations and other festivities. The band was an important part of Onarga. A makeshift merry-go-round was part of Onarga's Fourth of July celebration. The park benches that were used on the merry-go-round were also used for lawn concerts and other Onarga festivities. The Fourth of July in Onarga was also a good time for pranks: stealing outhouses, removing porch steps, and disassembling and reassembling wagons, which ended up on top of the mercantile building roofs!

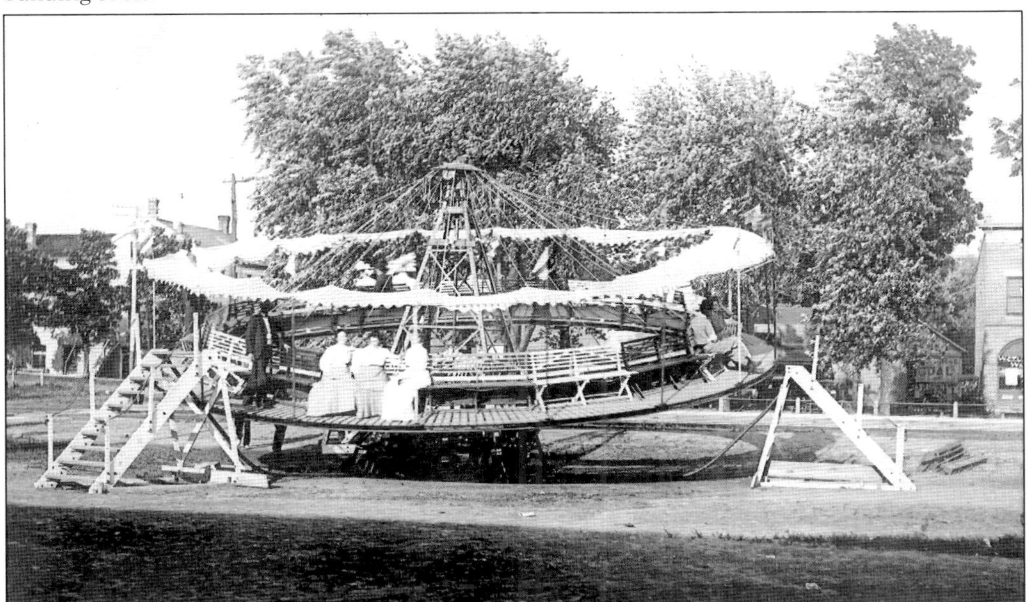

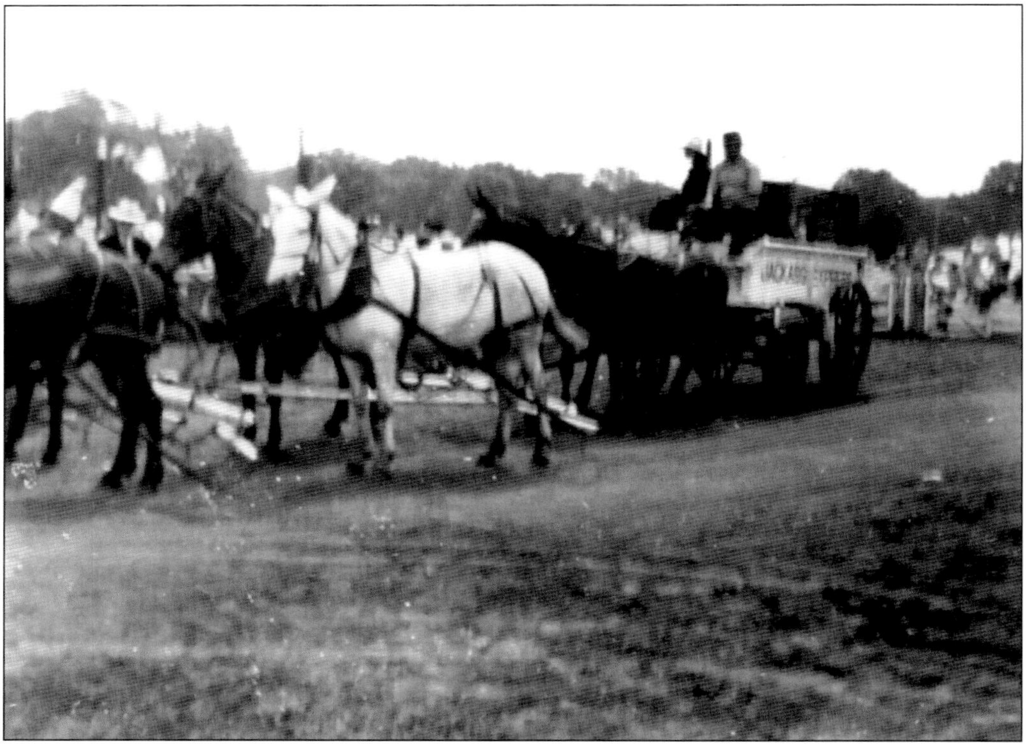

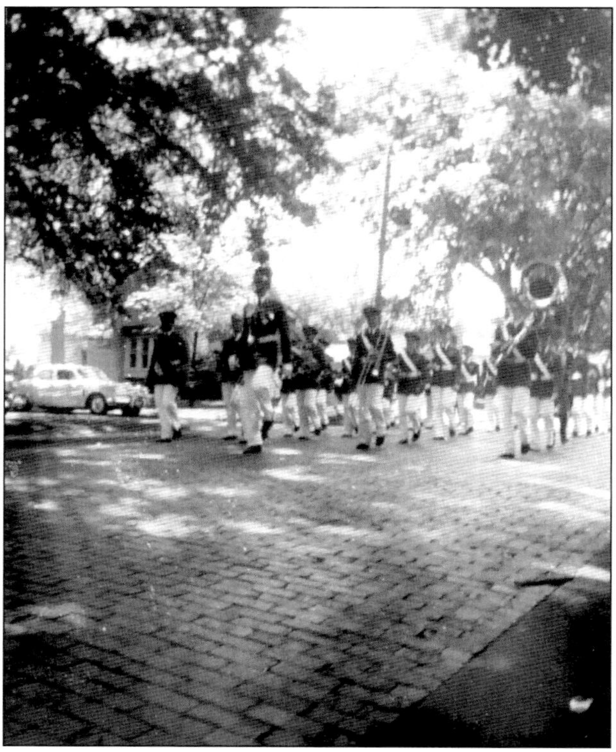

The 1954 Onarga centennial celebration was a grand success. Appropriately named the Princess Onarga Festival, the celebration opened Friday, July 2 at Durham Park. The parade was held on Monday, July 5. The grand prize was $75 for the entry that best depicted the centennial motif. There was even a special category for horses, and the grand prize was $50. The entry "Jackass Express" was the grand prize winner. Onarga's oldest citizens were honored with a special place in the parade, as was the lucky girl chosen as "Princess Onarga." The grand parade wound through Onarga taking the route of south on Evergreen Street to U.S. Highway 54, east to Chestnut Street, north to Lincoln Avenue, with Durham Park as its final destination where the judging took place.

For the Onarga centennial celebration, everyone was encouraged to dig up an old-fashioned costume and "plan to come and have a good time." Besides the grand parade, the Woman's Club held a special centennial tea on Thursday, July 1 at the Onarga Grade School. Nostalgic memories were stirred by the presentation of the "Old-Fashioned One-Room School" and "An Evening at a Box Social." These skits depicted early schooling of the community and the social life built around the country schools. The children did folk dances. Almost 1,000 persons attended the afternoon and evening sessions of the Woman's Club Tea.

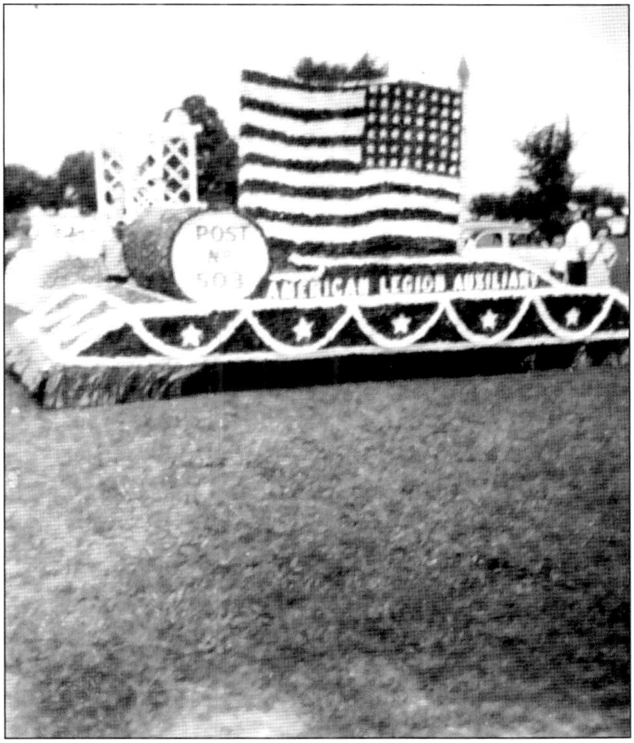

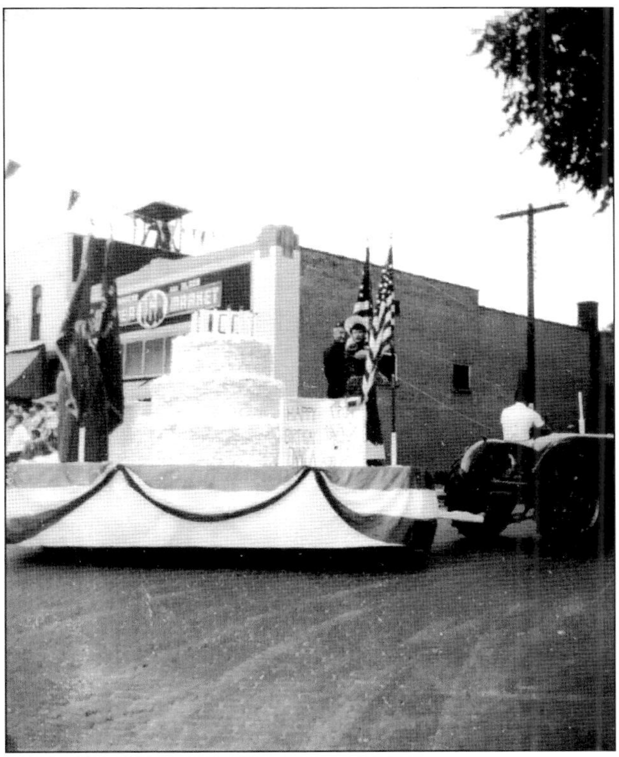

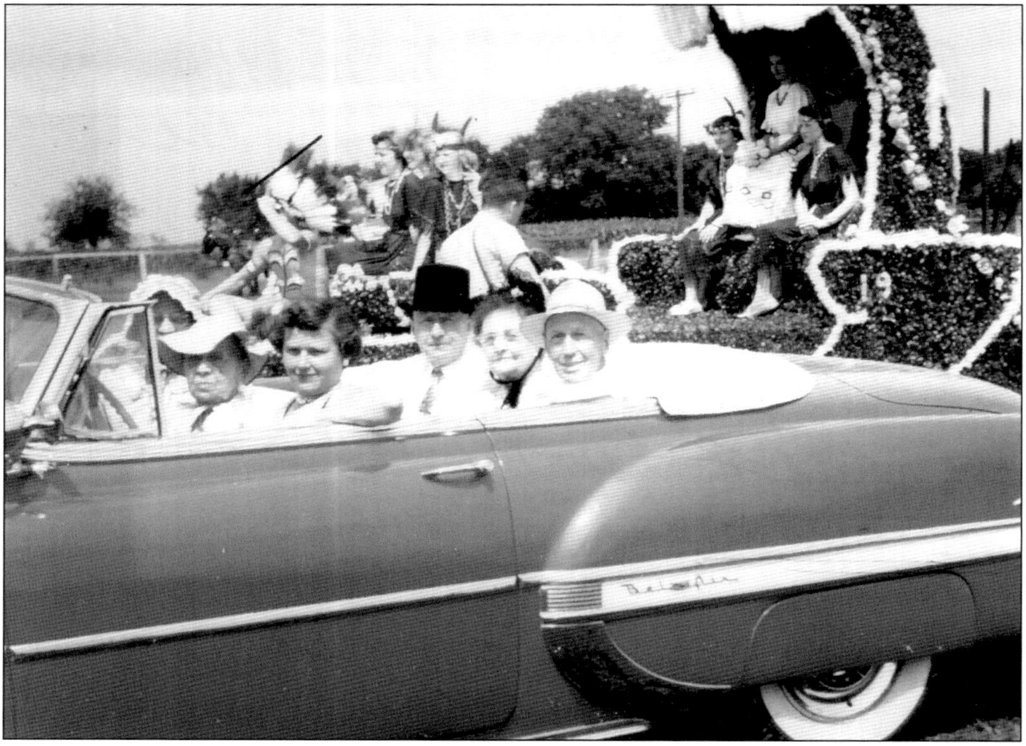

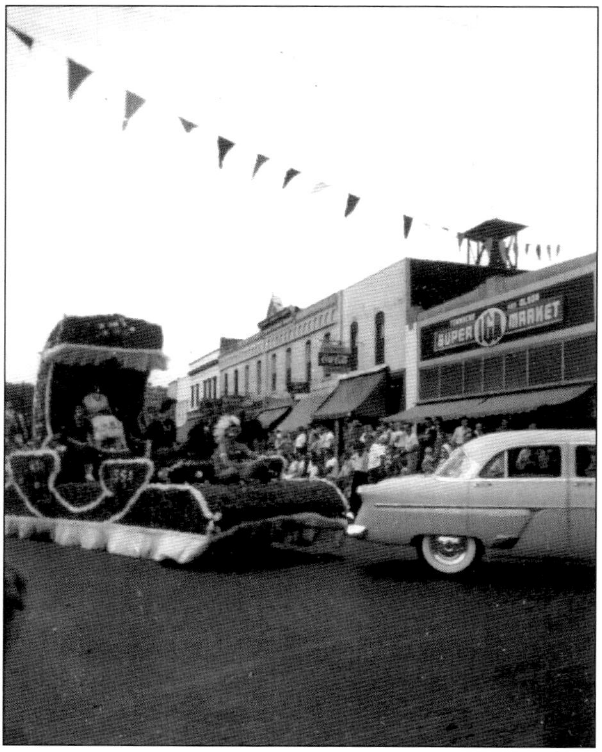

Time turned backward as Onarga celebrated its 100th birthday, July 2–5, 1954. Some of Onarga's oldest residents were honored guests in the centennial parade. From left to right in the rear seat are Mr. and Mrs. Frank Hockersmith and Ed Barber; Anna Dubbel is at left in the front seat with Julia Havens Smith to her right; and Donna Hall drove the car. The Princess Onarga float is also visible in this picture along with the American Indian chief, the school mascot.

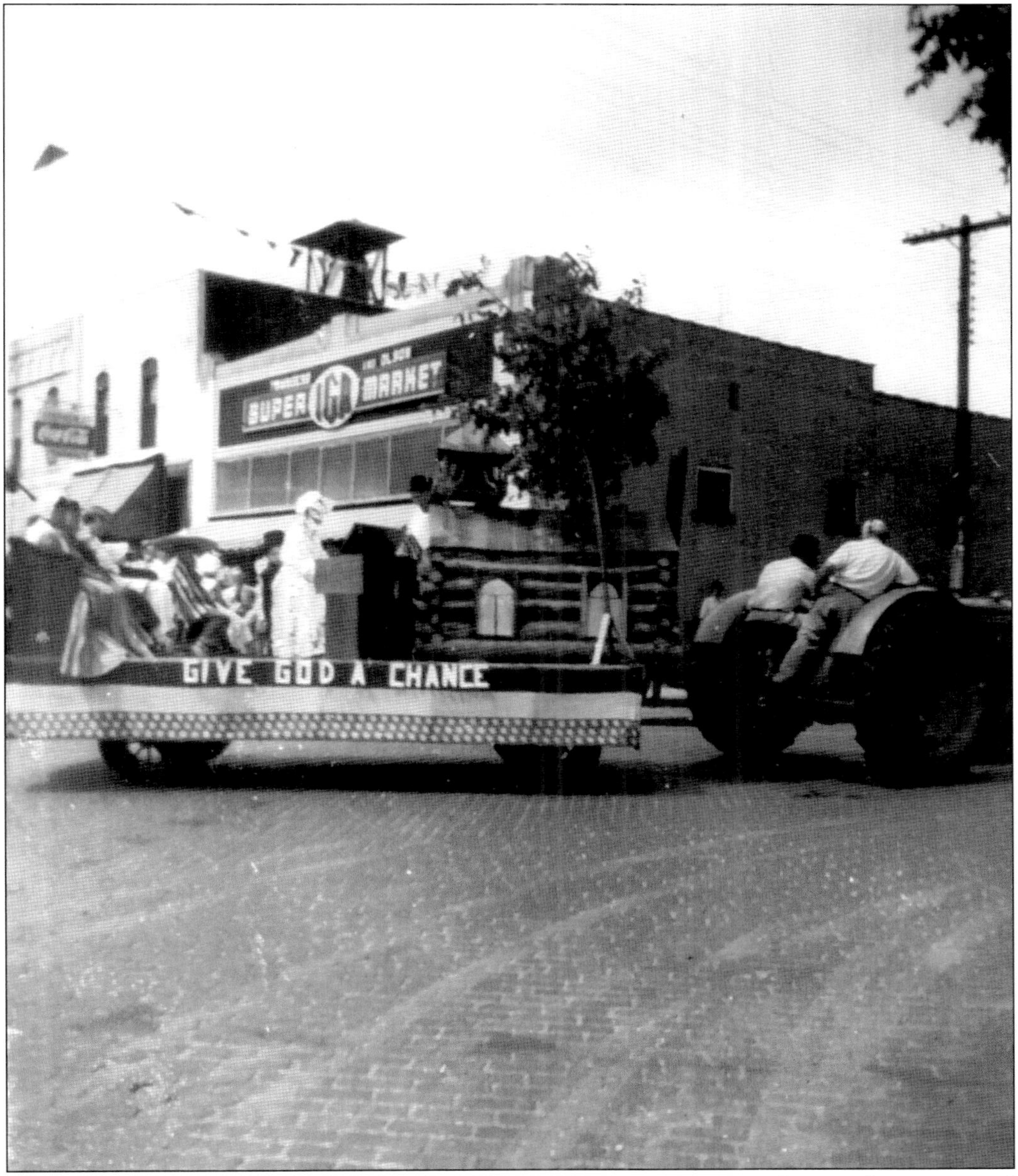

"The Bell and the Book" created the theme for the first prize–winning float in the centennial parade. The float was sponsored by the Onarga Christian Church. A miniature log church, a stump for a pulpit, a field organ, and an old pew were all combined to make a setting that reflected the centennial spirit and at the same time recalled the faith that made this country great and strong.

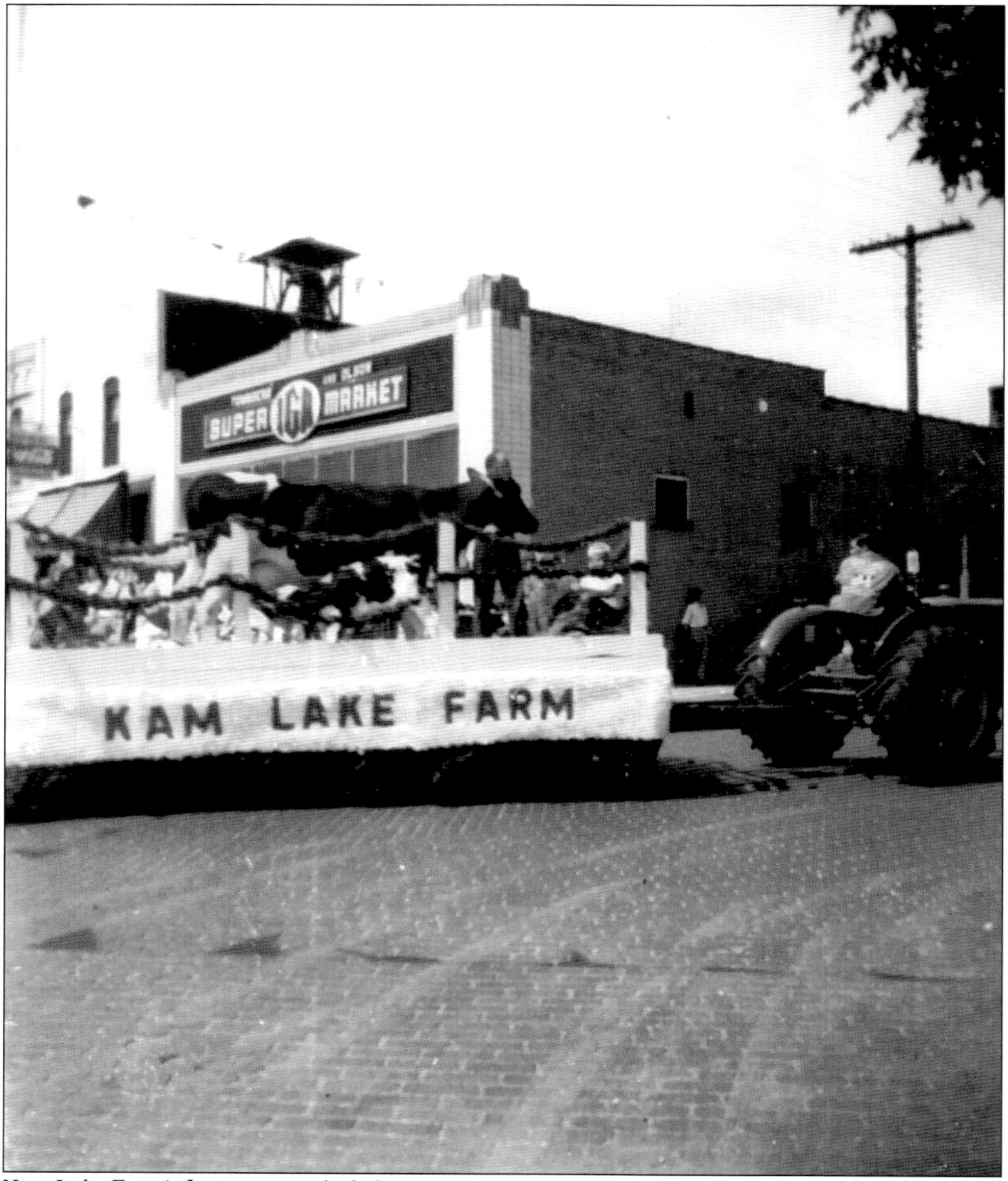

Kam Lake Farm's float consisted of a live cow and her new calf. How they stayed on the float was an oddity in itself! Kam Lake Farm was owned by Dr. Karl A. Meyer. Dr. Meyer was superintendent and chief surgeon at Cook County Hospital in Chicago for 50 years.

The 1954 100-year celebration was a grand success. After all the planning of the grand parade and tea and Princess Onarga Festival, all of Onarga had many wonderful memories. The photograph on the right depicts the Onarga Nursery Company's float. The photograph below is of Sam Moon's Funeral Wagon, which in 1954 was a unique antique.

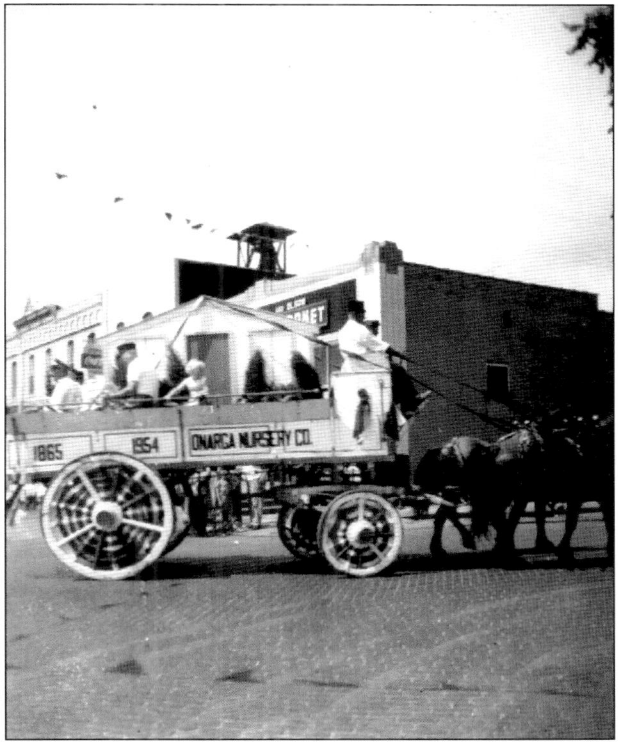

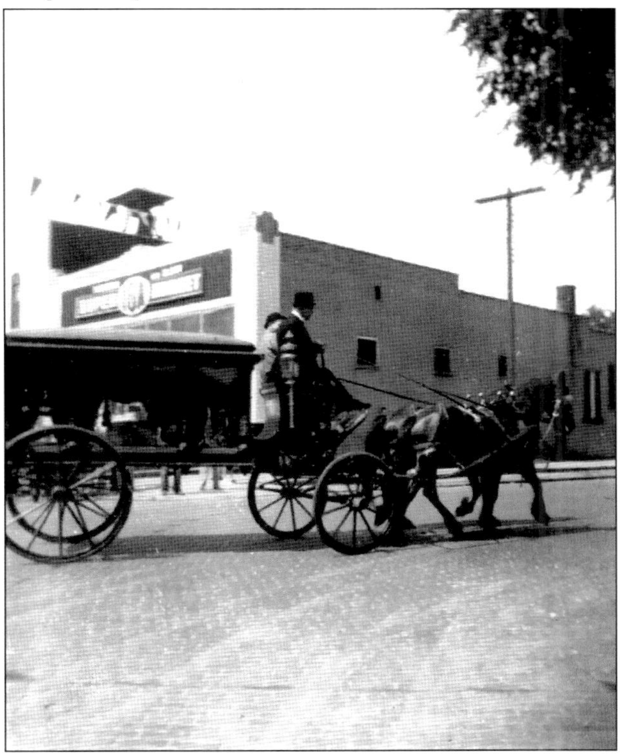